Disaster Recovery Planning

Roopendra Jeet Sandhu

Disaster Recovery Planning

Premier

Press

The Premier Press logo and related trade dress are trademarks of Premier Press, Inc. and may not be used without written permission. All other trademarks are the property of their respective owners.

Cisco, Cisco Secure IDS, Cisco 2514 Router, and Cisco 2501 Router are either registered trademarks or trademarks of Cisco Systems, Inc. in the U.S. and other countries. NFR NID and AFJ are either registered trademarks or trademarks of NFR Security in the U.S. and other countries. Symantec NetProwler is either a trademark or a registered trademark of Symantec Corporation in the U.S. and other countries.

All other trademarks are the property of their respective owners.

Important: Premier Press cannot provide software support. Please contact the appropriate software manufacturer's technical support line or Web site for assistance.

Premier Press and the author have attempted throughout this book to distinguish proprietary trademarks from descriptive terms by following the capitalization style used by the manufacturer.

Information contained in this book has been obtained by Premier Press from sources believed to be reliable. However, because of the possibility of human or mechanical error by our sources, Premier Press, or others, the Publisher does not guarantee the accuracy, adequacy, or completeness of any information and is not responsible for any errors or omissions or the results obtained from use of such information. Readers should be particularly aware of the fact that the Internet is an ever-changing entity. Some facts may have changed since this book went to press.

ISBN: 1-931841-98-5

Library of Congress Catalog Card Number: 2002106534

Printed in the United States of America

02 03 04 05 BH 10 9 8 7 6 5 4 3 2 1

Premier Press, a division of Course Technology
2645 Erie Avenue, Suite 41
Cincinnati, Ohio 45208

Publisher:
Stacy L. Hiquet

Marketing Manager:
Heather Hurley

Project Editor/Copy Editor:
Karen A. Gill

Technical Reviewer:
Rajat Sehdev

Interior Layout:
Danielle Foster

Cover Design:
Phil Velikan

Indexer:
Sharon Shock

I would like to dedicate this book to my parents and my nephew
for cheering me and making me smile when I treaded through hard times.

Acknowledgments

Thank you, dear parents, for your support. I will always be grateful to you for standing by me at all times. It would have been impossible to complete this book without your motivation.

I would like to thank the development head at NIIT Ltd., Vineet Whig, for his excellent support and guidance to all development teams. I appreciate my project manager, Anita Sastry, for her support and her belief in me for authoring this book. I would also like to thank Stacy Hiquet for making this book happen in the first place.

My thanks to Rajat Sehdev for providing valuable input throughout the development of the book. Special thanks also go out to Nitin Pandey and Kuljit Kaur for valuable input while reviewing the chapters. It has been a pleasure working with you. I would also like to extend my thanks to Swati Roy for always being there. Finally, I thank Priyanka Verma for creating the excellent graphics in this book. Thanks.

About NIIT

NIIT is a Global IT Solutions Corporation with a presence in 38 countries. With its unique business model and technology creation capabilities, NIIT delivers software and learning solutions to more than 1,000 clients across the world.

The success of NIIT's training solutions lies in its unique approach to education. NIIT's Knowledge Solutions Business conceives, researches, and develops all the course material. A rigorous instructional design methodology is followed to create engaging and compelling course content. NIIT has one of the largest learning material development facilities in the world.

NIIT trains more than 200,000 executives and students each year in IT areas by using stand-up training, video-aided instruction, computer-based training (CBT), and Internet-based training (IBT). NIIT has been featured in the *Guinness Book of World Records* for the largest number of students trained in one year.

NIIT has developed more than10,000 hours of instructor-led training (ILT) and more than 3,000 hours of Internet-based training and computer-based training. IDC ranked NIIT among the top 15 IT training providers globally for the year 2000. Through the innovative use of training methods and its commitment to research and development, NIIT has been in the forefront of computer education and training for the past 20 years.

Quality has been the prime focus at NIIT. Most of the processes are ISO-9001 certified. NIIT was the twelfth company in the world to be assessed at Level 5 of SEI-CMM. NIIT's Content (Learning Material) Development facility is the first in the world to be assessed at this high maturity level. NIIT has strategic partnerships with companies such as Computer Associates, IBM, Microsoft, Oracle, and Sun Microsystems.

About the Author

Roopendra Jeet Sandhu is an instructional designer for the Knowledge Solutions Business (KSB) division of NIIT Ltd. During her two-year tenure at NIIT Ltd., she has developed content for computer-based training, Web-based training, and instructor-led training for clients such as Course Technology, NetVarsity, and ITT. She has independently developed a couple of Web-based training projects. In addition, Roopendra has been developing content on technical areas, such as operating systems, security, and database management systems. She has also developed a project on Netscape 6.0 and co-authored the book *.NET Framework*, published by Premier Press.

Contents at a Glance

Contents

Chapter 7   **Testing and Maintaining the Recovery Plan** 161

Introduction

Man has always attempted to evade the forces of nature and the destruction they cause. Industrialization and the rapid advance in technology have led to new threats and tremendous increase in their potential to cause damage. As a result, man has developed strategies to overcome or minimize the impact caused by disasters. Man's efforts have been channeled toward planning for disaster recovery.

To plan, it is essential to understand the underlying needs and concepts. To this effect, *Disaster Recovery Planning* begins by answering the question, "Why must I plan for disaster recovery?" Besides detailing the planning considerations and the organizational structure required to plan, this book distinguishes among various disasters and their consequences. You can find detailed information on risk analysis that can be used to prevent and control risks. The important concepts in avoiding and handling disasters, such as access control, anti-viruses, and firewalls are covered. With the required input for planning, the book guides you through the rigorous cycle of creating a disaster recovery plan. It also presents valuable information that is related to testing and maintaining the plan. Finally, the book details the strategies for the recovery of centralized and decentralized systems. Here, you learn about systems recovery, network and communication links recovery, and data recovery. In the end, you review a case study to trace the steps involved in an organization's recovery.

How to Use This Book

Chapters 1, 2, and 3 discuss preliminary knowledge about disaster planning and classification of disasters, whereas Chapters 4, 6, and 7 discuss distinct phases in disaster recovery planning. You can learn about the baseline measures in Chapter 5. Chapters 8 and 9 teach you the recovery of centralized and decentralized systems, and Chapter 10 steps through a case study so you can review how a company can implement a plan.

To facilitate learning, this book uses specific aids such as Notes, Tips, and Cautions. Any additional or related information about concepts is covered in Notes, and Tips provide useful information or shortcuts so that you can perform tasks more efficiently. Caution state warnings that are related to procedures or facts.

Chapter 1

**Disaster
Recovery
Planning:
An Overview**

With the rapid advancement in the field of information technology (IT), organizations are increasingly relying on IT to perform mundane as well as critical tasks. This dependency often results in the interruption of the normal functioning of organizations when unplanned events occur. Such unplanned events that result in the interruption of an organization's normal business operations are known as *disasters*.

Disasters abound in the IT scenario, the impact of which can range from mere annoyance to complete destruction of business. Fortunately, you can minimize the impact of a disaster and continue operations in the face of them by implementing the appropriate disaster recovery plans and procedures. A recent survey conducted by Booz Allen Hamilton revealed that 9 out of 10 CEOs of companies with yearly revenue of $1 billion or more have personally reviewed disaster recovery plans since September 11, the day the World Trade Center was attacked.

Disaster recovery is the process that ensures the continuity of an organization's business operations when a disaster strikes. This process not only focuses on the recovery of the essential functions and systems of an organization, but it also emphasizes their recovery within the shortest possible time. To achieve maximum recovery in minimal time, you create a route map that details the actions to be performed before, during, and after a disaster. This route map is known as a *disaster recovery plan*. A disaster recovery plan is a comprehensive set of statements created to address any disaster that could damage an organization.

The process by which you create a disaster recovery plan is called *disaster recovery planning*. Disaster recovery planning is performed to ensure a quick, efficient, and cost-effective resumption and recovery of business operations regardless of the cause of the disaster. Considering that it is impossible to predict with certainty the time, place, and manner in which a disaster will occur, it becomes essential to plan for the unforeseen. The importance of planning is aptly emphasized in the following words of President Eisenhower, *"The plan is nothing. Planning is everything."*

This book builds on the significance of the disaster recovery planning process. This chapter teaches you to appreciate the need for disaster recovery planning.

It covers the benefits and strategies of implementing the planning process, as well as the considerations to keep in mind while planning for disaster recovery. Finally, it instructs you on the phases of disaster recovery planning and the recovery objectives that are commonly used in disaster recovery planning.

Need for Disaster Recovery Planning

An organization must contemplate disaster recovery planning because it might not be able to withstand the onslaught of a disaster. After a disaster occurs, for how long can the organization sustain itself without its mission-critical systems, applications, and data? Several types of disasters can strike an organization, including the following:

♦ **Natural calamities.** These include natural disasters, such as floods, tornadoes, and earthquakes. Japan experiences terrible earthquakes, but it has learned to live with these catastrophes by using well-designed disaster recovery plans. Extreme climatic conditions, such as heavy snowfall or hurricanes, also can hamper the normal functioning of a business. As an example, Hurricane Floyd of September 1999 brought Eastern United States to a standstill. It's important to account for such contingencies.

♦ **Link and power failures.** Link and power failures can lead to serious business losses. These might be the side effects of natural calamities or manmade disruptive activities, such as strikes or terrorist activities. Think of the impact on businesses and individuals in the aftermath of the World Trade Center attack. Telecommunication and network links are the lifelines for any business, and any disruptions to these lead to dissatisfied customers, partners, and suppliers.

♦ **Criminal and disruptive activities.** Cyberterrorism and criminal hacking belong to this category. These activities can lead to theft or leakage of confidential data or marketing strategies. An organization might have to face serious embarrassment as a result of such disasters. For example, an e-commerce firm might go out of business if the database that stores confidential customer records, such as credit card information, is compromised.

♦ **Civil unrest.** Civil unrest, strikes, or a politically volatile environment can hamper businesses. The disturbances created at the World Trade

Organization conference in Seattle in 2000 are an example of how civil unrest leads to business disruptions.

To ensure the continued survival of an organization, you need to plan for disaster recovery. In doing so, you should address all the disasters in the IT scenario that could impact the organization by creating a disaster recovery plan. Some other factors that necessitate disaster recovery planning are as follows:

◆ **Severe losses caused to an organization by disasters.** As discussed earlier, the increasing dependency on IT can result in severe consequences when IT-related disasters occur. Based on the nature of work performed, an organization might lose a considerable amount of money for every hour of downtime. Downtime caused by an IT disaster can result in the loss of revenue, customers, clients, or business partners. It would be difficult to convince customers and clients about the state of affairs in an organization caused from a disaster. A client would be reluctant to accept such excuses for non-performance. In addition, a prolonged downtime would reduce the profitability and the market value of the organization, which ultimately could result in business failure.

In addition to business losses, it is often a legal necessity for an organization to maintain all the essential information. The loss of information can be calamitous, so it's essential to protect records.

◆ **Rapid technological advancements leading to the development of new types of disasters.** The requirement of 24×7 availability of products and services forces organizations to increasingly rely on IT for every aspect of their business. As a result, innovative methods of performing business operations are being implemented and renewed by the hour. Practices such as remote connection to offices for round-the-clock connectivity make an organization vulnerable to external attacks and susceptible to disasters. In addition, data is dispersed across sites and networks spanning geographical boundaries, making it vulnerable to attacks from unauthorized users. Further, the occurrence of disasters such as earthquakes can damage the data center. The need for planning for disaster recovery in such cases cannot be overlooked.

◆ **Survival of business depending on its recovery in the shortest possible time.** In the event of a disaster impacting the IT setup, all the important functions that are dependent on IT, such as communication and transactions, are hampered. Although it might be possible for an organization to sustain itself in the absence of its critical operations for a day or two, prolonged interruption could spell the end for the organization. To prevent such a calamity, you can implement disaster recovery planning and prepare policies and procedures that ensure the recovery of the organization in the shortest possible time in the event of a disaster.

◆ **Contractual obligations.** Organizations that are directly involved in supplying products and services to customers or clients are bound by *Service Level Agreements* (SLAs) to perform their duties. These agreements seek assurance from the suppliers that in the face of disasters, the supply of deliverables will continue unhindered. When a commitment to high availability and quality is made, it takes special effort on the part of the supplier to honor the SLAs. This can only be achieved through disaster recovery planning.

◆ **Effective coordination of recovery tasks.** In a disaster recovery plan, you list the recovery procedures to ensure that the organization resumes its operations within the shortest possible time. Because these procedures are defined prior to the occurrence of disasters, the entire disaster recovery plan reflects the effectiveness and preparedness of the organization to meet the challenges of disasters. A preplanned list of the recovery procedures, therefore, helps in easy and effective recovery of the organization from a disaster.

After you examine the need for disaster recovery planning, you have a greater appreciation of the benefits of the planning process.

SLA

An SLA is a contract that specifies the services provided by an organization to its customers or clients. This contract lists the parameters used to measure the performance of the supplier and the consequences of not abiding by the contract. Often, the contract states that the supply of products and services should continue as and when required no matter what the circumstances are at the supplier end.

Benefits of Disaster Recovery Planning

In disaster recovery planning, you identify the means of dealing with the temporary unavailability or inaccessibility of technology. What benefits does disaster recovery planning have for an organization that implements this process?

Following are the benefits of disaster recovery planning:

◆ **Maintenance of business continuity.** The main objective behind implementing disaster recovery planning is to ensure business continuity and availability of critical resources and systems. This results in continued service to customers and clients.

◆ **Protection of critical resources and activities.** To ensure business continuity, all the critical resources and activities are identified and protected. This enhances the organizational stability, thereby safeguarding the interests of business partners. Further, the employees of an organization don't need to worry about the consequences if the organization comes to a standstill.

◆ **Reduced expenditure.** Planning and identifying recovery measures is wise when performed before a disaster occurs rather than after. With effective disaster recovery planning, you can minimize the financial loss that disasters can cause.

◆ **Identification of single points of failure.** An important activity in disaster recovery planning is assessment of the business functions of an organization. This is done to identify the single points of failure. In other words, you identify the functions or processes with a high dependence on a single resource. As a result, if the resource is affected by a disaster, the effect on the functions or processes is calamitous. For instance, if an organization stores its data at a single data center, the data is lost if a disaster occurs that affects the entire data center. The identification of such points of failure can be used to estimate the risks to the functions of the organization. You can use this information to ensure high availability of data by making backups of the data at an alternative site.

◆ **Avoidance of panic during a disaster.** Disaster recovery planning helps reduce the panic associated with a disaster occurrence. Prior to a disaster occurring, you identify all the tasks required to put an organization back on track in the event of a disaster. As a result, all tasks that involve decision making at the time of the occurrence of the disaster are significantly reduced. This eliminates the need to plan and invest money in disaster recovery when the organization is affected by the disaster. It also means that you do not need to await decisions of key personnel during a disaster. As a result, you achieve a smooth and orderly recovery within the shortest time frame.

In this section, you learned about the benefits of disaster recovery planning. You can achieve these benefits by employing different strategies to the planning process. These strategies, which are discussed in the next section, are aimed at minimizing the negative impact of disasters.

Disaster Recovery Planning Strategies

The primary aim of disaster recovery planning is to efficiently respond to and recover from a disaster. To achieve this aim, disaster recovery planning focuses on minimizing the impact of the disasters facing an organization by implementing three strategies. These strategies are as follows:

- **Preventive strategy.** As the name suggests, in this strategy, all efforts are geared to prevent disasters from happening. To accomplish this, you implement baseline measures to secure and make reliable the activities and systems on which the existence of an organization is dependent. In addition, you use tools and techniques to eliminate bugs, configuration errors, and hardware failures. In other words, you attempt to reduce the probability of occurrence of disasters that are IT related and under your control. You will learn about preventive strategies in Chapter 5, "Baseline Measures."

- **Anticipatory strategy.** In the anticipatory strategy, you identify the procedures to respond to and recover from disasters. For this purpose, you predict the scenarios that are likely to result in a disaster, their likelihood of occurrence, and their impact. You can obtain this information from experience and the information related to the systems deployed in the organization. You can use the configuration of these systems and the problems that are expected to affect them to obtain information about the scenarios that are likely to result in a disaster and their impact. You will learn more about this strategy in Chapters 4, "Risk Analysis," and 6, "The Recovery Plan."

◆ **Mitigatory strategy.** While you're planning for mitigation strategy, you implement measures to minimize the impact of an unavoidable disaster. You will learn more about this strategy in Chapter 6 and the implementation aspect in Chapters 8, "Recovery Plan for Centralized Systems," and 9, "Recovery Plan for Decentralized Systems."

To implement these three strategies, you must ensure that your disaster recovery planning follows a project-oriented approach. While you implement the disaster recovery planning strategies, you need to bear in mind certain considerations. These considerations are described in the next section.

Planning Considerations

While planning for disaster recovery, it is essential to keep in mind all disaster response procedures and the alternatives to recover from disasters. Further, you must be aware of all the assumptions for disaster recovery to help you create a comprehensive disaster recovery plan. Following are some other considerations to bear in mind while planning for disaster recovery:

◆ **Creation of a planning structure.** The creation of a planning structure is vital to the success of disaster recovery planning. This is because the process of disaster recovery planning involves multiple individuals and considerable expenditure. The planning structure should be multi-level to ensure coordination between the different levels and various departments of an organization. You can learn about the planning structure for disaster recovery planning in the later section "Organizational Planning Structure."

◆ **Support from management.** It is important to seek the support and involvement of management in the planning process and throughout the creation and maintenance of the plan. Management can not only help by providing financial support, but also by allowing personnel to devote time to the successful completion of the planning process. Management should coordinate the implementation and maintenance of the disaster recovery plan to ensure its effectiveness throughout the organization. The underlying support for disaster recovery planning ensures the necessary involvement of the organization's departments and employees.

The key to gaining the support of management is communication about the need and benefits of the planning process. You can adopt various other approaches to get the support of the management. For instance, you can state facts related to disasters to make management aware of the expenses likely to be incurred and other repercussions.

◆ **Incorporation of disaster recovery as part of the organizational processes.** To ensure the maximum benefit from disaster recovery planning, you need to incorporate disaster recovery as an organizational process. To retain a plan's effectiveness and relevance in an uncertain environment, you must also ensure that disaster recovery planning is an ongoing process. In other words, you should incorporate any changes in the organization into the disaster recovery plan. This ensures that appropriate measures are taken to reduce the impact of disasters.

◆ **Time consideration.** It is important to understand the time when disaster recovery comes into effect. Disaster recovery is the last effort to restore the operations of an organization after a disaster. Typically, organizations decide to create and implement a disaster recovery plan when an important activity or function of the organization is threatened for an unacceptable period of time. This decision is dependent on the type of organization, its business operations, and its dependence on IT setup. In addition, the level of service promised by IT setup decides the time when the disaster recovery plan should be implemented. For instance, the IT department has assured you that the disruption of business operation will be rectified within a stipulated time period. However, if the disruption of the operation continues beyond the stipulated time, you need to implement the disaster recovery plan.

◆ **Evaluation of the existing emergency plans and procedures.** You must review and assess all the plans and procedures currently in place in the organization—such as backup plans, archiving procedures, and security procedures—before you plan for disaster recovery. You also should evaluate the contingency planning for different types of disasters. Such an evaluation is performed to identify the existing plans and procedures that can be directly incorporated in disaster recovery plans.

It is wise to revert to the process owners or the creators of these plans and procedures for more valuable input. In addition, you can use documents such as departmental process flowcharts and organization charts to collect useful resources for disaster recovery planning.

◆ **Involvement of all departments of the organization.** A disaster is unlikely to impact a single department. Therefore, it becomes essential that all departments play an active role in the planning process to make it a success. The support of management is a definite drive toward the participation of employees in the planning process. You can achieve interdepartmental coordination by communicating and educating employees about the purpose of disaster recovery planning and its significance. In addition, you can state facts to specify how disasters can impact the employees and the organization. Consider innovative ideas that achieve the participation of the employees. You can, for instance, reward all the employees who successfully complete a disaster test drill.

In addition, you must analyze the activities and functions that each department performs to ensure an adequate representation of the risks and possible disasters in the disaster recovery plan. It is important that representatives from various departments review decisions that the planning team has taken to ensure analysis of the effect of each planning step on the department and its activities. Consequently, the disaster recovery plan will be realistic and effective. You will learn about the planning team in the later section titled "Planning Team."

◆ **Knowledge about disasters.** It is important to gain an accurate and in-depth understanding of disasters to make the entire exercise of creating disaster recovery plans a worthwhile effort. While planning, you should consider the worst-case scenario wherein the entire facility is destroyed and focus your plans around such an eventuality.

 NOTE

Although it is wise to plan and prepare yourself for all disasters, time and financial constraints might restrict you to planning for a few. The driving force behind disaster recovery planning is the balancing of business requirements and the realities the organization faces.

◆ **Role of external specialists.** Organizations often employ specialists who are external to an organization, such as consultants or vendors, to gather information for use in creating a disaster recovery plan. You can use the expertise of a consultant to create the disaster recovery plan. An organization will employ external specialists only when it lacks the capability to perform disaster recovery planning or system audits on its own. In this case, external specialists can perform the activities that contribute to disaster recovery planning. Disaster recovery consultants are trained to identify the vulnerabilities and risks of an organization. Based on the information gathered, the consultants can identify the activities required to perform disaster recovery. In addition, they can identify the personnel, budget, and timeframe required to perform disaster recovery. These specialists can define the scope for a disaster recovery plan, evaluate the existing plans, and direct disaster recovery efforts to management for approval.

 NOTE

To perform their task, external specialists assess the existing plans and procedures for disaster recovery of the organization. An important source that the specialists use to identify and gather information about the organization, its functions, and assets are the key personnel of the organization. In addition, these specialists refer to the local community services to identify the natural disasters in the area.

Apart from the planning considerations described previously, disaster recovery is implemented using different methodologies. These methodologies of disaster recovery planning vary across organizations, but two are most commonly used.

In the first methodology, the procedural format methodology, you record details of the planning process as complete sentences. In the second methodology, the checklist methodology, you record planning details in the form of bullet points. Each methodology has advantages. Therefore, it's your decision to use either of these methodologies or a combination of them.

Despite the difference in the methodologies that the different organizations use, the phases of the planning process are common to all methodologies.

Phases of Disaster Recovery Planning

The disaster recovery planning project is approached in phases, keeping in mind the time and resources that the project involves. A phased approach ensures that all the key areas of an organization that are likely to be impacted by a disaster are considered. A phased approach also ensures that the planning process is systematic and simple.

NOTE

The phases and the activities therein serve only as guidelines. You can modify them to meet the requirements of your organization. Similarly, you can use your discretion to classify the activities performed under each phase.

Each phase of the planning process relies on seeking answers to questions and using the answers to achieve a timely recovery. For instance, what are the critical activities of an organization or department? Similarly, what is the current level of preparedness of the organization to face disasters?

Each phase utilizes the output of the preceding phase as input. The phases of the disaster recovery planning process are as follows:

◆ Initiation

◆ Risk analysis

◆ Creation and implementation of the plan

◆ Testing of the plan

◆ Maintenance of the plan

In the subsequent sections, you will learn about each of these phases.

Initiation

The initiation phase is when you conceptualize the disaster recovery planning project. In this phase, the planning team is formulated. Upon creation, the team decides the goals and objectives of the planning process. The planning team reaches a consensus on the assumptions for the planning project. For this purpose, the team analyzes different aspects of the organization, such as the requirements, environment, and exposure to calamity. For instance, the team can assume that the key personnel of an organization will not be affected by a disaster to an extent that the organization comes to a standstill.

The assumptions that the team arrives at help decide the aspects that should be covered in the plan. For instance, the team can assume that the geographical area in which the facility is located is prone to natural disasters. In such a case, the team will assess the regional disasters to plan for recovery of the organization from them. In other words, the team defines the scope for the project based on the assumptions. The team can then use the scope of the project to identify disaster recovery strategies and solutions. While defining the scope for the project, the team performs the following activities:

◆ **Identify for whom it is planning.** For instance, the team identifies whether the scope of the project is the entire organization or its specific departments.

◆ **Consider the nature and the impact of the disasters for which it is planning.** For this purpose, the team considers the worst-case scenario involving the destruction of the main facility as well as disasters that are specific to departments.

In addition to defining the scope for disaster recovery planning, the team identifies the resources required for the project. As the first step to this effect, the team finalizes the budget for the planning activity. The budget should include expenses that are likely to be incurred for activities such as the mitigation of disasters, the replacement of assets, and the recovery and resumption of activities. It is a good idea to revise the budget with every change to the project requirements.

After identifying the resources, as a member of the team, you garner support and resources from management. As mentioned earlier, management plays a vital role in the success of the planning process. Management is not only responsible for providing the required assistance and support to the planning team in the organization and its departments, but it also allocates funds for the planning, development, and implementation of the plan.

The creation of a schedule is also important for the project. Like the budget, the schedule also needs to be modified as and when the priorities of the planning process are modified.

The planning team identifies the resources available within the organization that can be utilized during a disaster. For instance, the team identifies all the personnel who have adequate knowledge of medical aid. In addition, the team members identify the organization's equipment that is available for fire protection and warnings. After identifying the internal resources, the team identifies the resources outside your organization that might be needed during a disaster. The team gathers information such as the name, contact person, and address of the external resource. The team members also identify the need for formal agreements to define the resources to be provided during a disaster. Some examples of external resources are the American Red Cross and the Fire Department.

Having performed the preplanning tasks, the risk analysis team identifies all the activities that the organization and its departments carry out. The risk analysis team also identifies the risks to an organization and their impact and occurrence. In addition, the team lists all the strategies that other organizations implement to mitigate these risks.

Risk Analysis

During risk analysis, the risk analysis team identifies the requirements for disaster recovery. For this purpose, the team analyzes the data gathered in the initiation phase. The team also identifies all the interdependencies between activities and departments. Following the analysis, the team obtains the list of prioritized activities, functions, resources, and risks on which the planning process should focus. The planning team then ensures that disaster recovery is directed toward the prevention or mitigation of the risks that are on a high priority.

 NOTE

Why is it important to prioritize activities, functions, and resources? An organization typically performs numerous activities and functions. In addition, many resources comprise an organization. Although it is possible to defer the recovery of some activities, functions, or resources to a later time, the same cannot be done for the others. In addition, planning for disaster recovery of all would not only be expensive, but it also would prove futile.

Based on the assigned priority, you identify the recovery strategies and the resources required to recover from the disasters within acceptable time frames. As the next step, the risk analysis team identifies the current standing of the organization with respect to the identified risks. The team lists all the measures that are commensurate with the requirements identified earlier. Consequently, the team sets baseline measures for the security of the organization to improve the existing disaster prevention measures of the organization. These measures are implemented to prevent disasters that can be avoided. For instance, the team can recommend implementation of an *Uninterruptible Power Supply* (UPS) to prevent power outages. In addition, the team can identify the alternative facilities for use in the event of a disaster.

As a result of this phase, the planning team prioritizes disaster recovery planning.

Creation and Implementation of the Plan

In the next phase, the planning team creates the disaster recovery plan. This plan documents all the procedures necessary for effective and timely recovery of the organization if a disaster occurs. The planning team formulates all the strategies required to replace critical application hosts, which can be centralized as well as distributed, after a disaster. This phase also involves the creation and assignment of roles and responsibilities to recovery teams. You will learn about the recovery team in the later section titled "Recovery Team."

Key personnel of the organization, such as the CEO and senior management, review and approve all the decisions that the planning team makes. After the plan is approved, the recovery team incorporates the plan into the business operations of the organization. Therefore, this phase also includes imparting training to the required personnel to execute the processes for service resumption.

After the planning team creates the plan, the recovery team tests it to ensure that if a disaster occurs, recovery will be efficient and speedy.

Testing of the Plan

During the testing phase, the recovery team evaluates the procedures that are documented in the disaster recovery plan for effectiveness and appropriateness. This phase helps identify and correct the weaknesses in the plan while examining the completeness and timing of the plan. In addition to testing the scenarios that contribute to a disaster, the team must test the applicability of the disaster recovery plan to the worst-case scenario: the entire facility being destroyed.

In this phase, the team also assesses the ability of the organization to implement the disaster recovery plan. The team develops a test program to evaluate and monitor the plan and then establishes the test goals and a testing strategy. Next, the team creates a test procedure to test the disaster recovery plan.

The team must regularly update the testing plan to ensure that evaluation of the disaster recovery plan adds value and helps to keep it live and applicable to the current scenario. This task constitutes the maintenance of the plan.

Maintenance of the Plan

In this phase, the recovery team performs the maintenance of the disaster recovery plan as an ongoing process. After the team tests the disaster recovery plan, it should incorporate the suggested improvements into the plan based on the analysis of the results of testing. Changes in the organizational environment should be reflected in the plan. Modify the existing change management procedures to conform to the disaster recovery plan. If these procedures are unavailable, create them.

To ensure regular maintenance of the disaster recovery plan, seek assistance from the employees of various departments of the organization.

You will look at each of these phases in detail in the later chapters of this book. Different teams perform these phases. These teams form part of the organizational structure that is involved in disaster recovery planning.

Organizational Planning Structure

As discussed earlier, it is essential to follow a planning structure to develop, implement, and manage disaster recovery plans. This structure is multilevel and includes the following:

- ◆ Planning team
- ◆ Recovery team

A coordinator leads each team in the planning structure. In the subsequent sections, you will learn about the role of these teams and the responsibilities of individuals with respect to disaster recovery planning.

 NOTE

The roles and responsibilities discussed here are recommendations. Organizations can customize these roles and responsibilities to align with their business needs. The members of these teams might be the employees of the organization or external specialists.

Planning Team

The planning team is formulated to define strategies to develop a disaster recovery plan for the organization. The planning team decides and approves the procedures that are performed for recovery during and after a disaster. In addition, this team approves all the unplanned activities, such as hiring a site to temporarily relocate employees. This team also ensures that the plan caters and adheres to the business and service goals of the organization.

To ensure the plan's adherence to the organization's goals, the planning team is composed of individuals who have a vast knowledge of the organization. In addition, the team includes individuals who perform the critical activities and represent the various support groups of the organization. The planning team also comprises key individuals from the various departments of the organization. The groups of individuals who represent the departments of an organization within the planning team are known as *functional teams.*

A separate functional team represents each department in the organization. It is vital to ensure representation in the planning team from all the departments—such as finance, security, and telecommunications—that are likely to be affected by disasters. This ensures that the input and needs of all the departments are incorporated into the disaster recovery plan.

You can include the representatives from community services who need to be integrated into the disaster recovery plan, such as firefighters and police officers. You also can ensure the success of the planning process by involving users and senior personnel in the development, implementation, and maintenance of the plan.

 NOTE

You can consider the participation and input from the users of the services and products of an organization in the planning process. The input from users is likely to provide you with valuable information based on the role and perspective of the users to the services and products. Consequently, you can obtain invaluable information about the various aspects of a disaster, such as impact and duration.

A planning coordinator is identified to lead the planning team. The responsibilities of the planning coordinator include these:

- ◆ Convincing the decision makers about recovery-related procedures
- ◆ Coordinating the disaster response and recovery activities
- ◆ Assessing the disaster situation and authorizing the activation of disaster response activities

◆ Handling the communication between the planning team and senior management

◆ Assigning responsibilities to the members of the planning team

Key personnel of the organization, such as the CEO and senior management, review and approve all the decisions that the planning team makes. After approval, the recovery team implements the plan in the organization.

Recovery Team

The recovery team performs the activities related to the recovery and restoration of critical activities, functions, and resources during and after a disaster. Following the occurrence of a disaster, the recovery team implements the disaster recovery plan. Subsequently, the team tests and maintains the plan. Teams divide work among themselves, and different teams perform different functions. Following a team approach facilitates smooth and fast disaster recovery. Following are some examples of disaster recovery teams:

◆ Damage Assessment team

◆ Departmental Recovery team

◆ Off-Site Storage team

◆ Public Relations team

◆ Logistics Support team

One or more disaster response coordinators lead the recovery team. The disaster response coordinators assess and notify the planning team of the damage that the disaster caused and accordingly decide the recovery steps to implement. In addition, the coordinators report the status of the disaster recovery to the planning coordinator.

Typically, a group of individuals (subject to change based on circumstances and the availability of resources) performs the activities of a recovery team. Therefore, it is advisable not to associate individuals with specific tasks. You must simply identify the skills and requirements needed to perform the recovery activities.

Now that you know about the functions and the role that each team plays in disaster recovery planning, you will learn about common concepts and terminology related to disaster recovery.

Recovery Objectives

Because disaster recovery planning is a complex process, it uses certain terms to define important concepts. These recovery objectives are used to make decisions related to the recovery of critical activities, functions, or resources. Following are the most commonly used recovery objectives in the industry:

- ◆ **Recovery Point Objective (RPO).** RPO refers to the point in time to which data must be recovered.
- ◆ **Recovery Time Objective (RTO).** RTO refers to the acceptable time period within which the business functions should be restored and made available to ensure normal functioning of the organization.

The RPO and RTO values collectively help you to specify how current the data should be and estimate the time frame within which a disrupted activity or resource should be restored. Consider Figure 1.1. The figure denotes the disruption of a resource, Web server, and a service, e-commerce, of an organization. The scale in the figure represents time periods. From the figure, you can see that although the RPO for the Web server can range from days to weeks, the RTO cannot be more than a few seconds. Similarly, if the disruption of e-commerce is prolonged beyond a few seconds, the organization will suffer considerable financial loss.

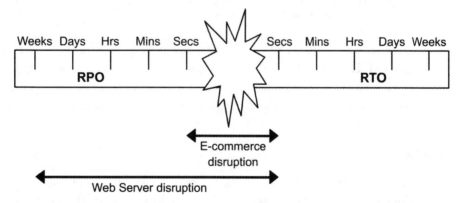

FIGURE 1.1   *RPO and RTO for Web server and e-commerce disruption.*

The values for RPO and RTO are decided in consultation with the management. You will learn about these concepts in the subsequent sections.

RPO

RPO helps you resume business operations from—or close to—the point of interruption. Simply stated, the data restored should not be older than the RPO value. A low RPO is relevant for an organization in which operations rely on the high accuracy of data. The prolonged unavailability of data indicates increasing losses to the organization, as displayed in Figure 1.2.

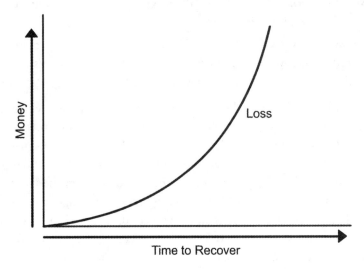

FIGURE 1.2 *Graph displaying increasing loss due to prolonged unavailability of a critical activity or resource.*

In other words, for an RPO value of 1 day, the acceptable state of data is one day old. However, the loss of data beyond one day negatively impacts the organization. The organization, therefore, implements measures to restore data to meet its RPO value through disaster recovery planning.

RTO

RTO helps you define the acceptable time to restore the critical activities, functions, or resources of an organization to ensure that the normal business operations of an organization are unaffected. In other words, if the time taken to restore a resource is beyond its RTO value, it adversely impacts the organization.

A low RTO is relevant for organizations that are dependent on short recovery time periods for business operations and demand their high continuity.

For instance, it is essential for an e-business organization to restore its e-commerce Web site in the shortest possible time. Therefore, in this case, the RTO will range between seconds and minutes.

It is important to ensure that the RTO value is realistic and based on the worst-case scenario. In addition, a longer RTO for an activity or resource indicates reduced costs of its recovery. This is displayed in Figure 1.3.

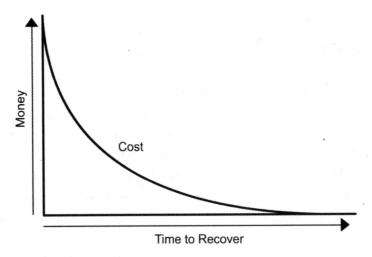

FIGURE 1.3 *Graph displaying the cost of recovery.*

Summary

In this chapter, you learned that to achieve disaster recovery, you must create a detailed plan of action to perform before, during, and after a disaster. This plan is known as a disaster recovery plan. The process by which you create a disaster recovery plan is called disaster recovery planning.

You learned about the need and benefits of disaster recovery planning. Disaster recovery planning employs three strategies: preventive, anticipatory, and mitigatory. You must bear in mind certain considerations while planning for disaster recovery. The process of disaster recovery planning follows a phased approach that makes it a systematic process. The following are phases of disaster recovery planning:

◆ Initiation
◆ Risk analysis

◆ Creation and implementation of the plan

◆ Testing of the plan

◆ Maintenance of the plan

You also learned about the organizational planning structure to create and implement disaster recovery plans. Finally, you learned about the recovery objectives commonly used in the industry.

Check Your Understanding

Multiple Choice Questions

1. Two organizations in the state of Texas are contemplating the implementation of disaster recovery planning. Identify the correct statements about the need for disaster recovery planning.

    a. The organizations seek to reduce the losses caused by disasters.

    b. An organization is legally bound to maintain critical information.

    c. An organization is bound by SLA to supply products and services to its customers.

    d. An organization needs to identify the minimum configuration of resources required to sustain its business operations.

2. Which of the following is the correct definition of RTO?

    a. It's the maximum time period before which the unavailability of a critical resource has disastrous consequences for an organization.

    b. It's the time period for which an organization can manage without a resource.

    c. It's the time period for which strategies to replace critical application hosts must be implemented.

    d. It's the point in time to which data must be restored to resume vital business operations.

3. Identify the statement that correctly defines the strategy of implementing disaster recovery planning.

    a. The strategy should be preventive to minimize the probability of a deliberate attack.

    b. The strategy should be mitigatory to prevent disasters from occurring.

    c. The strategy should be deterrent to detect the occurrence of disasters.

    d. The strategy should be anticipatory to identify procedures to recover from and respond to disasters.

4. Identify the statements that correctly define the activities performed in the initiation phase of disaster recovery planning.

    a. Define the assumptions for the planning project.

    b. Impart training to key personnel to execute the processes for business resumption.

    c. Identify the baseline measures for the security of an organization.

    d. Identify the resources external to an organization that can be required during a disaster.

Short Questions

1. Mucarz, Inc. has decided to implement disaster recovery planning. For this purpose, a planning team has been created. List the role of the planning team.

2. List the strategies followed to implement disaster recovery planning.

Answers

Multiple Choice Answers

1. a., b., and c. The two organizations need to implement disaster recovery planning to minimize the losses caused by disasters. In addition, if an organization is legally bound to maintain critical information and supply products and services to its customers, it needs to implement disaster recovery planning.

2. a. RTO is defined as the maximum time period before which the unavailability of a critical resource has disastrous consequences for an organization.

3. d. In the anticipatory strategy, you identify procedures to recover from and respond to disasters.

4. a. and d. During the initiation phase of disaster recovery planning, you define the assumptions for the disaster recovery planning project. In addition to defining the assumptions, you identify the resources that can be used during a disaster but are located outside an organization.

Short Answers

1. The main purpose of the planning team is to create the disaster recovery plan. The team ensures that the disaster recovery plan caters and adheres to the business and services goals of the organization. The planning team is led and coordinated by a planning coordinator. In the initiation phase, the team decides the goals and objectives of the planning process. The team also defines the assumptions and scope for the planning project and identifies the resources required for the project. In addition, the team gathers the support of management for the planning project. All the available resources that can be utilized during a disaster are identified within and external to an organization.

    The planning team identifies the resources for which disaster recovery needs to be planned and the measures required to prevent or mitigate the impact of the disasters.

2. The three strategies for implementing disaster recovery are as follows:

    ◆ **Preventive.** The preventive strategy aims at preventing the occurrence of disasters. To achieve this, you ensure that the activities and systems on which the existence of an organization is dependent are secure and reliable.

    ◆ **Anticipatory.** In the anticipatory phase, you predict the scenarios that are likely to result in a disaster, their likelihood of occurrence, and their impact. In addition, you identify the procedures to respond to and recover from disasters.

    ◆ **Mitigatory.** In the mitigatory strategy, you implement measures to minimize the impact of a disaster.

Chapter 2

What Constitutes a Disaster?

Susan will never forget the cold and windy December evening in 2001. Her family had gathered for dinner when the county sheriff called to inform her that the department store she owned had been destroyed in a fire. The fire had been caused by a short circuit in the neighboring shop and had engulfed all the shops in the area. Susan was now faced with the daunting task of rebuilding the business from scratch. Although the insurance would cover the costs of rebuilding, the loss of business transaction details would impact her business seriously.

Susan is a victim of a disaster. This chapter introduces you to the various types of disasters, their causes, and their repercussions.

What Is a Disaster?

Susan's tragedy is not an isolated case. Every year, entrepreneurs and businesses the world over suffer heavy losses due to disasters. The *Disaster Recovery Journal* defines a disaster as "any event that creates an inability on an organization's part to provide critical business functions for some predetermined period of time." Business interruption, outage, and catastrophe are some of the synonyms for this term.

Susan was back in business in less than a month. It was not merely the insurance that helped her put her business back on the rails, but a practice that she had adhered to for many years. Susan used to back up the daily transactions on a rewritable CD and take it home with her. In this way, she had a copy of all business transactions at a location far from the department store. Susan had merely implemented a simple disaster recovery plan (DRP) that saved her the pain of starting from scratch.

Computers have changed the face of business. With the emergence of e-commerce, businesses have begun to cater to a wide variety of people spread over large geographical distances. It is, therefore, necessary for a company to be up and running all the time. One of the biggest causes of loss in this scenario is computer downtime. In the event of a node failure, companies must plan for keeping the business functional and recovering the failed node. The former is known as *business continuity planning* and the latter is known as *disaster recovery*. This book concentrates on disaster recovery in the IT scenario.

Disaster recovery planning is not a new phenomenon and is fast becoming a specialized science. Companies are spending millions of dollars to develop disaster recovery plans. When planning for disaster recovery, you need to identify the continuity elements that any business depends on for its critical operations. These continuity elements are as follows:

- ◆ **Data.** Every organization maintains confidential information that can be stored as data in databases or servers. Such data comprises data assets. Based on the type of information that is stored, data assets are classified as follows:

  - ◆ **Financial.** This includes budget reports, balance sheets, and shareholder information.

  - ◆ **Logistics.** This includes information about hardware, equipment, supplies, and personnel.

  - ◆ **Operations.** These are processes and applications that relate to various departments, such as payroll that maintains employee details.

  - ◆ **Strategic.** These are long-term plans for various business units.

    It is vital to ensure appropriate security of data assets because the employees of the organization can readily access and alter them. Intruders also can alter the data by hacking the databases that are meant only for organizational use. For instance, intruders can hack into and misuse confidential information about an organization's financial operations.

- ◆ **Hardware and software.** Hardware assets include computers, storage media, and a network interface, such as router, cables, and I/O devices. Hardware assets are prone to physical damage and theft. They are indispensable to the resumption of computer-based activities. For instance, system failure and the accompanying loss of data can be a source of disaster for hardware assets. In addition, hardware assets can be subject to threats, such as power failure, denial of service attacks, and hacking. Software assets include the operating systems, system software, applications, development tools, and utilities that an organization uses. These assets are prone to threats, such as piracy, theft, unauthorized modification, and virus infection.

◆ **Buildings.** The building or the facility where employees work forms the physical assets of an organization. Besides the building, the utilities and supplies—such as power, water, and furnishings—are categorized as physical assets. This category of assets is classified into two subcategories:

  ◆ **Communication links.** This subcategory consists of all the equipment required to communicate within and outside the organization. The equipment that is required for organizations to communicate includes telephones, fax machines, and computers that are equipped with Internet access.

  ◆ **Support services.** All services, such as water and electricity, that the employees of an organization require to work make up the support services. All IT-dependent activities require an uninterruptible power supply (UPS).

◆ **Personnel.** The employees of an organization make up the personnel assets. Skilled personnel form the backbone of any organizational activity. It is impossible, for example, to replace a network administrator with a data entry operator.

◆ **Documentation.** All the organizational policies and procedures, licenses and contracts, program code, and manuals form the documentation assets of an organization. The documentation of an organization might be available on paper or in electronic form. These must not only be protected from physical damage, such as fire and theft, but also unauthorized use. Loss of documentation, such as contracts, can cause immense damage to an organization. In addition, disclosing documentation that is confidential to an organization can result in direct losses to the organization or to its reputation.

Causes of Disasters

Disasters can be categorized as natural and manmade. In this section, you will look at the causes of the two types of disasters.

Natural Disasters

Disasters that are caused by extreme weather and geological conditions are known as *natural disasters*. The common natural disasters are as follows:

◆ Floods

◆ Hurricanes

◆ Tornadoes

◆ Earthquakes

◆ Volcanoes

◆ Wildland fires

◆ Thunderstorms and lightning

Floods

Floods are common and widespread natural disasters. They are generally caused by seasonal events such as rains, thunderstorms, and winter snow thaws. Floods caused by seasonal events are slow rising and can be predicted by weather satellites. However, floods are not always slow rising. Flash floods, caused by intense storms, can occur within minutes.

Floods can also be caused by accidents such as dam failures. Floods caused by dam failures have disastrous consequences. When a dam fails, the water from the reservoir flows at a high velocity, destroying everything in its path. The time available for evacuating the victims is short, so expediency is essential.

Table 2.1 lists 10 states in the U.S. that have incurred the highest losses over a period of five years due to floods.

 NOTE

The data depicted in the tables and graphics in this chapter has been referenced from the sites http://www.fema.org/ and http://www.storagetek.com/.

Table 2.1   Losses Caused by Floods

State	Losses Per Year (in Millions of USD)
Pennsylvania	$682.3
California	$521.8
Louisiana	$320.5
Iowa	$312.9
Texas	$276.9
Missouri	$272.2
Connecticut	$219.4
Illinois	$218.7
New York	$218.2
Colorado	$198.9

Figure 2.1 shows the damage caused by floods in the U.S. over the past 45 years.

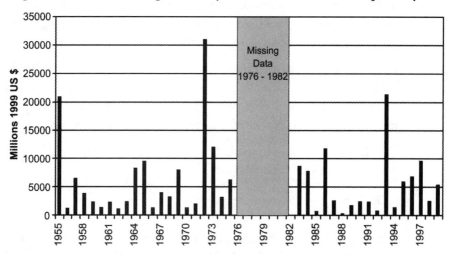

FIGURE 2.1   *Damages due to floods in the U.S. over the past 45 years.*

Hurricanes

Hurricanes are tropical storms with wind speeds in excess of 80kph. The characteristic feature of a hurricane is the "eye"—an area of relative calm around which the storm winds blow. The diameter of an average storm is 400 miles, whereas the eye might have a diameter of about 25 miles. A hurricane can extend inland for hundreds of miles, creating tornadoes, storm surges, and torrential rains, which add to its destructiveness. A storm surge is a dome of ocean water that can be 20 feet at its peak and 50–100 miles wide. The surge can devastate coastal communities as it sweeps ashore. Torrential rains cause floods and flash floods. Following a hurricane, inland streams and rivers can flood and trigger landslides. The hurricane season in America falls between June and November, with August and September being the peak months.

The areas vulnerable to hurricanes include the Atlantic and the Gulf from Texas to Maine; territories in the Caribbean; and tropical areas of the western Pacific, including Hawaii, Guam, American Samoa, and Saipan coasts. Table 2.2 lists 10 states that have incurred the highest losses in the U.S. over a period of five years due to hurricanes.

Table 2-2   Losses Caused by Hurricanes

State	Total Normalized Damage (Millions USD)
Florida	$238,900
Texas	$100,500
North Carolina	$34,200
Louisiana	$33,850
New York	$18,460
South Carolina	$17,400
Mississippi	$16,500
Connecticut	$16,430
Alabama	$12,400
Rhode Island	$10,330

Table 2.3 lists the 10 most damaging hurricanes in the past century.

Table 2.3 The 10 Most Damaging Hurricanes in the Past Century

Rank	Hurricane	Year	Damage (in Millions USD)
1	SE Florida/Alabama	1926	$87,170
2	Andrew (SE FL/LA)	1992	$39,900
3	N Texas (Galveston)	1900	$32,090
4	N Texas (Galveston)	1915	$27,190
5	SW Florida	1944	$20,330
6	New England	1938	$20,050
7	SE Florida/Lake Okeechobee	1928	$16,630
8	Betsy (SE FL/LA)	1965	$14,990
9	Donna (FL/Eastern US.)	1960	$14,530
10	Camille (MS/LA/VA)	1969	$13,220

Figure 2.2 shows the damage caused by hurricanes in the U.S. from 1900–1999.

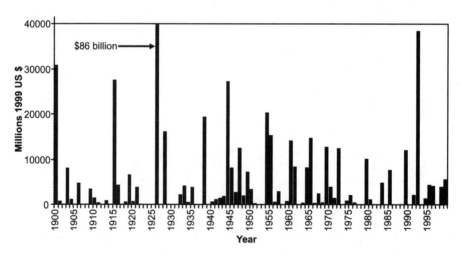

FIGURE 2.2 *Damages caused by hurricanes in the U.S. from 1900–1999.*

Tornadoes

A tornado is a violent windstorm with wind speeds of about 300 miles per hour. Tornadoes carry objects over a large area. The swirling winds turn these objects into missiles. A tornado is characterized by a twisting, funnel-shaped cloud that reaches heights greater than 60,000 feet above the ground and travels distances of more than 100 miles. Tornadoes are produced when cool air overrides a layer of warm air, forcing the warm air to rise rapidly. A tornado is often spawned by a thunderstorm (or sometimes as a result of a hurricane). The damage from a tornado is a result of the high wind velocity and wind-blown debris. Tornado season is generally from March–August, although tornadoes can occur at any time of year. They tend to occur primarily in the afternoons and evenings.

The intensity of a tornado is expressed on the Fujita–Pearson Tornado Scale. Figure 2.3 shows this scale.

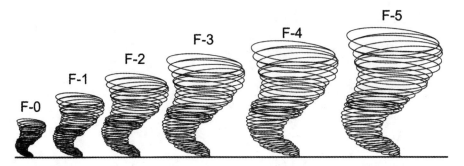

FIGURE 2.3   *Fujita–Pearson tornado scale.*

Table 2.4 lists the various categories of tornadoes and their descriptions.

Table 2.4   Categories of Tornadoes

Category	Speed	Description
F-0	40–72 mph	Chimney damage; tree branches broken
F-1	73–112 mph	Mobile homes pushed off foundation or overturned
F-2	113–157 mph	Considerable damage; mobile homes demolished; trees uprooted
F-3	158–205 mph	Roofs and walls torn down; trains overturned; cars thrown
F-4	207–260 mph	Well-constructed walls leveled
F-5	261–318 mph	Homes lifted off foundation and carried considerable distances; autos thrown as far as 100 meters

On an average, the U.S. experiences 100,000 thunderstorms each year. Approximately 1,000 tornadoes develop from these storms. The areas that are most vulnerable to tornadoes are the Midwest, Southeast, and Southwest. The states of Alabama, Arkansas, Florida, Georgia, Illinois, Indiana, Iowa, Kansas, Louisiana, Mississippi, Missouri, Nebraska, Oklahoma, South Dakota, and Texas are at the greatest risk. Table 2.5 lists the losses caused by tornadoes from 1950–1999.

Table 2.5   Losses Caused by Tornadoes from 1950–1999

State	Av/Yr (Millions of 1999 USD)
Texas	$88.60
Minnesota	$84.84
Oklahoma	$81.94
Missouri	$68.93
Illinois	$62.94
Indiana	$53.13
Alabama	$51.88
Georgia	$51.68
Iowa	$49.51
Kansas	$49.28

Figure 2.4 shows the losses caused from tornadoes from 1950–1999.

Earthquakes

An earthquake is caused by a rapid shifting of rock plates on either side of a fault beneath the earth's surface. This shifting generates an enormous amount of energy. The energy produces seismic waves that radiate outward in all directions from the initial point of rupture and cause the ground to shake at the earth's surface. This shaking can cause buildings and bridges to collapse; disrupt gas, electric, and phone service; and sometimes trigger landslides, avalanches, flash floods, fires, and huge, destructive tidal waves (tsunamis). The area over which these seismic waves propagate depends on

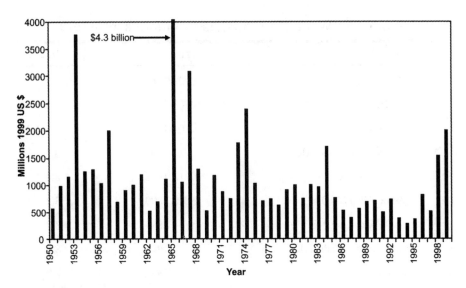

FIGURE 2.4   *Tornado property damage from 1950–1999.*

the amount of total energy released and the characteristics of the underlying rocks in the region. Geologically young rocks dampen wave propagation. California is such a region. Geologically older rocks, in contrast, are harder and propagate seismic waves over a longer distance. The New Madrid Seismic Zone (NMSZ) is one such region in the U.S. Although the most severely damaged areas are usually confined to relatively short distances from the fault, the total area impacted is significantly higher in the case of the NMSZ than in the western U.S. Buildings that have foundations resting on unconsolidated landfill, old waterways, or other unstable soil are at the greatest risk. Buildings, trailers, and manufactured homes that are not tied to a reinforced foundation anchored to the ground are also at risk because they can be shaken off from their mountings during an earthquake. Earthquakes can occur at any time of the year.

Areas west of the Rocky Mountains are most vulnerable to earthquakes, although historically, the most violent earthquakes have occurred in the central U.S.

Table 2.6 shows the 20 worst earthquakes in America's history.

Table 2.6 Worst Earthquakes in America's History

Location	Date	Intensity
Prince William Sound (AK)	03/28/1964	9.2
Andreanof Islands (AK)	03/09/1957	8.8
Rat Islands (AK)	02/04/1965	8.7
Shumagin Islands (AK)	11/10/1938	8.3
Lituya Bay (AK)	07/10/1958	8.3
Yakutat Bay (AK)	09/10/1899	8.2
Cape Yakataga (AK)	09/04/1899	8.2
Andreanof Islands (AK)	05/07/1986	8.0
Fort Tejon (CA)	01/09/1857	7.9
Ka'u District (HI)	04/03/1868	7.9
Kodiak Island (AK)	10/09/1900	7.9
Gulf of Alaska (AK)	11/30/1987	7.9
Owens Valley (CA)	03/26/1872	7.8
Imperial Valley (CA)	02/24/1892	7.8
San Francisco (CA)	04/18/1906	7.7
Pleasant Valley (TX)	10/03/1915	7.7
Kern County (CA)	07/21/1952	7.5
Lompoc (CA)	11/04/1927	7.3
Dixie Valley (NV)	12/16/1954	7.3
Hebgen Lake (MT)	08/18/1959	7.3

Volcanoes

Volcanoes are sudden or continuous releases of energy. The energy release can occur in the form of earthquakes, gas-emissions at the surface, release of heat, explosive release of gases, and the nonexplosive extrusion of magma. An event could be destructive without the release of solids or magmatic fluid, or it could be destructive with voluminous lava flows or explosive activities. Volcanic activity is caused from the intense heat built up inside the earth. Volcanic eruptions can spawn earthquakes, flash floods, landslides, mudflows, thunderstorms, and tsunamis. Another feature of volcanic eruptions is a lateral blast. A lateral blast is a volcanic explosion directed sideways. A lateral blast can shoot large pieces of rock at high speeds for several miles. These explosions can kill by impact, burial, or heat. They have been known to flatten entire forests. The majority of deaths attributed to the Mount St. Helen's volcano were a result of lateral blasts.

Pacific Rim states of Hawaii, Alaska, Washington, Oregon, and California are most vulnerable to volcanic eruptions. Active volcanoes of the Cascade Mountain Range in California, Oregon, and Washington have erupted recently.

Wildland Fires

Wildland fires are a common phenomenon during hot summer months in wildland areas. These fires are often caused by overheating of the dry vegetation. Nevertheless, careless human beings also have caused fires. These fires are of three kinds:

- ◆ Surface fire
- ◆ Ground fire
- ◆ Crown fire

Surface fires are the most common. They move slowly along the forest floor killing or damaging trees. Ground fires burn on the forest floor. These fires are often caused by lightning. Crown fires, as the name implies, burn the tops of the trees. They are spread by winds.

Although the impact of forest fires on industrial establishments has been minimal, fire's impact on the animal and human population has been extremely damaging. Wildland fires cause wide-scale pollution and kill many animals and birds. The animals that are driven from the forests during such fires become a menace to the local human population; the larger animals like tigers kill cattle and humans, and the other animals like snakes enter people's houses. These fires destroy the ground cover and leave the ground barren. The areas might not return to prefire conditions for decades, and erosion becomes one of several potential problems. Heavy rains following the fires can cause landslides, mudflows, and floods because ground cover isn't available to hold soil in place on steep slopes and hillsides.

All wooded, brush, and grassy areas—especially those in Kansas, Mississippi, Louisiana, Georgia, Florida, the Carolinas, Tennessee, California, Massachusetts, and the national forests of the western U.S.—are vulnerable to wildland fires.

Table 2.7 lists some of the worst wildland fires in recent times in the U.S.

Table 2.7   Recent Wildland Fires

Year	Location	Losses
1988	Yellowstone National Park (WY, MT, ID)	No records of financial damage
1990	Santa Barbara County (CA)	$200 million
1991	Oakland (CA)	$1.5 billion

Manmade Disasters

Manmade disasters, or technological disasters, are a result of human failure. We can categorize the causes of these disasters as follows:

- Hazardous materials
- House and building fires
- Nuclear power plant emergency
- Terrorism

Hazardous Materials

Hazardous materials are substances that can cause damage to life and property when misused. Poisons and petroleum products are common examples of hazardous materials. Accidents due to hazardous materials can occur anywhere. Communities who live near chemical plants or on the transportation routes of these materials are the most vulnerable to accidents caused by these materials. Many hazardous materials, such as fuel, liquid cleaners, and pesticides products containing hazardous chemicals, are used and stored in homes routinely. The improper use of these substances can cause death, serious injury, long-lasting health effects, and damage to buildings, homes, and other property.

Table 2.8 lists the number of accidents involving the transportation of hazardous chemicals from 1983–1990.

Table 2.8 Number of Accidents Involving Transportation of Hazardous Chemicals from 1983–1990

Mode of Transportation	Number of Accidents	Associated Deaths	Associated Injuries
Air	1,220	0	153
Highway	41,781	79	1,569
Railway	7,886	1	423
Water	83	1	35
Other	29	0	2
Total	50,999	81	2,182

House and Building Fires

Fires are among the worst technological disasters because they can engulf a structure in a matter of minutes and also create several other disasters, such as chemical accidents and explosions. According to the U.S. Fire Administration, fires kill more people than hurricanes, earthquakes, floods, and all other natural disasters combined. Fires can be caused by various sources. Figure 2.5 shows the various causes of building/house fires in the U.S.

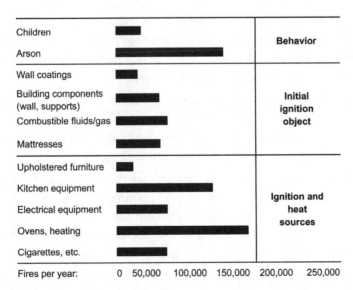

FIGURE 2.5 *Causes of building/house fires in the U.S.*

Nuclear Power Plant Emergency

Nuclear disasters are rare, but the few that have occurred have had disastrous consequences. In the U.S., the Nuclear Regulatory Commission (NRC) closely monitors the construction and operation of nuclear plants. Despite stringent regulations, the possibility of a nuclear disaster cannot be overlooked.

The typical threat posed by nuclear plants is radiation leakage. Exposure to leaked radiation could come from the release of radioactive material from the plant into the environment, usually characterized by a plume formation. The area that is affected by the leakage is determined by the amount of radiation released from the plant, wind direction, and speed and weather conditions, which would quickly drive the radioactive material to the ground.

All of us are exposed to a normal level of radiation every day. The common sources of radiation are the sun, radioactive elements in the soil and rocks, household appliances, such as television sets and microwave ovens, and medical and dental x-rays. Even the human body emits radiation. Radiation exposure is expressed in rem. An average American receives 360 millirems of radiation each year—300 from natural sources and 60 from manmade activities. Radiation can be detected and measured with sophisticated instruments, the most common of which is the Geiger counter.

An emergency in a nuclear plant can be classified at one of four levels:

◆ **Notification of unusual event.** This is the least serious of the four levels. Events that fall under this category typically pose no threat to the plant or the employees. Nevertheless, emergency officials are notified. Such events do not affect the public.

◆ **Alert.** An alert is declared when an event that can reduce the plant's level of safety occurs. Such events do not affect the working of the backup plant systems. Although emergency agencies are notified and kept informed, these events do not affect the public.

◆ **Site area emergency.** Malfunctioning of the plant's safety systems might cause radiation leakage. A site area emergency is declared when this leakage is not expected to exceed Environmental Protection Agency (EPA) Protective Action Guidelines (PAGs) beyond the site boundary. Thus, no action by the public is necessary.

◆ **General emergency.** A general emergency is the most serious of the four classifications. It is declared when safety systems collapse and radiations are released beyond the site boundary. During a general emergency, people in the affected areas could be advised to evacuate promptly or, in some situations, to seek refuge in a shelter.

Terrorism

Terrorism has been a major challenge to law enforcement agencies throughout the world. The Federal Bureau of Investigation (FBI) categorizes terrorism in the U.S. as one of two types:

◆ Domestic terrorism
◆ International terrorism

Domestic terrorism involves groups or individuals whose terrorist activities are directed at the elements of the local government or population without foreign direction.

International terrorism, as the name implies, involves groups or individuals whose terrorist activities are foreign-based or directed by countries or groups outside the U.S. or whose activities transcend national boundaries.

Figure 2.6 shows the number of casualties over the years due to terrorism.

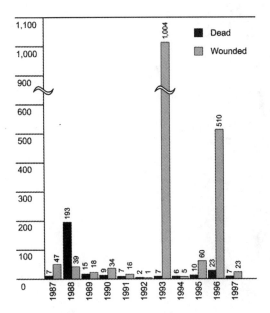

FIGURE 2.6 *Number of casualties due to terrorism from 1987–1997.*

Disasters and Their Consequences

The term disaster is a relative one, but the consequences are similar. Disasters lead to outage and downtime, which leads to losses in revenue. The following pie charts show two dimensions of the same problem—downtime. Figure 2.7 compares the cost of an hour of downtime for different companies.

Figure 2.8 shows the maximum downtime that a company can survive.

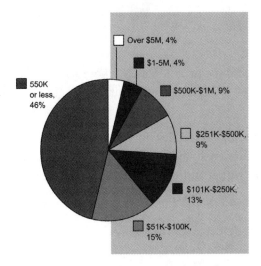

FIGURE 2.7   *Cost of an hour of downtime.*

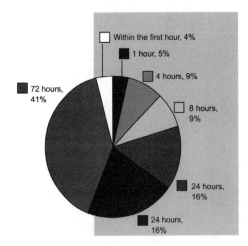

FIGURE 2.8   *Maximum downtime that a company can survive.*

Figure 2.9 shows the leading causes of computer downtime for more than 12 hours.

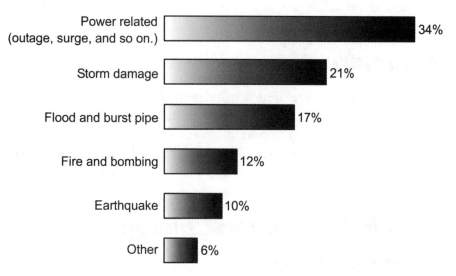

FIGURE 2.9 *Leading causes of computer downtime.*

One of the worst disasters of this century was the World Trade Center (WTC) terrorist attack on September 11, 2001. This attack reduced the twin towers of the WTC to rubble, killing hundreds, and destroying millions of dollars' worth of office space and equipment.

Losses incurred during the WTC disaster can be attributed to the following sources:

- ◆ Fire
- ◆ Massive projectile debris
- ◆ Airborne debris
- ◆ Pressure wave
- ◆ Vibration and ground deformation

The National Association of Insurance Commissioners estimated the losses to reach or even surpass $20 billion. On the other hand, Munich Reinsurance, Swiss Reinsurance, and Berkshire-Hathaway pegged the figure between $44–73 billion.

Trading firms lost an estimated $1.7 billion worth of computer hardware and $1.5 billion software. Approximately 50,000 computers were destroyed.

Professionals and research analysts used these computers. The insurance claims could even surpass the costs of Hurricane Andrew in 1992, and U.S.-based insurers, as well as international providers, are expected to make the payments.

Summary

Although disaster recovery is still viewed as a discretionary expense, the market for disaster recovery services is expected to experience positive growth in the near future. At the current growth rates, this industry can generate in excess of $1 billion annually. This chapter provided an overview of what constitutes a disaster and explained the various types of disasters and their impacts.

Check Your Understanding

Short Questions

1. The data in the _____ category contains information about hardware, equipment, supplies, and personnel.

2. The data in the _____ category contains processes and applications that relate to various departments, such as payroll, which maintains employee details.

3. The plan to ensure that a company is up and running all the time is known as the _____.

4. The plan for keeping the business functional and recovering the failed operations is known as the _____.

5. Define disaster as defined in the *Disaster Recovery Journal*.

6. Briefly discuss the continuity elements of a business.

7. What are the types of disasters? List some of the causes of each type of disaster.

8. Briefly discuss the four emergency levels in a nuclear plant.

Answers

Short Answers

1. Logistics.
2. Operations.
3. Business continuity plan.
4. Disaster recovery plan.
5. A disaster is any event that creates an inability on an organization's part to provide critical business functions for a period.
6. The continuity elements are as follows:

   ◆ **Data.** Every organization maintains confidential information that can be stored in databases or servers. Such information comprises data assets. It is vital to ensure appropriate security of data assets because the employees of an organization can readily access and alter the data assets. Intruders can also alter the data by hacking database that are meant only for organizational use, such as the details of financial operations of an organization.

   ◆ **Hardware and software.** Hardware assets include computers, storage media, and a network interface, such as routers, cables, and I/O devices. Hardware assets are prone to physical damage and theft. They are indispensable to the resumption of computer-based activities. These assets can be subject to threats, such as power failure, denial of service (DoS) attacks, and hacking. Software assets include the operating systems, system software, applications, development tools, and utilities that an organization uses. These assets are prone to threats, such as piracy, theft, unauthorized modification, and virus attacks.

   ◆ **Buildings.** The building or the facility where employees work is the physical assets of an organization. Besides the building, the utilities and supplies, such as power, water, and furnishings, are also categorized as physical assets. This category of assets is classified into two subcategories: communication links and support services.

   ◆ **Personnel.** The employees of an organization compose the personnel assets of the organization. Skilled personnel form the backbone of any organizational activity.

◆ **Documentation.** All the organizational policies and procedures, licenses and contracts, program code, and manuals form the documentation asset of an organization. The documentation of an organization might be available on paper or in electronic form. You must protect this documentation not only from physical damage, such as fire and theft, but also from unauthorized use. Loss of documentation, such as contracts, can cause immense damage to an organization. In addition, disclosing documentation that is confidential to an organization can result in direct losses to the organization or to its reputation.

7. The two types of disasters are natural and manmade. Disasters that are caused by extreme weather and geological conditions are known as natural disasters. The common natural disasters are as follows:

◆ Floods

◆ Hurricanes

◆ Tornadoes

◆ Earthquakes

◆ Volcanoes

◆ Wildland fires

◆ Thunderstorms and lightning

Manmade disasters, or technological disasters, are a result of human failure. The causes of these disasters can be categorized as follows:

◆ Hazardous materials

◆ House and building fires

◆ Nuclear power plant emergency

◆ Terrorism

8. An emergency in a nuclear plant can be classified at one of four levels:

◆ **Notification of unusual event.** Events that fall under this category typically pose no threat to the plant or the employees. Nevertheless, emergency officials are notified. Such events do not affect the public.

◆ **Alert.** An alert is declared when an event that can reduce the plant's level of safety occurs. Such events do not affect the working of the backup plant systems. Although emergency agencies are notified and kept informed, these events do not affect the public.

◆ **Site area emergency.** Malfunctioning of the plant's safety systems might cause radiation leakage. A site area emergency is declared when this leakage is not expected to exceed Environmental Protection Agency (EPA) Protective Action Guidelines (PAGs) beyond the site boundary. Therefore, no action by the public is necessary.

◆ **General emergency.** A general emergency is the most serious of the four classifications. It is declared when safety systems collapse and radiation is released beyond the site boundary. During a general emergency, people in the affected areas could be advised to evacuate promptly or, in some situations, to seek refuge in a shelter.

Chapter 3

Categorizing Disasters

In Chapters 1, "Disaster Recovery Planning: An Overview," and 2, "What Constitutes a Disaster?," you learned about the different types of natural and manmade disasters, such as floods, volcanoes, and terrorism. These disasters can affect the essential elements—such as people, buildings, applications, data, and equipment—required to sustain critical business operations. This chapter categorizes the disasters depending on the severity and impact that they have on your business or IT operations. Organizations categorize disasters to prepare recovery plans and manage recovery activities during and after disaster events. The disaster type determines the risk reduction measures that an organization deploys to counter the threat of the disasters. In addition, knowledge about the disaster type helps organizations select appropriate recovery measures.

Disasters: Impact and Severity Level

It is possible to categorize disasters based on different factors, such as the financial loss that they cause, the time for which there is an outage of critical operations, or the time taken for recovery. Categorizing disasters helps you compare the severity of various disaster scenarios. In addition, after you know the potential severity of a disaster, you can plan for appropriate measures and devote the necessary resources to the process of disaster recovery.

The following is an example of a scheme that you can use to categorize disasters based on the severity of their impact:

- **Severity Level 1.** Severity Level 1 (SL1) disasters lead to outage of business operations for extended periods, such as 2–10 hours. Such disasters are the least severe disasters.

- **Severity Level 2.** Severity Level 2 (SL2) disasters are those that cause partial or complete loss of critical resources. An organization needs to determine its critical resources based on factors such as the business that it is in, the business operations that are vital for the organization, and the resources that are required to support these operations. For example, for a bank, treasury operations are essential; therefore, resources such as a communication link that support the treasury operations are a critical resource. The loss of a critical server during a fire in the server room can be classified as an SL2 disaster if the server hardware cannot be replaced within an acceptable time.

◆ **Severity Level 3.** The damage caused by Severity Level 3 (SL3) disasters extends beyond the confines of the organization. These disasters can affect an entire geography, such as a city or state, and are also known as city-level disasters. Natural disasters are categorized as SL3 disasters. Riots that disrupt a city are also SL3 disasters.

Note that different organizations can use different schemes to categorize disasters based on their needs. A disaster's speed of onset and timing of occurrence and the organization's level of preparedness are factors on which organizations can base a scheme for categorizing disasters.

Categorizing Disasters: Severity of Impact

Now that you have learned the criteria used to categorize different disasters based on the severity of their impact, it's time to look at real-world scenarios. Each of these scenarios depicts a specific disaster. You will learn how to identify the category to which the disaster belongs.

Some of the disaster scenarios that you will look at include hard disk subsystem failure, power crisis, and virus attack.

Hard Disk Subsystem Failure

Sam is the owner of a car rental store. He had installed a high-end computer in his office to store all business transactions. He noticed that the computer was making a clicking sound, and of late, the sound had grown more frequent. Sam ignored this sound because he thought it was due to the fan in the computer's cabinet.

One Monday morning, when Sam switched on his computer, he received a `Hard disk not accessible` message. Sam later learned that the boot disk had failed and as a result, the computer was unable to boot. Sam wasn't tech savvy, and it never occurred to him to save his data at an alternative location. A few frantic calls later, he was able to contact a data recovery specialist who charged him $500 to recover his data. The computer vendor was able to get Sam's computer up and running by the end of the day, and the data recovery expert was able to retrieve all the data the next day. Sam had the computer up and running in less than a week.

In this case, the disaster, namely hard disk subsystem failure, caused a downtime of one working day. Therefore, it can be categorized as an SL1 disaster. However, if the transaction data stored on the hard disk had been permanently lost, this disaster would be classified as SL2.

Not all businesspeople are as lucky as Sam. Every year, American businesses lose thousands of dollars due to failure of hard disk drives. Losses due to hard disk failure can be segregated into three components:

◆ Cost of employing technicians to repair the computer

◆ Loss of productivity due to downtime

◆ Losses associated with lost data

Disk drive failures can either be unpredictable or predictable. Unpredictable failures occur without warning and are generally caused by external sources, such as electronic and mechanical problems. A power surge can cause a chip or circuit failure. You can reduce unpredictable failures by improving the quality and design of hard disk drives.

Predictable failures, on the other hand, are often caused by internal sources. The typical cause of predictable failure is degradation of components over time. Certain other circuits that are built into the hard disk drive are capable of monitoring these components and predicting failures. Mechanical failures are the most easily predictable ones. Mechanical failures account for 60 to 70 percent of drive failures. Degradation of the flying height of the head indicates a potential head crash. The monitoring circuits can monitor this height and display an alarm before the height decreases below a safe level.

You can minimize data losses due to predictable failures by implementing reliability prediction technologies. The most prevalent reliability prediction technology is Self-Monitoring Analysis and Reporting Technology (S.M.A.R.T.). S.M.A.R.T., first developed by Compaq, is now being jointly enhanced by the top five disk drive manufacturers in the world: Seagate Technology, Inc.; IBM; Conner Peripherals, Inc.; Western Digital Corporation; and Quantum Corporation.

The most prevalent and damaging result of disk failure is data loss. The following are the chief causes of data loss:

- User error
- Software error
- Malicious damage

The hard disk subsystem is one of the most critical components of a computer.

Server Failure

On Monday morning, Rob, the network administrator at Presco, Inc., was hassled. The mail server was down and he felt like the whole world was yelling at him. All the external mail was blocked and no one was able to receive mail. Outgoing mail was stuck in the Outbox on the mail clients. Employees couldn't receive mail from any source. Inbound messages from clients and business partners started bouncing back to the originator, causing loss of both business and business opportunities. Rob was at his wit's end.

Rob was finally able to correct the problem at the end of the day, but communication was blocked for an entire working day. Because no critical resource was either partially or fully destroyed, this was an SL1 disaster.

Server failure, as the name implies, describes the malfunctioning of a server. In the client-server environment, the server plays a central role either as a repository of data or as a service provider. Mail servers and DNS servers are some of the critical nodes in a network. Some of the common causes of server failure are as follows:

- CPU or memory fault
- PCI adapter fault
- Hard-disk drive or controller fault
- LAN controller fault
- Power fault

A report on Intel's Web site pegs the cost of server downtime at more than $75,000 per year for less than 1 percent downtime. The report further states that every hour of downtime translates to $4,000 in losses. A report compiled by the Standish Group reveals that 41 percent of site outages, caused by server downtime, last between 9 hours and four days.

Power Crisis

Power crisis describes all the situations "when power fails you." Electrical power is the lifeblood of computer systems. Any malfunctioning of the power system can have disastrous effects on poorly protected systems.

Alan is the network administrator at a small software organization. He is also in charge of the maintenance of the facilities. Alan had always been proud of the setup and the way things moved. The company successfully survived many major power breakdowns without a single minute of downtime due to the excellent backup facilities. A week ago, a totally unexpected disaster struck. The systems in the company were struck by a major power surge. Alan had never anticipated a surge and had not planned for one. Not only did the developers lose data, but the servers containing important data were shut down. The code for several critical projects was lost or damaged.

Because the power failure disaster damaged and destroyed the organization's critical resources, this disaster can be classified as SL2. If the power failure had happened because of a natural disaster, such as a tornado or an earthquake, then the impact of the disaster would extend to the entire city, making it an SL3 disaster.

Many of us tend to think the way Alan did. We are familiar with power shortage and tend to plan for power shortages only. Power crisis can occur either due to excess or lack of electrical power. The various instances of power crisis are as follows:

- Spike
- Surge
- Sag
- Brownout
- Blackout

Spikes and surges are the two forms of dangerously high voltages. A spike is an extremely quick rise in supply voltage. Spikes typically last for a few seconds. A surge, on the other hand, is a rise of the voltage level that is long lasting. Spikes and surges are caused by the starting and stopping of compressors and electric motors. Spikes are more dangerous than surges because they have higher voltage levels.

Sags, brownouts, and blackouts are the three forms of power shortage. A sag, as the name implies, is a fall in voltage level. It lasts for a few seconds or even less. A brownout is a longer version of a sag. The best indicator for brownouts is dimming of the lights. A blackout is a complete power failure.

Power problems are not unavoidable. Here is a list of devices that will help you avoid the ill effects of power crisis:

♦ Surge suppressors

♦ Generators

♦ Uninterruptible Power Supplies (UPSs)

Accidental Deletion/Modification of Critical Data

Bob is the team leader of a group of software developers who are working on a prestigious project for a bank. The project has reached the critical beta level stage, and the team worked all night to finalize the beta version. This version is due for presentation at a meeting that will be attended by senior managers of the client organization. Bob is excited because he met all deadlines and the imminent success of this project will make him a project manager.

Bob reaches his workplace early. The beta release is a few days away, but the testing is still pending. He takes a deep breath and gets down to work. It will take him all day and a good portion of the night to review the software, but it is worth the effort. The computer seems to take forever to boot up, but after it is ready, he hurriedly opens the folder where the final version of the software is stored. He cannot believe it at first. The team members must have inadvertently stored the files somewhere else. Bob hunts frantically for the critical files. Exasperated, he runs a global search on his computer and reaches for the phone to call the lead developer, Andy. The project files are missing, and all he has with him are two-day-old project files, which are practically useless. The testing team had pointed out a few critical bugs that had been painstakingly removed.

Andy finally answers the phone, and the results of his late-night stay are evident in his voice. He swears to have backed up the final version of the project files on Bob's computer, but Bob's frantic tone convinces him to rush to the office. Bob is devastated because somebody deleted the project files. Whether the deletion was accidental or malicious, it will take him another four days to re-create the version they created the previous day. With five days left for the presentation, Bob cannot afford to waste time.

This disaster can be categorized as SL1. Accidental or intentional deletion of data can have disastrous consequences. Not all victims are as lucky as Bob. Deletion of data can cripple the working of data-driven organizations, such as banks and defense labs.

Intentional damage to computers can be thwarted by the implementation of intrusion detection systems and by defining access control for critical data. Accidental deletion of data, on the other hand, is often unavoidable. The best an organization can do is maintain a procedure for data backup at regular intervals.

Theft or Sabotage

Saboteurs have always existed. Disgruntled employees, mischievous teenagers, and greedy business partners are the common faces of saboteur. Theft and sabotage have become a common cause of concern in the IT world today.

Ronnie Davis had been a systems administrator at NetKrafts, Inc. for six years. He is now serving a 10-year prison sentence for having sabotaged the network that he helped develop over the six-year period he was there.

Ronnie had joined the organization as a systems associate. His hard work and brilliance helped him climb the corporate ladder quickly, but not as quickly as he had wanted. Rob was the other "bright young lad " in the organization. He was Ronnie's competitor and was climbing just as quickly as Ronnie. Things finally came to pass when Rob was made the chief technology officer. Ronnie could take it no longer, and he decided to sabotage the network and destroy it. NetKrafts, Inc. had been completely dependent on the network for all business transactions, and Ronnie knew every nook and corner of the network. He created code that crippled the network in a matter of hours, bringing NetKrafts, Inc. down. It took Simon, the chief operating officer of NetKrafts, Inc., no time to figure out the culprit, but the damage had already been done. NetKrafts, Inc. suffered heavy losses.

In this case, the disaster caused damage to a critical resource of the organization, namely the network. Therefore, this disaster can be classified as SL2.

Virus Attack

Sarah is an editor for a newspaper. She has just returned from maternity leave and is finding it difficult to cope with the working hours. Seeing her difficulty, her boss Bill advised her to take her work home. This solution turned out to be perfect for Sarah. She began to copy all her work on floppy disks and edit them at home. This enabled her to leave the office early and spend more time with her baby. The arrangement worked perfectly for more than a month until her computer crashed mysteriously one day. By the end of the day, most of her colleagues began complaining of computer failure of some sort or the other. Sensing a major virus attack, Brenda, the systems administrator, ordered all employees to disconnect their computers from the network until she detected the problem. A virus scan on one of the computers revealed that the network was under siege by a file virus. Brenda now worked quickly. She downloaded the latest virus description file from the Internet and ordered everyone to update their antivirus software and scan their computers.

Brenda was now curious to know the source of infection. A discussion with Sarah, the first victim, revealed the cause of the virus attack. Sarah had been taking work home and returning it to work on floppy disks. These floppies had become infected on her home computer, and the virus was passed on to her office computer. The virus quickly spread to the other computers. To top it all, Brenda was at fault for not having updated the employees with the latest virus description file.

In this case, the disaster, namely virus attack, did not permanently damage critical resources of the organization. Therefore, it can be classified as an SL1 disaster. However, viruses can severely damage the computers and servers of an organization. In the past, several large-scale virus attacks have damaged organizational resources all over the world. Some of these infamous virus attacks include the Code Red worm and the Melissa virus. Such large-scale virus attacks can be categorized as SL3 disasters.

A *virus* is a computer program that attaches to an executable file on your computer—that is, to any file that has the extension .EXE or .COM—without your knowledge. Every time the host program is run, the virus copies itself to another location on your floppy or hard disk. Although some viruses are benign, most are designed to cause damage to your computer, usually by deleting files or corrupting data. After a virus has been activated, it usually resides in memory, infecting all subsequent programs that are run.

The four different types of viruses are as follows:

◆ **File viruses.** These viruses infect executable files. When you execute one of these executable files, you activate the virus as well. These viruses spread when you share infected files, either by disk or through network transfer.

◆ **Boot sector viruses.** A boot sector virus moves to a new computer when an infected diskette, accidentally left in the disk drive when the computer is shut down, is still in place when you turn on the computer. The computer tries to boot from the disk, and the virus moves from the disk to your computer.

◆ **Multipartite viruses.** Multipartite viruses possess the characteristics of both file and boot sector viruses. Therefore, these viruses can affect files as well as boot sectors.

◆ **Macro viruses.** A *macro* is a piece of code that is embedded in a data file. Macros enable users to perform repetitive tasks at the click of a button or key. Macros also can be programmed to execute every time a document is opened, closed, or saved. This feature of macros is used to create macro viruses.

Network Failure

Arthur is a project manager at a content development organization. He had a hard time the previous night. He spent the whole night with his team testing and adding final tweaks to the Web site they had been creating for a client. The morning greeted them with disastrous news—the network was down. Not only would the team be unable to upload the content to the client site, but they also would not be able to send or receive samples to/from the client. All the effort spent the previous night seemed a waste, and the client was angry. Bill, the network administrator, informed Arthur that the network failure was linked to failure of a domain controller due to a virus attack. In addition, the emergency repair disk was outdated, and the necessary documentation for restoring the domain controller was misplaced. Ultimately, after a lot of trouble, the network was finally restored after three days.

In this case, the disaster damaged a critical resource of the organization; therefore, this disaster can be classified as SL2. On the other hand, if the emergency repair disks and documentation for restoring the domain controller were available, then the impact of the disaster could have been less painful and time consuming, and the disaster could be classified as SL1.

Note that network failure is a broad term that encompasses all the events that might cause a network to stop functioning. When a network fails, a user cannot access it. These failures are rare but damaging. According to Chevin, a British network management company, the 10 most common causes of network failures are these:

- Misconfigured routers
- Faulty Ethernet cards
- Broadcast storms
- Unwanted protocols
- Poor switch allocation
- Server overloading
- Faulty devices
- SNMP management tools
- Rogue equipment
- Power outages

Systems Software Failure

Roger is a graphic designer with PQR Corp. One day after arriving at work, he found that his computer wouldn't start up. He asked the systems administrator at PQR Corp. to help him out. After investigating, the systems administrator informed him that the operating system (OS) of the computer had crashed and that the only solution was to reinstall it. Roger had recently created some graphics for a client. Fortunately, he stored backups of his work on another computer.

In this case, because no permanent damage was caused, this disaster can be categorized as SL1. System software failure is said to occur when the OS or some component of the OS, such as a device driver, fails.

Summary

In this chapter, you learned how disasters can be categorized based on factors such as the time for which there is an outage of critical operations or the critical resources of an organization that are damaged. Any disaster recovery plan that you create must keep in mind the severity of a potential disaster to enable you to effectively deal with the disaster.

Check Your Understanding

Multiple Choice Questions

1. What is the major loss that disk failure causes?
   a. Loss of connectivity
   b. Memory loss
   c. Loss of productivity
   d. Data loss

2. Which of the following terms implies a long period of fall in voltage?
   a. Blackout
   b. Sag
   c. Brownout
   d. Spike

3. Statement A: Misconfigured routers are a common cause of network failure.

   Statement B: Software errors can lead to data loss.
   a. Both statements are true.
   b. Statement A is true, and Statement B is false.

   c. Statement A is false, and Statement B is true.

   d. Both statements are false.

4. Statement A: Surge suppressors are devices used to combat system software failure.

   Statement B: A virus is a computer program that attaches to files that have the extension .EXE or .COM—without your knowledge.

   a. Both statements are true.

   b. Statement A is true, and Statement B is false.

   c. Statement A is false, and Statement B is true.

   d. Both statements are false.

Short Questions

1. Rita, a project manager at PQR Corp., was unable to access critical data from a server. She contacted the systems administrator, John, to help her. John told Rita that the server was down and the entire technical team was trying to fix the problem. Fortunately, Rita had anticipated such problems and had made backups of this data on another computer. Therefore, she did not face much problem. After much effort, the technical team found that the root of the problem was a virus. The server was up and running by the end of the day. To what category (SL1, SL2, or SL3) does this disaster belong?

2. XYZ University is situated on the banks of the Mississippi River. Due to a rise in the water level, the river flooded. The data center of the university, located in the basement of a building on the campus, suffered a lot of damage. Other companies in the city also suffered different degrees of damage. To what category (SL1, SL2, or SL3) does this disaster belong?

Answers

Multiple Choice Answers

1. d. Data loss is the major loss that disk failure causes.

2. c. A brownout implies a long period of fall in voltage.

3. a. Both statements are true.

4. c. Statement A is false, and Statement B is true.

Short Answers

1. The disaster, namely server failure, did not cause permanent damage to critical resources. In addition, the downtime for the disaster was not more than one working day. Therefore, it can be categorized as an SL1 disaster.

2. The disaster, namely flood, affected the entire city. Therefore, it is an SL3 disaster.

Chapter 4

Risk Analysis

When you're in an elevator, you unconsciously move away from the door to a safe distance. Similarly, when you're standing on the terrace, you stay away from the edge. In both of these cases, you are aware of the risk involved and its associated impact. In a majority of situations, critical or noncritical, it is beneficial to have prior knowledge of the risks involved so that you can take the appropriate preventive measures. Let's extrapolate these real-life scenarios to the organization level. Organizations, like individuals, are vulnerable to risks that often threaten to destroy the very existence of the organization. Therefore, it is essential for organizations to identify and plan to mitigate these risks.

In risk analysis, you identify and analyze all the risks that can potentially harm an organization. Risk analysis helps organizations identify and devise the measures to implement to successfully mitigate and contain risks so that they do not transform into unavoidable disasters. Risk analysis forms a vital aspect of the planning involved in disaster recovery.

Keeping in mind the importance of risk analysis in disaster recovery planning, this chapter introduces you to the concept of risks as well as risk analysis and its phases. It also covers the benefits of performing risk analysis.

Defining a Risk

According to the American Heritage Dictionary, a *risk* is defined as "the possibility of suffering harm or loss; danger." In other words, a risk has an element of adversity associated with it. It is this element of accompanying fear and loss that drives you to take precautionary measures against it. The degree of adversity associated with risks enables you to assess a risk's impact and create a suitable disaster recovery plan.

In other words, you can say that a risk is an event comprising the following elements:

◆ **Risk event.** A *risk event* is defined as the adverse event that results in a risk. Such an event can range from natural hazards to disasters that humans cause.

◆ **Risk probability.** *Risk probability* is defined as the likelihood or uncertainty of a risk to occur. It is based on data about the past occurrences of the risk event.

◆ **Risk impact.** The *risk impact* is defined as the loss or extent of damage caused by a risk.

We will illustrate the elements of a risk by using the two examples stated in the introduction to this chapter. Table 4.1 lists the required information.

Table 4.1   Elements of a Risk

Example	Risk Event	Risk Probability	Risk Impact
1	Getting caught in the elevator door	Negligible	Injury
2	Falling from the terrace	Medium	Severe injury or loss of life

For the first example, the probability of occurrence might range from negligible to medium. For instance, the presence of an elevator operator can reduce the probability of occurrence of the risk event. Similarly, the presence of safety bars on the terrace will help to minimize the risk of your falling from the terrace.

To identify the nature of the elements on which the occurrence of a risk is dependent, you might classify risks in three different ways:

◆ Voluntary and involuntary risks

◆ Inherent and acquired risks

◆ Insurable and uninsurable risks

Besides these classifications, you can use many other means of classification. You can use a classification listed here, a combination of these, or an entirely new classification. For instance, you might want to classify risks as simply critical or noncritical, in which all the risks that might impact an organization are classified as critical. However, the purpose of risk classification remains the same—to help you focus and prioritize your planning efforts toward what is most critical for you to protect. In the subsequent sections, you will learn about the classification mentioned earlier.

Voluntary and Involuntary Risks

Voluntary risks are associated with the activities that someone performs. In other words, they are the result of an action. For instance, driving a car without wearing a seat belt is a voluntary risk.

On the other hand, involuntary risks are associated with unpredictable events. Such risks are beyond someone's control. For instance, the risks due to floods and earthquakes are involuntary risks because their occurrence cannot be predicted with certainty.

Inherent and Acquired Risks

All built-in risks are referred to as *inherent risks*. For example, for an organization that deals with inflammable chemicals, fire is an inherent risk.

Acquired risks are those caused as a result of external factors, such as the methodologies, skills, experience, or tools applied. An example of an acquired risk is assigning untrained employees to a project that is critical to an organization.

Insurable and Uninsurable Risks

Insurable risks are those for which you can plan measures to control risks based on their probability of occurrence. For all insurable risks, you can calculate the probability of occurrence based on historical data. For instance, the past records of earthquakes in a locality can be used to predict their occurrence in the future.

All risks for which appropriate measures cannot be planned based on the probability of their occurrence are called *uninsurable risks*. Often, the occurrence of such risks is occasional. As a result, the probability of occurrence cannot be calculated. For instance, the probability of occurrence of terrorist attacks cannot be predicted based on any calculations.

You learned what a risk is and the ways in which risks can be classified. To be able to understand risks and take appropriate measures for their prevention or mitigation, you need to analyze them. You analyze and understand risks and their associated impact by using a process called risk analysis.

Defining the Process of Risk Analysis

An organization can implement numerous measures and spend millions to safeguard its interests. Yet, how many such measures are commensurate with the actual risks it faces? You can evaluate the proportionality between risks and their corresponding security measures through risk analysis. To accomplish this, the process of *risk analysis* involves defining and analyzing the risks that can jeopardize the existence of an organization. Risk analysis also involves an analysis of the security measures currently in place. In other words, risk analysis is a detailed process that involves the following activities:

- Identifying the activities, functions, and assets of an organization without which the existence of the organization is not possible
- Identifying and measuring the magnitude of the risks associated with the aforementioned activities, functions, and assets
- Analyzing the threats and vulnerabilities in the existing setup
- Recommending measures to mitigate the identified risks

To perform these activities, risk analysis involves systematic scrutiny of an organization's environment. This enables you to define the probable risks and assess their impact and likelihood of occurrence. Therefore, organizations can identify the scope and impact and prioritize risks by performing risk analysis.

Such quantification of risks helps management make decisions related to security and disaster recovery. The risk analysis process assesses the cost effectiveness of security measures and recommends measures to mitigate the risks that are not addressed by the existing security measures. The recommended measures might include certain baseline measures that are required to prevent a risk from transforming into a disaster. The recommendations might also include the creation of plans and recovery procedures to ensure the recovery of all that is critical to the organization in the shortest possible time. Therefore, this process can be used as the basis for creating an effective security program to preserve the organization's operations and status in the market. For instance, the risks that are identified as having maximum impact can be allocated a budget for implementing immediate security measures. On the other hand, the risks with minimal or no loss can simply be ignored.

Risk Management

Risk management is a cyclic practice that aims to manage and effectively control the risks that an organization faces. This practice involves the following activities:

◆ Identifying and analyzing the loss due to risks

◆ Selecting measures to control the risks

◆ Implementing the selected measures

◆ Regularly monitoring the decisions made and making appropriate changes, if required

The output of risk management is essentially the determination of the risks that an organization should deal with and the strategies to deal with those risks.

Timely and extensive risk analysis can help an organization ward off the ill effects of a risk. The success of this phase determines the success of the entire risk management cycle, of which risk analysis is an integral part.

Now that you know what risk analysis is, let's talk about its benefits.

Benefits of Risk Analysis

Before proceeding with a process, answer the following question: What benefits will this process provide to my organization? This section answers this question with respect to risk analysis. Following are some benefits of risk analysis:

◆ **Ease of data comprehension.** The output of risk analysis allows decision makers to understand risks well. This is because the data related to the impact and the loss caused by risks is presented in simple figures. In addition, the output of risk analysis does not involve complex mathematical calculations or complex graphs.

◆ **Identification and prioritization of critical activities and functions.** Risk analysis plays a vital role in identifying the activities and functions without which an organization would be unable to sustain its operations. The organization can channel all its efforts and resources toward the successful sustenance and resumption of these activities and functions in the event of a disaster.

◆ **Identification of areas where policies and procedures need to be enhanced and implemented.** In any organization, expansion and acquisition offer prospects for lapses in the implementation of security policies and procedures. By performing risk analysis, you can identify all such areas where the policies and procedures are either inadequate or not implemented. Then you can take appropriate measures to enhance the existing procedures or implement new ones.

◆ **Justification of cost of implementation of measures.** The implementation of security measures is usually costly. Therefore, management is often reluctant to implement these measures. However, with risk analysis, you can evaluate the necessity and the proportionality of a risk to its corresponding measures. In other words, you can better justify the implementation of measures to control a risk.

With risk analysis, you can ensure that the security measures implemented to control risks are appropriate. In risk analysis, you perform a one-to-one mapping of the risks with the security measures. In this way, you also avoid unnecessary expenditure.

◆ **Assessment of the preparedness of an organization with respect to the risks.** In risk analysis, you identify the risks that are likely to harm an organization and then check the level of preparedness of the organization to face the onslaught of the identified risks. Therefore, by performing risk analysis, you can assess whether the organization is capable of facing disasters in the near future.

◆ **Assessment of the security awareness among employees.** Risk analysis provides a way for employees to learn about the risks that their organization can face. This helps employees avoid errors on their part and report early signs of danger. The employees might also help identify new risks that have been ignored until now.

Now that you know about the benefits of risk analysis, it's time to look at implementing the process of risk analysis.

Performing Risk Analysis

A successful disaster recovery plan is created by considering all the risks that will severely impact an organization. To ensure the adequate consideration and representation of risks in disaster recovery planning, you need to perform risk analysis. While performing risk analysis, you need to consider certain guidelines and select a methodology. As discussed earlier, the entire risk analysis process is a detailed process that involves a set of activities. These activities can be grouped into distinct phases.

In the subsequent sections, you will learn about the guidelines, methodologies, and phases of risk analysis. To begin, we will discuss the guidelines for performing risk analysis.

Guidelines for Performing Risk Analysis

Just like any other process, you need to follow certain guidelines for successful risk analysis. These guidelines are explained in the following list:

◆ **Set up a risk analysis team.** Create a team that is devoted to performing the task of risk analysis. This team, known as the risk analysis team, should consist of a team leader and representatives from all the affected groups of the organization or those involved in a project. Ideally, the risk analysis team should consist of individuals from all organizational units. You also can include users in the risk analysis team. The input from users helps you gain an understanding about the use of information to which the owners or custodians of the information would otherwise be oblivious.

When selecting the team members, consider their experience and knowledge of risk management. The team members should be well informed about their unit, its activities and processes, and the relationship of their unit to the entire organization. The team leader should be an experienced member who has knowledge of the tools and techniques required to perform risk analysis.

◆ **Ensure that management actively participates in risk analysis.** Management plays a vital role in the success of risk analysis. At all times, management should support fully the risk analysis exercise. Management is responsible for creating the risk analysis team and delegating roles and responsibilities to the team members. Management also reviews the findings of the team and decides whether to accept recommendation that are made.

◆ **Conduct risk analysis during the initial phases of disaster recovery planning.** Include risk analysis during the initial phases of disaster recovery planning. The purpose of including risk analysis in the preliminary phases of development is to identify and successfully mitigate risks before they harm the organization.

◆ **Consider all the functional areas of an organization and the interdepartmental dependencies.** Risk analysis can be best utilized when applied holistically to the entire organization, inclusive of all its departments and business units. Therefore, you must include all the functional areas and the dependencies between the departments in an organization.

◆ **Decide the level of risk acceptance at the beginning of the process.** It is important to arrive at the degree of risk acceptance for each resource or activity of an organization. In other words, identify the loss that an organization can handle without jeopardizing its existence before you proceed with risk analysis. This helps you devote resources toward the mitigation of high-risk events to reduce their impact to an acceptable level.

◆ **Define all the baselines in the beginning to decide the priorities.** Identify and decide the baseline for security before you categorize risks. Set the minimum security level for activities and resources below which security would be detrimental to an organization.

◆ **Conduct risk analysis whenever a significant change occurs.** Risk analysis is an ongoing process that you should perform regularly to retain the essence of risk management. It is important to conduct and revisit risk analysis whenever an organization experiences change. For instance, with every new acquisition of the organization, the nature and the scope of the risk might change.

◆ **Document the results of all the phases.** Document the results of all the phases of risk analysis in the form of reports. In addition to maintaining a permanent record of all the work done, this allows you to reuse the results. You can create templates or use the existing ones for this purpose.

Now that you know about the guidelines for successful risk analysis, you can decide the methodology to follow for performing risk analysis.

Risk Analysis Methodologies

You can perform risk analysis by using two methodologies to measure risks. It is important to measure risks so that you can analyze and understand them.

You can use these methodologies to compare the loss caused by a risk with the cost of the measures required to mitigate the risk impact.

The risk analysis methodologies are as follows:

◆ Quantitative risk analysis
◆ Qualitative risk analysis

You will learn about these methodologies in the subsequent sections.

Quantitative Risk Analysis

In quantitative risk analysis, you measure risks in monetary terms. In other words, the enormity of a risk is expressed as its cost to an organization. For instance, assigning a recently recruited employee to set up a firewall is fraught with risks such as the incorrect configuration of the firewall. To measure the enormity and the associated impact of the risk, the loss caused to the organization by the inappropriate configuration of the firewall can be measured in terms of dollars.

In this methodology, you calculate the exposure to risks and the Annual Loss Expectancy (ALE).

You can define the exposure to risks as the product of two elements of risk: the risk probability and the risk impact. You can calculate the exposure to a risk by using the following equation:

Exposure to risk = risk probability * risk impact

We will now explain the methods to calculate the risk probability and the risk impact.

Calculating the Risk Probability

The probability of occurrence of risks is expressed mathematically as a fraction between 0.0 and 1.0, in which 0.0 indicates the nonoccurrence of the event contributing to the risk. In contrast, 1.0 indicates a strong probability of the occurrence of the risk event.

We can illustrate the method of calculating the probability of occurrence of a risk by using an example. Given two dice, if the sum of the numbers on the faces of the dice is 5, you need to pay $500. However, if the sum of the numbers is not 5, you are credited $1,000. What is the probability that the sum of the numbers will be 5?

In this example, the risk is the possibility that the sum of the numbers will be 5. To calculate the probability of occurrence of this risk, you use the following equation:

Probability of occurrence = Total number of possible cases / Number of possible combinations

For this example, the possible cases that result in a sum of 5 are listed in Table 4.2.

Table 4.2   Possible Cases That Result in a Sum of 5 on Two Dice

Dice 1	Dice 2
1	4
4	1
2	3
3	2

Note that four possible cases can result in a sum of 5, and the total number of combinations is 36. Therefore, the probability of occurrence is 4/36 or 0.111.

You can convert the decimal value that represents the risk probability into a percentage value for convenience. For example, in this case, the probability of occurrence of the risk can be expressed as .111, or 11.1 percent. This implies that there is 11.1 percent chance that the sum of the numbers on the faces of the dice will be 5.

Calculating the Risk Impact

Just as the probability of a risk event is unique, its impact is also unique. You calculate the impact of risks to identify the risks that are likely to cause the maximum loss. You can judge the enormity of the risk impact based on the type of risk and its probability of occurrence. Consider the aforementioned scenario. If the sum of the numbers returned by the dice were 5, you must pay $500, but if the sum were not 5, you are credited $1,000. In this case, the probability of the risk's occurrence was calculated as 0.11. In this example, the impact of the risk is a loss of $500 if the risk occurs. This implies a probability of 11.1 percent that you will lose $500 on rolling the dice.

The cost in terms of loss helps you assess and compare the potential monetary impact of a risk with the cost of implementing measures to mitigate it. While you're assessing the impact of a risk, consider the cost to repair, replace, and set up a temporary replacement for the damaged entity. Based on the potential impact of a risk, you can allocate appropriate funds toward its mitigation.

At this point, we will illustrate the method to calculate the exposure to a risk by using the example discussed in the earlier section, "Calculating the Risk Probability." For this example, the probability of occurrence was calculated as 0.11 and the impact as $500.

Therefore, as stated earlier, the risk exposure for the example is 0.11 * $500, in which 0.11 is the risk probability and $500 is the risk impact.

The calculated value of risk exposure is known as the Single Loss Expectancy (SLE). You can define SLE as the quantitative or monetary representation of the loss caused by a single risk. You can calculate the SLE by using the following equation:

SLE = Asset value * Exposure factor

Note the following in the preceding equation:

◆ *Asset value* indicates the value of the asset that is likely to be damaged by a risk to an organization. You will learn about valuating assets in the later section titled "Valuating Critical Assets."

◆ *Exposure factor* is defined as the degree of loss in the value of an asset as caused by a risk. It is expressed as a percentage of the asset value ranging from 0–100.

You can express the annual loss caused by a risk by calculating the Annual Loss Expectancy (ALE), also referred to as Annual Loss Exposure, of a risk. *ALE* is defined as the loss likely to be caused in a year by a risk. Using ALE, organizations can plan budgets for risk management.

ALE is also useful in evaluating the cost effectiveness of a security measure to mitigate a risk. You will learn about evaluating the cost effectiveness of a security control in the later section, "Recommendation Phase."

You can calculate ALE by using the following equation:

$$ALE = (SLE) * (ARO)$$

In the preceding equation, ARO is the Annualized Rate of Occurrence of a risk. *ARO* is defined as the annual frequency at which a risk is expected to occur. For instance, if a risk occurs every three years, the ARO for the risk is 1/3.

We can illustrate the concept of ALE by using the example of an organization situated in an area that is prone to earthquakes. Two earthquakes have occurred in the past year, causing $17,500 damage to the equipment.

In this case, because two earthquakes have occurred in the past year, the ARO is 2/1, or 2.

Therefore, you can calculate ALE as follows:

$$ALE = \$(17,500 * 2) = \$ 35,000$$

However, it is unlikely that you can measure the probability of all risks in realistic terms. The data in such cases can be unreliable and inaccurate. An important drawback of this methodology, therefore, is the use of precise estimates even in cases where reliable input data is unavailable. Consequently, when it is not possible to measure risks quantitatively, you should use qualitative risk analysis.

Qualitative Risk Analysis

Qualitative risk analysis is the most widely used type of risk measurement. You measure risks qualitatively when it is not possible to calculate them accurately and they are subjective in nature. In qualitative risk measurement, you describe the elements of risks in qualitative terms. While evaluating the probability of occurrence of risks, you must consider factors such as the topography of the area, its geography, and its proximity to highways that transport hazardous material. Consider this example to illustrate the point. You need to measure the risk associated with the occurrence of fire in an organization's facility. You cannot predict the occurrence of a fire with certainty. For such events, you can measure the associated risks—of uncertainty—by using the qualitative method.

For risks that cannot be quantified or measured, such as the dissatisfaction of a supervisor, you can rate the risk as low, medium, or high. The categorization of risks as low, medium, and high forms the basis of qualitative risk measurement. Qualitative risk measurement advocates the use of descriptions and includes the analysis of threats, vulnerabilities, and security measures. For instance, you can express the vulnerabilities caused by a risk through fuzzy reasoning or as estimates of magnitude.

Based on the qualitative measurement of risks, you can decide on the investment required to implement measures to mitigate the risks. For a risk categorized as high, you need to take prompt action toward mitigation. For a risk categorized as moderate, you take appropriate measures to mitigate the risk. You can simply ignore risks with minimal criticality.

You can implement either qualitative or quantitative methodology described earlier or use a methodology that is a combination of the qualitative and quantitative approaches.

You can conduct risk analysis by using any methodology manually or by using risk analysis software packages. These software packages automate the different phases of risk analysis. The next section discusses the phases of risk analysis.

Phases of Risk Analysis

Risk analysis is a systematic and detailed process that involves various activities. These activities can be grouped and categorized into the following phases:

- ◆ Identification
- ◆ Analysis
- ◆ Recommendation

The output of each phase forms the input for the next phase. In the subsequent sections, you will learn about the activities for each phase of risk analysis.

Identification Phase

In the identification phase of risk analysis, you perform the following activities:

- ◆ Identifying critical activities
- ◆ Identifying critical assets
- ◆ Valuating critical assets
- ◆ Identifying risks

You will learn about these activities in the subsequent sections.

Identifying Critical Activities

The existence of an organization depends on the smooth operation of its activities and processes. Certain activities and processes might cause irreparable damage to an organization when they're disrupted. Such activities are known as the *critical activities* of the organization. The disruption of critical activities causes immense loss in terms of revenue and profits. In addition, these activities are required to sustain the operations of the organization in the event of a disaster. In other words, after a disaster, the survival of an organization depends on the resumption of its critical activities in the shortest possible time. For instance, the maintenance of treasury operations is a critical activity for banks.

 NOTE

Noncritical activities do not impact an organization significantly. Such activities do not result in financial loss or the disruption of vital business operations. Often, noncritical activities can be conducted manually or by using the minimum organizational resources. Although the resumption of critical activities is always a priority, you can delay the resumption of a noncritical activity to a later period. The maintenance of an organization's intranet Web site is an example of a noncritical activity.

Therefore, the objective behind identifying the critical activities is to identify all the activities that are essential for the organization to sustain its business continuity, both during and after a disaster. To identify the critical activities of an organization, simply answer this question: What is important to the organization? You can gather information about the critical activities in the following ways:

- ◆ **By gaining a thorough knowledge of the business, the processes, and the technology used to run the organizational processes and systems.** You can gather information about critical activities by understanding the organization's purpose and business strategy. Often, the policy statements, Web sites, and other guides to the organization can be helpful in identifying the required information.

- ◆ **By assessing parameters, such as financial loss.** As stated earlier, the disruption of critical activities causes loss of revenue and profits. You can use this as a parameter to identify the criticality of activities. Table 4.3 displays an organization's loss in monetary terms that a disruption of activities causes.

Table 4.3 Financial Loss Caused by Disruption of Activities

Activity	Financial Loss
A	$100
B	$100,000
C	$50,500
D	$800

From Table 4.3, you can clearly see that the disruption of activity B would cause the maximum loss to the organization. Therefore, activity B is a critical activity for the organization.

Apart from the financial loss caused due to the disruption of activities, you must also consider other factors, such as the humiliation the organization faces. In addition, consider factors such as the users, the suppliers, and the contracts that support the activities. Finally, consider all the legal implications.

◆ **By documenting the daily activities within each department.** For this purpose, you must consider all the important activities that a department performs. Such activities can include the information, processes, activities, equipment, and personnel that are essential to maintain the functioning of a business unit or a department in the face of a disaster.

You can then analyze the activities over a period of time—preferably one month—to identify the main activities that a department performs.

After identifying the critical activities, you determine their degree of dependency on Information Technology (IT). You can express the dependency of the activities on IT as high, medium, or low, where high dependency indicates dedicated support from IT systems. To derive these dependencies, you need to interview the personnel who are involved in performing the activities. This helps you segregate the activities that can be resumed easily and manually and those that rely extensively on IT. All activities that rely extensively on the availability of the IT setup require time to be performed. Therefore, you can focus on the recovery of these IT activities while planning for disaster recovery.

The next step is to identify the critical functions performed within these activities. Each activity comprises functions that are required to perform and maintain the activity. Consider the example of an activity that includes five functions. Among these functions, only two might be critical and required to maintain the critical activity. These functions are known as *critical functions*. It is these critical functions that you need to focus on and protect from risks.

Think about a bank as an example. In a bank, communication links are vital for treasury operations. The disruption of communication links for weeks on end would severely hamper the treasury operations of the bank and would be a disastrous situation. Therefore, whereas treasury operations form a critical activity of the bank, communication forms a critical function for this activity. It is important to prioritize such critical functions within a critical activity of the organization so that you can plan and implement appropriate measures.

After you assign criticality to activities, you obtain a list of activities that an organization must sustain to resume operations after a disaster. Only assess and analyze the activities with the highest criticality in subsequent activities.

An organization's critical activities and functions depend on certain resources. These resources, called *assets*, are required for the successful sustenance and resumption of activities during normal circumstances and after a disaster, respectively. Therefore, as the next task in the risk analysis process, you map the critical activities with the critical assets.

Identifying Critical Assets

An *asset* is defined as any resource that is essential for an organization to sustain its operations. Some examples of organizational assets include personnel and buildings. An organization can be considered a collection of assets that help it achieve its purpose and sustain its activities and operations.

As stated earlier, the sustenance and resumption of critical activities and functions depend on the availability of certain assets. These assets are known as *critical assets*. Inevitably, the loss of or damage to a critical asset disrupts the normal business operations of the organization. Therefore, an adequate knowledge about these assets helps you to better understand the risks to these assets and to implement the appropriate measures to mitigate these risks.

To achieve a better understanding of the assets, you can categorize the assets of an organization as one of the following:

◆ **Tangible.** You can identify and assess such assets easily. Some examples include hardware and documentation.

◆ **Intangible.** You cannot identify or evaluate these assets easily. Some examples include the reputation of an organization and the morale of the employees.

You also can categorize assets based on their deployment and use under five categories. These categories comprise the five areas discussed in Chapter 1: viz. data and applications, systems and equipment, buildings, communication links, and personnel.

 NOTE

You must track the assets of an organization by location, use, and ownership. All the assets owned or under the custody of the organization should be included in the list of assets.

Organizations often maintain a detailed list of their assets. However, before using the list of assets, you should ensure that it is up to date with the new acquisitions. In addition, it is vital to track the movement of all the assets within an office and within an organization. Changes in the location and configuration of the assets, if applicable, make tracking assets an arduous task.

After you identify and categorize the assets, you need to map each critical activity to the asset required and specify an estimate for the quantity and cost of the required asset. This helps you determine the minimal level of resources required to sustain the critical activities. In addition, it helps you assign criticality to the assets. Following are some other factors that you can consider while assessing the criticality of an asset:

◆ **Elimination causes complete destruction of the organization or data.** All the assets that, when eliminated, cause the complete destruction of the organization or the data are considered critical assets.

◆ **Elimination causes loss of integrity and availability of data.** All the assets that, when eliminated, lead to loss of integrity and availability of data in the organization are considered critical assets. In addition, if the assets are involved in sending and receiving large volumes of information, they are classified as critical.

◆ **Elimination causes loss of confidentiality of information.** If the loss of an asset leads to the disclosure of confidential information to unauthorized users, it is referred to as a critical asset. Confidentiality of information is critical, especially in military organizations and government agencies.

NOTE

You can classify assets as critical, essential, or normal. The essential assets include all the assets that the organization can operate without for some time but which would have to eventually be replaced after a disaster. Normal assets are resources that an organization can do without and whose replacement can be deferred.

Consider the example of the documents in an organization. You can classify the records that are not replaceable as critical. You can classify records as essential if they can be reproduced but with considerable expense and delay. All the records that do not affect the working of a department when lost are classified as normal records.

Consider the example of a fictional organization named Mucarz, Inc. The organization has developed an automated tool to process the firm's transactions. All the organization's business transactions depend on the tool. In such a case, the criticality of the tool, which is an asset to the firm, is high. This is because the loss of the tool will adversely impact the working of the firm and can lead to heavy financial losses.

After you identify the critical assets, you need to valuate them.

Valuating Critical Assets

When you *valuate* critical assets, you assess their importance to the organization. The valuation of assets is important to determine the protection and replacement costs for them. During asset valuation, you identify the importance of an asset based on parameters such as cost, sensitivity, mission criticality, or a combination of these. You also might consider legal and ethical issues. In addition, management might perform the valuation of assets, keeping the objective of the organization in mind.

To arrive at the monetary value of assets, you calculate the following:

- ◆ **The fair market value of the fixed asset and equipment.** This is defined as the price of the asset in the open market. The current price of the asset is surveyed and compared with the historical trends to assess its fair market value.

- ◆ **Leasehold improvements.** All the changes to an asset to be considered part of the asset when it is sold or when a lease is not renewed are considered as leasehold improvements.

◆ **Owner benefit.** The discretionary cash of the seller for one year is accounted for in the owner benefit. You can obtain this information from the adjusted income statement.

◆ **Inventory.** This includes the wholesale value of inventory. It includes the raw materials, the finished product, and the products that are being manufactured.

The sum of all these figures returns the monetary value of an asset.

 NOTE

Some tools that you can use for asset valuation include statistics, ratio analysis, and fundamental analysis.

You also can use the list of assets generally maintained by organizations to access the corresponding values and criticality of the assets.

To ease the mammoth task of risk analysis for all assets, first analyze the critical assets—the assets with the highest priority—for risks. After you complete the risk analysis for critical assets, proceed with risk analysis for the assets with medium priority and finally, move to the assets with the least priority.

From there, identify the risks that are likely to adversely affect the organization's critical activities and assets.

Identifying Risks

During risk identification, you identify all the probable risks that are associated with the critical activities and assets identified earlier. The activity of risk identification requires the complete cooperation of all the departments of an organization and cannot be performed in isolation by a single department. In addition, the importance of performing risk identification at the start of an activity cannot be ignored. However, it is essential to revisit the list of risks identified at the beginning of a project to evaluate any changes in the risks identified earlier or to list new risks. With every change in the scope, requirements, budget, or structure of an organization, the emphasis of the organization might undergo a change.

NOTE

A risk identification team can be created to provide input to the risk analysis team for identifying risks. This team consists of personnel who are capable of identifying risks based on their valuable experience, such as project managers and stakeholders.

It might not be possible to list all the probable risks. Nevertheless, it is a good practice to list as many risks as possible. You also must include long-term risks. An exhaustive list of risks will help you plan better to mitigate the effects of a risk and safeguard the interests of the organization.

You can obtain potential risks from past experience and documentation. In addition, the experience of the representatives from different units of an organization forms a valuable source for risk identification. Following are some other sources for identifying risks:

◆ **Face-to-face interviews.** The ideal method for identifying risks is face-to-face interviews. It is a good idea to interview a large number of employees. You should consider all the concerns that the employees raise.

◆ **Brainstorming.** For brainstorming purposes, you can gather a group of people who represent the business units of an organization and then conduct an information gathering session.

◆ **Information sharing.** A vital source for identifying risks is the sharing of information. You must approach all those who have successfully analyzed risks before you. You can visit seminars and consult various sources, such as weather services or other businesses. Similarly, you must not hesitate to give your own insights to another risk analysis team.

◆ **Questionnaires.** You can create questionnaires for risk identification. This questionnaire should be created with the organization's requirements and environment in mind. You can include questions pertaining to each area of risk. It is also important to consider the importance of an asset and the magnitude of the loss caused by a risk to the organization. You also can consider a specific aspect of the risk in detail in the questionnaire.

 NOTE

Although we have listed a few sources, in the course of performing risk analysis, you might identify many more. Don't restrict yourself to these sources only.

After you obtain a comprehensive list of risks, you can group the related risks. This grouping helps you to categorize all the related risks and aids the analysis process. Next, you need to determine the cause, the possibility, and the expected consequence of each risk in financial and nonfinancial terms. In this way, you can identify the risks that are likely to cause maximum impact and should, therefore, be addressed on a priority basis.

While assessing the impact of a risk, you need to consider the type and the scope of the risk. The types of risks are discussed in the section titled "Defining a Risk," earlier in this chapter. When you define the scope of a risk, you assess all the critical assets and define a logical boundary within which the impact of the risk is most severe and the occurrence is the highest. In other words, you state the areas of risk and the implications for the organization. This enables you to concentrate the mitigation efforts within the identified area. For example, you can limit the scope of a risk to the geographical area of a call center. In this case, all the measures to mitigate the risk will be limited to the call center.

To define the scope of a risk, you can consider the listed parameters:

◆ **Physical area.** While considering the physical area for defining the scope of a risk, you need to consider all the physical assets of your organization. You can also demarcate a physical location that is most vulnerable to the risk. For instance, call centers can be the scope for a risk. After you define the scope for a risk, it is essential to monitor the scope regularly for changes. For instance, it is possible that with the opening of a new branch office, the scope for the risk increases to include the new branch office.

◆ **Organizational units.** You also can define the scope for a risk as a unit of an organization. Such a definition is based on the data flow between the different units of an organization.

Apart from defining the scope for risks, you also identify and categorize the threats to critical assets during risk identification. A threat is defined as an element, event, or object that causes imminent harm to an asset, thereby causing the loss or unavailability of the asset. In other words, a risk is the outcome of the existence of a threat.

NOTE

The term *threat* is often used in the risk analysis process in place of the word *risk*. In this chapter, however, you will notice a distinct relationship between risks and threats as mentioned.

You can categorize threats based on the objective behind them as:

◆ **Intentional.** *Intentional threats* are described as deliberate threats, such as fraud and misuse. They are caused by people such as hackers, disgruntled employees, and terrorists. Some intentional threats include the following:

  ◆ **Distributed Denial of Service.** In distributed denial of service, multiple systems are used to communicate with a specific system simultaneously and for an extended period of time. As a result, the targeted system might crash due to excessive inbound traffic. In addition, the targeted system cannot service authorized users.

  ◆ **Malicious code.** Code can be used to infect programs, systems, or networks with the intention of damaging the systems or the programs and rendering them inoperable. Such code is called *malicious code*. As a result, such code can threaten the reliability, availability, and confidentiality of data. A few examples of malicious code include viruses, Trojan horses, and worms.

  ◆ **Eavesdropping.** Often, unauthorized users monitor and access confidential information without the consent of the information owner. This practice is known as *eavesdropping* or *sniffing*. Eavesdropping jeopardizes the confidentiality of data.

  ◆ **Sabotage.** During their service or interaction with an organization, the employees or contractors of an organization amass immense knowledge about the organization. This information about the assets, policies, and infrastructure of the organization can be misused. For instance, employees can share confidential information with other organizations on purpose. Such an activity that is performed with the intention of damaging an organization or a set of people is called *sabotage*.

  ◆ **Social engineering.** An individual can obtain vital confidential information by misleading a person. This practice of misleading someone to obtain vital information without raising any suspicion is known as *social engineering*. For example, an individual can impersonate a credit card agent and obtain confidential information from you on the pretext of launching a new service.

◆ **Unintentional.** *Unintentional threats* are described as accidental threats that people might cause. The primary causes of such threats are human error and inadequate knowledge about software and procedures. Often, such threats are caused by negligence, errors, and omissions. For example, flooding caused as a result of torrential rains can be an unintentional threat. Some accidental threats include these:

  ◆ **Accidental fire.** This might harm the assets of the organization, such as personnel.

  ◆ **Communication services failure.** In this age of communication, the failure of communication services such as satellite systems, telephone lines, or e-mail systems can hamper business operations. A faulty satellite link, an unstable server, or power failure can cause such a failure.

  ◆ **Key personnel loss.** Certain employees play a pivotal role in the strategies of the organization. Such personnel have knowledge about the organization, such as its new ventures and customer requirements. These key personnel hold immense value for the organization; therefore, their loss costs the organization dearly. The loss is compounded when documentation for the tasks solely performed by the key personnel is not available. Such a loss is also compounded when new entrants take time to adjust to the work and other daily activities.

  ◆ **User errors.** The errors that users cause can contribute extensively to the loss that an organization faces. For instance, the accidental deletion of critical files can cause immense loss to the organization. To tackle this, an organization might consider increasing employee awareness about such threats.

  ◆ **Software or programming bugs.** Data is also subject to threats and risks if errors have been introduced in the coding, installation, or maintenance phase of the product life cycle. This affects the availability, integrity, and reliability of the data.

◆ **Environmental.** The environmental threats include natural disasters and conditions such as extreme temperature, as discussed in Chapter 1, "Disaster Recovery Planning: An Overview." Natural disasters and environmental conditions can lead to data loss. This could delay critical tasks, thus leading to the loss of customer confidence and money. The possibility of a natural disaster looms large as a consequence of the location of the office or data storage center. Disasters such as fires can be caused from within the premises of an organization. A fire can be started accidentally or intentionally.

 NOTE

An organization's valuable assets are often at risk from disgruntled employees. Having worked with the organization, these employees have knowledge of just about all the confidential information that an outsider requires to harm the organization in any way.

You can also classify threats based on their impact on assets, as follows:

◆ **Hardware threats.** These threats affect the hardware assets. Some examples include theft and fire.

◆ **Software threats.** These threats affect the software, documents, and data assets, and in some cases, the hardware assets. Some examples include viruses and system failure.

◆ **Physical threats.** These threats affect the physical assets. Some examples include ineffective cooling systems and easy access to the data center.

A threat can impact the business, disrupt operations, and damage an organization. In addition, a threat can endanger the financial position of the organization and its public image. Threats can compromise the confidentiality, integrity, and availability of critical assets. While assessing the impact of a threat, you should consider the interruption of business, contract obligations, critical supplies, and production distribution. You need to ask questions such as these: How much will the business be affected? Will the organization be able to continue its operations? Such questions can help you ensure that appropriate time, effort, and money are devoted to mitigate the threat. The impact of a threat depends on the type of outage that occurs and the time that lapses before normal operations can be resumed.

This data about the consequences of a threat to an asset is recorded in a table known as the threat impact table. In addition to including the fiscal value of the assets in a threat impact table, you also can include fields such as asset description, asset value, existing preventive measures, threat description, type of effect, and impact.

The information listed in the threat impact table forms a vital input for the risk identification table. The risk identification table is generated at the end of risk identification. This table lists the details of a risk, such as the description, the source, the frequency of occurrence, the scope, and the expected impact of all identified risks.

The activity of risk identification forms the last in the series included in the identification phase of risk analysis. The details of the risk identification table are analyzed in the analysis phase.

Analysis Phase

In the analysis phase, you analyze the vulnerabilities that make an asset susceptible to risks or threats. Based on the analyzed vulnerabilities, you prioritize the risks to the critical activities and assets. The activities included in the phase are as follows:

- Analysis of vulnerabilities
- Prioritization of risks

You will learn about these activities in the subsequent sections.

Analysis of Vulnerabilities

You can define *vulnerability* as the susceptibility of a system—such as the applications, the information setup that the organization uses, and the hardware server—to risks. Often, the vulnerability of an asset leads to the disruption of service, unauthorized access, or loss, depending on the asset. In other words, risks materialize from the exploitation of the vulnerabilities that exist in assets. Therefore, you need to identify and analyze the vulnerabilities of all critical assets. The output of this activity is a list of all the vulnerabilities identified at a given point in the critical assets and activities of an organization.

While performing vulnerability analysis, you check for all the vulnerabilities that the critical assets and critical activities are susceptible to. In other words, you test for all the situations that are likely to cause damage to or disrupt the critical assets and critical activities, respectively. For instance, you test your network to check for design or access control flaws that might permit unauthorized change of content at the intranet site.

All factors that are likely to result in the materialization of the identified threats and risks are given due consideration. Often, vulnerabilities are inherent within the software, such as a software bug, or caused by the misuse of software. The other causes of vulnerabilities are misconfiguration, mismanagement, or inherent system bugs that have not been tested. In addition, vulnerabilities result from the lack of awareness among employees about security issues and the lack of enforcement of appropriate security measures by security personnel.

You can perform vulnerability analysis by using numerous methods. In each of these methods, the scenarios that can happen in real life are simulated. In addition, the vulnerabilities are assessed for exploitation from internal as well as external sources. To this effect, testing is done onsite as well as remotely. You can perform vulnerability analysis by using the following methods:

◆ **Penetration testing.** In penetration testing, the risk analysis team conducts tests that simulate the techniques deployed by hackers to access a network or critical assets. In this way, all vulnerabilities that are likely to be exploited by hackers in real life are checked and evaluated. For instance, to check the vulnerabilities of a firewall, the risk analysis team tries to access a network across the firewall, as a hacker would do. In addition, the misconfiguration of the assets that can be used to gain unauthorized access to the assets are analyzed. Penetration testing also involves testing the known and unknown bugs, configuration problems, and unnecessary network services.

◆ **Scanning systems for misconfiguration.** While scanning systems such as a network for misconfiguration, you need to check for all the open and unused ports. In addition, all the services and ports that are accessible to users are tested to authenticate trust relationships and analyze the bugs and misconfiguration.

◆ **Security audit.** You also can audit the existing security measures in place to test their efficiency. For instance, you can check and test your servers for protection against unauthorized use. While auditing the servers and networks, you can test for all the ports that are open and unused that can act as potential connection points for unauthorized access. You also can audit the use of access control specified for confidential data. As part of the audit procedure, you can interview the employees about the security policies and procedures to check their awareness.

In vulnerability analysis, you identify the factors that determine the vulnerability levels. You can determine the vulnerability levels from the following:

◆ **The complexity (and scope) of an asset.** Vulnerability is directly proportionate to the complexity of an asset. For instance, a large network is more vulnerable to an intruder attack than a small and simple network. This is largely because with the increased load of personnel accessing information, the chances of unauthorized access is greater. In addition, in a large network, it is impossible to ensure adequate access controls, thus leaving the network vulnerable to intruder attack. Networks that are dispersed across cities are also vulnerable to damage by natural threats.

◆ **Existing security measures.** Keeping in view the threats to assets, management implements security measures to protect them. However, with every change in assets, the security measures might prove inadequate or obsolete. In addition, these security measures might have become ineffective with the recurrence of threats. Therefore, you must regularly examine the existing security measures to evaluate their effectiveness against threats and update them, if required.

Therefore, the level of vulnerability is expressed as a function of the complexity of assets and the existing security measures.

You can calculate the vulnerability level of an asset by using the following equation:

Vuln level = f (AssetCompl, ExSecMeas)

where `Vuln level` is the vulnerability level, `AssetCompl` is the complexity of the asset, and `ExSecMeas` is the existing security measure.

In vulnerability analysis, you also analyze the relationship between the threats and the vulnerabilities. Simply stated, you map the threats with the vulnerabilities. It is not uncommon to find a threat exploiting multiple vulnerabilities of an asset. In this case, the risk to the asset multiplies.

As an example, Table 4.4 lists details about the threat of earthquakes and the vulnerabilities exploited.

Table 4.4 Threats and Vulnerabilities Exploited

Information About Threat	Details
Threat Description	Earthquake
Type of Threat	Natural
Scope of threat assessment	Study the threat from earthquakes in the region of the facility
Frequency (based on historical data)	Twice a year
Impact	Devastated data center
Vulnerabilities exploited	Infrequent offsite backups
	Absent or malfunctioning detection systems
	High-rise building

In Table 4.4, the threat of an earthquake exploits the vulnerability of malfunctioning or absent detection systems. Additionally, the fact that the building is a high-rise building with infrequent offsite backups compounds the risk to the assets of the data center. You can see from the example that multiple vulnerabilities can compound a threat.

In the earlier section titled "Identifying Risks," we listed a couple of threats. Table 4.5 lists some of these threats and the vulnerabilities that they exploit.

To identify the vulnerabilities in a system, you also can interview the employees about the physical, system, and personnel security. It is essential to interview, on a regular basis, all the employees who work with the system that is identified as vulnerable and who are familiar with the system's problems.

The information obtained from the analysis of the vulnerabilities associated with the critical assets is then used to prioritize the identified risks. This indicates the risks that require immediate action and those for which action can be deferred or is not required. This activity is explained next.

Prioritization of Risks

As emphasized earlier, it's imperative to identify the risks that have the maximum severity level. The security measures to control risks are decided and implemented accordingly. All the risks that pose maximum danger need to be managed early to prevent disasters. Keeping this in mind, you need to prioritize risks based on their calculated impact and probability of occurrence.

Table 4.5 Threats and Vulnerabilities Exploited

Threat	Vulnerabilities
Distributed Denial of Service	No firewall
	Laxity in network administration
	Personnel who have malicious intent
Malicious code	Nonimplementation of anti-virus software
	Absence or nonimplementation of updates for anti-virus software
	Inadequate knowledge among employees about viruses
	Unmonitored download of software from the Internet
	No policy regarding the management of e-mail messages and attachments
	No policy on scanning floppy disks before use
Eavesdropping	Insecure data communications closets or hubs
	Leaving confidential information, such as logon passwords, accessible to all
	Leaving a system that stores sensitive data unlocked
	Sending data over the network in an unencrypted form
Sabotage	Nonimplementation of physical security
	Absence of change management controls
	Incorrect access rights
Social engineering	No policies to restrict employees from providing information over the phone
	No policies to verify customer calls for identity

You can calculate the probability and the impact of a risk by using the method described in the earlier section titled "Quantitative Risk Analysis." To assess the probability of risks and their potential impact, you can adopt a multitude of approaches. We will discuss risk maps as a methodology to prioritize risks.

Risk maps are similar to any graph with two axes. The two axes of a risk map display the annual probability of occurrence of a risk and the monetary impact of the risk, respectively. Figure 4.1 displays a sample risk map.

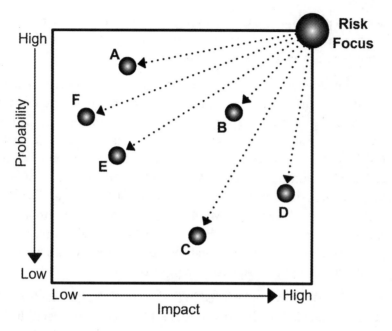

FIGURE 4.1   *A sample risk map.*

In the sample risk map, the points indicate the probability and the impact of risks. For instance, point B might represent the probability and the impact of an earthquake in the region. As you can see from the figure, the probability of occurrence of the risk is slightly higher than moderate. In addition, the risk has severe consequences.

In this way, you can categorize each risk according to its probability and impact. Therefore, you can use risk maps to assess the effectiveness of risk prevention measures. You also can use risk maps to prioritize the disaster recovery planning efforts based on the risks with the highest priority.

To create plans based on the risks with the highest priority, you need to order the risks based on priority. For this purpose, you need to identify and plot the scenario with dire consequences—destruction of the main facility—on the risk map. Such a scenario is identified by the highest probability of occurrence and the most severe consequences. Therefore, you plot this scenario at the extreme top-right corner of the risk map and label it as *risk focus*. The risk focus helps you to assess all the risks plotted on the risk map.

To assess the risks in relation to the risk focus, you need to draw lines from the risk focus to the points indicative of the risks. The distance between the risk focus and the points helps to arrange the risks in an orderly manner based on their probability of occurrence and severity. All the points located closest to the risk focus are assigned highest priority.

At times, individual risks combine to impact an asset. Such risks are known as *compound risks* and impact an organization on more than one front. For instance, the risk of a database server crashing is a compound risk. In this case, if there is no backup, then it is not possible to restore the latest database contents. In addition, the database server can crash in the event of a power outage. Therefore, in this case, the risk is compounded by the lack of testing of backup data on a regular basis and the absence of Uninterruptible Power Supply (UPS). It is advisable that you break a compound risk into manageable individual risks. However, if this is not possible or the impact of the compound risk is higher than the total impact of the individual risks, then compound risks should be assigned high priority.

The result of this activity can be listed in the risk identification table by simply adding a column labeled Priority or Rank. This column indicates the level of danger posed by each risk to the assets of an organization.

You can use the risk identification table to recommend the measures that satisfactorily mitigate the risks that have been identified as high-priority risks. This task is performed in the next phase of risk analysis.

Recommendation Phase

During this phase, you determine the measures that are required to protect the assets of an organization cost effectively from the identified risks. Such measures are known as controls, counter measures, security mechanisms, or safeguards. For the sake of consistency, the term *safeguard* is used in the chapter. You can define safeguards as the controls, mechanisms, procedures, and policies that are implemented to protect an asset from risks.

In this phase, you convert all the risk-related data into information that management can use to decide and plan the implementation of safeguards based on an evaluation of their cost effectiveness.

During this phase, you create a risk detail sheet that uses the results of threat identification, vulnerability analysis, and risk calculation. This sheet represents the overall effect of a threat. Management can utilize this sheet to make decisions regarding a threat. Figure 4.2 displays a sample risk detail sheet.

```
┌─────────────────────────────────────────┐
│ Catalog Number:                          │
├─────────────────────────────────────────┤
│ Threat Description:                      │
│                                          │
│ Threat Source:                           │
│                                          │
├─────────────────────────────────────────┤
│ Probability of Occurrence:               │
│                                          │
│ Expected Frequency of Occurrence:        │
│                                          │
│ Threat Level:                            │
│                                          │
├─────────────────────────────────────────┤
│ Threat Impact:                           │
│                                          │
│                                          │
│                                          │
├─────────────────────────────────────────┤
│ Authority Signature:                     │
└─────────────────────────────────────────┘
```

FIGURE 4.2   *A sample risk detail sheet.*

In the risk detail sheet, while listing the frequency of occurrence, you can state whether the risk event occurs often or seldom. You also can specify whether the risk event is accompanied by a forewarning that can be used to predict its occurrence. In addition to the impact of the risk event, you can note the duration of the impact.

As stated earlier, in the recommendation phase, you determine the measures required to protect an organization's assets. To achieve this purpose, you examine the existing safeguards for adequacy, and based on the gathered facts, you suggest additional safeguards.

In the subsequent sections, you will learn about assessing the existing safeguards and suggesting additional ones.

Assessing the Existing Safeguards

Keeping in mind the potential risks to an organization, the organization implements safeguards to mitigate the impact of risks to an acceptable level. For effective risk planning and appropriate security of critical assets, you must evaluate all the safeguards currently in place, keeping in mind the identified threats and vulnerabilities. You must consider and address each risk within the context of the impact that it is likely to have on the organization. Often, a highly critical risk for one organization might have a minimal impact on another organization.

The safeguards vary based on the asset to be protected and the risk being mitigated. Therefore, there is a different safeguard for different assets. For instance, denying access to confidential information can be a safeguard for personnel assets, and scanning for viruses can be a safeguard for software assets.

 NOTE

It is likely that during the evaluation process, you identify a significant vulnerability. In such a case, you need to revisit vulnerability analysis.

For this purpose, you identify all the internal resources—such as facilities, equipment, and capabilities—that can be used to mitigate the identified risks. In addition, you identify all the personnel who have specialized skills required during disasters, such as medical services.

Consider the example of earthquakes described in the earlier section titled "Analysis of Vulnerabilities." To mitigate the impact of earthquakes, an organization can perform offsite backups or install earthquake detection systems.

After you identify the existing safeguards implemented to mitigate risks, you need to evaluate their effectiveness. Often, the existing safeguards are implemented in accordance with the company rules and regulations. However, if you find the safeguards to be ineffective in mitigating the risks that potential threats pose, you must select additional safeguards to reduce the risk to acceptable levels.

Selecting Additional Safeguards

While examining the existing safeguards, if you find that the appropriate safeguards are not implemented or the existing safeguards are inadequate, you suggest additional safeguards. These additional safeguards are sometimes also referred to as *discretionary safeguards*. It is important to identify and document all possible safeguards.

The selection of safeguards depends on the kind of asset to be protected and the measure to which the protection is required. Based on the results of risk prioritization, you can implement any of the following categories of safeguards:

◆ **Protective measures.** Management decides on this category of safeguards for a risk that can be controlled. In this case, organizations invest money in the safeguards that help to mitigate the risk. You might also spread a risk to mitigate it. For example, you can distribute the valuable assets across facilities and locations.

◆ **Eliminating the risk.** Organizations adopt this category of safeguards when the risk is high. In this case, no safeguards are available to control the risk. Therefore, to mitigate the risk, the organization might not perform the activity that results in the risk.

◆ **Accepting the risk.** This category is implemented when the risk does not harm an asset. Therefore, safeguards to control the risk are not required.

◆ **Transferring the risk.** When an organization is unable to handle a risk appropriately, it might decide to transfer the risk to another entity— often a partner or another group. In this case, the risk can be handled by the subsequent entity cost effectively.

When you decide to eliminate a risk, you suggest the safeguards that are currently not in place and should be essentially implemented in accordance with the company rules and regulations. Next, you recommend the discretionary measures. To decide on the discretionary measures to implement, you need to consider the Return On Investment (ROI) value. A positive ROI indicates savings. If the cost of implementation of a safeguard is high, the ROI will be negative. In this case, safeguards that have a lower cost of implementation should be considered. Therefore, before implementing an additional safeguard, you need to consider the cost of its implementation.

An important consideration that goes into recommending safeguards is the budget within which the safeguards need to be implemented. The basic premise for selecting an additional safeguard is that the cost of controlling a risk should never exceed the potential loss caused by the risk. Therefore, to determine the safeguard to implement, you consider the dollar value of the impact of the risks and the cost effectiveness of the safeguards. To evaluate the cost effectiveness of the safeguards, you need to consider the vulnerabilities that the existing safeguards do not address. The new safeguards should address all the vulnerabilities identified during the vulnerability analysis but not addressed by the existing safeguards. Include the cost of developing, implementing, and maintaining additional safeguards. In addition, consider the life span of the safeguards. To evaluate the monetary benefit of an additional safeguard, you subtract the cost of maintenance of the safeguard from the monetary value of the risk impact.

It is likely that some additional safeguards map to vulnerabilities that do not compound the harm from a threat. It is also likely that the list of additional safeguards is extensive. How do you identify which safeguards to implement? In such a case, you must identify the vulnerability that is of the greatest concern to management. Then you simply identify the safeguards that mitigate the identified vulnerability. Additional safeguards are recommended to ensure that the baseline security level of the organization is met.

It is possible that one safeguard can mitigate the effect of multiple threats. A common example of such a safeguard is the backup of important server data to an offsite location. Not only can you ward off the risk due to power failures at the original site; you also can eliminate the threat to data from earthquakes.

 NOTE

When a single safeguard can mitigate the risk posed by multiple threats, you can calculate its benefit to the organization by integrating the risks from 1 to the last number before the safeguard is implemented to obtain A. Integrate the risk models, 1 to n, after the safeguard is applied to obtain B. Subtract B from A. Finally, subtract the annual cost of the safeguard from the net result. The following equation is used to calculate the benefit of a safeguard to an organization when a safeguard can mitigate multiple threats:

Net Benefit = (A-B) - Annual Cost of Safeguard

You might recollect that at the end of each phase, you derive a table that lists the results of the phase. You use this table in the next phase of the process. The result of each phase contributes to the final outcome of the risk analysis process. Now that you are familiar with the phases of risk analysis, we will discuss the output of the risk analysis process.

Output of Risk Analysis

Risk analysis involves examining the relationship between assets, threats, vulnerabilities, and safeguards to mitigate the risks with the highest criticality. The output of risk analysis is a report that summarizes the conclusions of all the phases of risk analysis. The report aids management in making decisions about the implementation of safeguards and planning for disaster recovery. In addition, the report consists of the detailed analyses and other documentation involved in the phases of risk analysis. After you have performed all the phases of the risk analysis process, the final output of the process is a report that includes the following:

♦ The critical activities and prioritized functions

♦ A prioritized list of the critical assets that support the critical functions

♦ The prioritized risks

♦ A description of the risks

♦ An evaluation of the existing safeguards

♦ The areas where safeguards are not implemented

♦ Recommendations for enhancement of the existing safeguards

♦ Recommendations for new safeguards

The result of risk analysis also helps to verify whether the safeguards in place are commensurate with the identified risks. Based on the analysis results, the organization can appropriately streamline its operations and business decisions to meet the present and the future of an uncertain environment.

As you can see, the output of the analysis helps you scope the efforts of disaster recovery planning. The output of successful risk analysis helps you plan disaster recovery budgets. You also can identify the possible catastrophes and take appropriate actions to prevent them. This aids not only in alerting management about the risks, but also in prioritizing the sites for disaster recovery plans.

 NOTE

If you're short of time, you can perform a well-defined and crisp prioritization of the critical activities and their recovery strategies. In this case, the prioritization and planning activities are scoped and well defined.

Summary

In this chapter, you learned that a risk consists of a risk event, risk probability, and risk impact. Like all things in life, you must take preventive measures for the risk events that might impact an organization. Risk analysis is a detailed process that helps you take preventive measures for risks by analyzing the risks associated with the critical activities and functions of an organization.

You can perform risk analysis either qualitatively or quantitatively. For successful risk analysis, you need to consider certain guidelines. The entire process of risk analysis is divided into the identification, analysis, and recommendation phases.

In the identification phase, you identify the critical activities, the critical functions, the critical assets, and the risks. During the analysis phase, you analyze the vulnerabilities of the critical assets that make them susceptible to threats and prioritize the identified risks. In the recommendation phase, you examine the existing safeguards based on their effectiveness to mitigate the identified risks and suggest enhancements, if required. In the recommendation phase, you also suggest the implementation of additional safeguards if the appropriate safeguards are found to be lacking or inappropriate.

The output of successful risk analysis helps you ensure that appropriate safeguards are implemented to prevent risks from being transformed into catastrophes. Therefore, it is of great significance to implement effective risk analysis.

Check Your Understanding

Multiple Choice Questions

1. Identify the statements that correctly affirm the guidelines to be followed for performing risk analysis.

   a. You must decide the level of risk acceptance before you begin risk analysis.

   b. You do not need to revisit risk analysis when a significant change occurs.

   c. You do not need to include the interdependencies between departments when you're analyzing risks.

    d. You must set the baselines for deciding the priorities before you begin risk analysis.

2. What is SLE?

    a. The value of the asset likely to be damaged by a risk.

    b. The quantitative or monetary representation of the loss caused by a single risk.

    c. The degree of loss in value of an asset caused by a risk.

    d. The annual frequency at which a risk is expected to occur.

3. What is ARO?

    a. The annual frequency at which a risk can occur.

    b. The loss likely to be caused by a risk in a year.

    c. The monetary representation of the loss caused by a single risk.

    d. The value of the asset that is likely to be damaged by a risk.

Short Questions

1. The risk analysis team at Mucarz, Inc. has created a risk identification table. As the next step, the team needs to recommend safeguards. List all the factors that the team should consider to make the recommendations.

2. How does the output of risk analysis play a significant role in disaster recovery planning?

Answers

Multiple Choice Answers

1. a. and d. Before you perform risk analysis, you need to decide the level of risk acceptance. In addition, you must set the baselines for deciding the priorities before you perform risk analysis.

2. b. You define SLE as the monetary representation of the loss caused by a single risk.

3. a. ARO is defined as the annual frequency at which a risk can occur.

Short Answers

1. While recommending safeguards, the team should consider the budget within which the safeguards need to be implemented. The team should ensure that the cost incurred to implement the safeguards does not exceed the potential loss caused by the risk. The recommended safeguards should address all the vulnerabilities identified during vulnerability analysis and not considered by the existing safeguards.

2. Risk analysis helps to verify whether the safeguards in place are commensurate with the identified risks. The output of risk analysis is a report that details the output of all the activities performed therein. This report helps management make decisions regarding the implementation of safeguards and plan for disaster recovery. Based on the report, an organization can appropriately streamline its operations and business decisions to effectively deal with risks before they result in disasters. Therefore, management can scope its efforts at disaster recovery planning. In addition, management can plan disaster recovery budgets and prioritize the sites for disaster recovery plans.

Chapter 5

Baseline Measures

Disasters do and will continue to happen. However, you can implement certain baseline measures to avoid most disasters. Even if a disaster does happen, proper planning and policies can contain much of the damage. This chapter discusses some important concepts in avoiding and handling disasters. Baseline measures such as access control, anti-viruses, and firewalls go a long way in securing your network. Installing Intrusion Detection Systems (IDSs) can forewarn you of an impending disaster. Backups help you remain prepared for the worst. You must implement these as a minimum to ensure that your organization is protected from disasters.

Access Control

Modern-day networks are like houses with lots of doors and windows in them, and the network administrators have the keys. The administrators must control access to various areas of the house by distributing the keys in a manner that provides people with what they need and denies them what they don't. The network administrators might want certain people to access only certain compartments in the house (network) or might want to use the "No Entry" board for some users.

Access control refers to any means, device, or feature that allows the network administrator to selectively grant or disallow access to a resource. The resource might be a file, an electronic document, or a sensitive area in the organization, such as the server room, servers, subnets, or any other network object.

Before moving on to the locks and keys, it is important to ascertain the following:

- ◆ What should be secured?
- ◆ What is the size of the network?
- ◆ What is the topology?
- ◆ How many subnets exist?
- ◆ Is the network connected to the Internet?
- ◆ What are the mission-critical servers that need to be secured?
- ◆ Do we need to provide access to external partners or suppliers?

Organizations need to answer these and numerous such questions before they can zero in on the resources that are to be secured. Armed with the list, organizations can then go about planning the locks that are required and the corresponding keys that should be distributed. Sound daunting already? It's better than having burglars take control over the house (organization).

TIP

Before organizations secure access to their network resources, it is important to find out what needs to be secured and lay out a comprehensive security plan accordingly. Never implement access control haphazardly.

Let's look at a scenario so that you can understand the importance of access control. Mike never shares a file without setting its permissions, and with good reason. It all began with an incident a month ago that nearly ruined the hospital's reputation. Mike is the system administrator at the computer data center of a large hospital. His team is in charge of maintaining the network. The data center contains highly confidential information about every patient admitted to the hospital. The center also contains employee details. Access to the data is highly regulated, or at least that was what Mike had thought. John, a young intern at the hospital, had noticed certain discrepancies in the symptoms of a heart patient. Abraham Livingstone, a rich industrialist, who had been admitted for a bypass, seemed healthier than what his report suggested. Moreover, Livingstone was still being administered strong medicines that his condition didn't warrant, which were doing him a lot of harm. John brought this to the notice of the authorities, who promptly ordered a covert inquiry. The inquiry revealed a shocking fact—the data had been tampered with. The inquiry further revealed that this had been possible due to the lack of a proper security policy governing the network. The data, although confidential, was accessible to all doctors, and worst of all, all doctors had write permissions to the data. This finding had disastrous possibilities. Any person having access to such data could jeopardize the lives of patients, as in this case.

Access control needs to be implemented in systems and networks to prevent unwanted or unauthorized intrusions. Almost all operating systems provide mechanisms to control access to shared resources. After the resources that need to be secured are decided upon, there are many ways to achieve them.

Physical access control is often implemented to mission-critical servers and domain controllers. Critical servers should be kept physically locked in a room, and access to the room should be severely restricted. This guards against direct access to the server console.

Access control can be divided into the categories discussed in the following sections.

Authentication

Authentication is one of the most important and common ways to implement access control. Users need to authenticate or prove their identity to the system, network, or service that they are trying to access. Thus, operating systems have the provision for user logins, as do many network servers and application services.

All operating systems have a class of users that is designated as administrators (or super user or root). These users have complete control over the system and can make system or network-wide changes. The administrators need to provide the administrative password to users to provide them with administrative privileges. Administrators can create user accounts that have limited rights. After an administrator has defined these rights, when a user logs on, the user account rights determine which resources and services the user can access.

In today's networked environment, users often need to authenticate to a server over the network. It might be a domain controller on a LAN or it might be a remote server across the Internet. In these cases, it is important that the authentication information doesn't get sniffed in between. This is where encryption technologies such as Kerberos and digital certificates come in. The former is typically used to authenticate over the LAN, whereas the latter is often used over the Internet.

Kerberos uses encrypted communication between the client and the server so that the conversation stays private. The password is not sent over the network. Only a hash of the password is sent, which is matched with the hash of the password stored at the server.

Digital certificates are a proof of user's identity and are typically guaranteed by a third party, whom both parties trust. This third party is known as the Certification Authority (CA). Digital certificates are handy when you're authenticating user IDs across the Internet. A Web site might verify the digital certificate before it allows the user to access content. Digital certificates can also be issued when a partner or supplier needs access to the organization network. In this case, the CA would belong to the trusting network.

Devices such as smart cards provide for greater security in authentication. They provide what is known as *dual authentication*. Someone might be able to guess a user password. To compensate, users have additional security in the form of the card. To authenticate themselves, users need to provide both the card and the password. If the card is stolen, users still have the password, and if the password is cracked, users still possess the card. The dual security ensures greater protection against impersonation.

Permissions

Permissions determine a user's access level after he has been authenticated. Thus, a user might have limited or no access to certain resources, and at the same time might have full access to others. For example, users need access to an enterprise-wide payroll database system. User permissions would determine whether the system could be accessed. The user might be allowed to read the data but not to modify it, or he might have complete access to the data.

Operating systems typically use Access Control Lists (ACLs) to list permissions on a network object for various users and groups. These ACLs determine the level of access that a user has on a given resource. For example, in UNIX, a user might have read (r), write (w), and execute (x) permissions granted or denied for a particular file or directory.

Permissions are inherited by default, which makes the task easier for the system administrator. Thus, if a user has read rights over a folder, he automatically has read rights for the files in the folder, unless the right is explicitly denied at the file level. Rights flow naturally from parent to child objects.

Permissions should be granted to a group of similar users, rather than to individual users. This makes the task of granting (and denying) permissions easier for the system administrator. Many operating systems have built-in groups with preassigned roles and rights, which the system administrator can modify according to his needs. For example, Windows 2000 has the built-in groups called administrators and backup operators. Administrators have complete control over the operating system, whereas backup operators can make file backups. Backup operators do not have sweeping rights like the administrators group. The domain users group might have even more restrictive permissions applied to them. Solaris uses Role-Based Access Control (RBAC) to implement the same concept. It's the same for other operating systems.

A user's permissions might be different when he logs in locally from when he logs in remotely. For instance, the finance manager might have access to a file called payroll.dat locally. However, he cannot access the same file when he logs on remotely over the Internet.

Encryption

Encryption is another way to implement access control. Data is encrypted to make it undecipherable for snoopers and also to store it safely. For example, Windows 2000 uses Encrypting File System (EFS) to encrypt data stored on a disk. Thus, even if a laptop is stolen, the data isn't compromised. Even sensitive data can be backed up.

Encryption also becomes important when communication takes place over an insecure network. Access to data can be restricted over the wire by encrypting the wire. For example, Virtual Private Networks (VPNs) use IPSec to provide encryption services at the network layer. This allows organizations to safely communicate over a highly insecure network, such as the Internet. PGP can be deployed to restrict access to confidential mail. Such software uses public key technology to implement encryption and decryption. Figure 5.1 depicts the process of encryption.

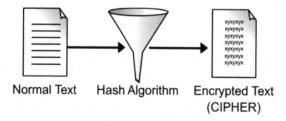

Normal Text   Hash Algorithm   Encrypted Text
(CIPHER)

FIGURE 5.1 *The process of encryption.*

You can deploy PGP to restrict access to confidential mails. Software such as these uses public key technology to implement encryption and decryption.

There are two common forms of encryption:

◆ **Symmetric encryption.** This involves the use of two identical keys for the encryption and decryption processes. These keys are known as *shared secret keys*.

Both the sender and receiver of the information share these keys prior to exchanging information via a network. The sender encrypts the message with his secret key. An identical shared key can only decrypt the message. When the receiver gets the message, she can easily decrypt it using his shared secret key.

Figure 5.2 illustrates the process of symmetric encryption.

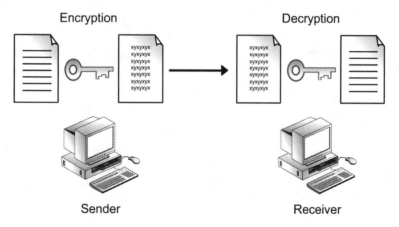

Encryption   Decryption

Sender   Receiver

FIGURE 5.2   *Symmetric encryption.*

◆ **Asymmetric encryption.** Asymmetric encryption involves the use of a public and private key pair. The theory behind this scheme is that what one key can encrypt, only the corresponding pair can decrypt. Thus, a message encrypted with the private key can be decrypted with the corresponding public key and vice versa.

In a typical scenario, an entity would distribute its public key freely, while only it has access to the private key. Anyone who wants to send confidential information to the entity can do so by encrypting it with his public key. Only the corresponding private key can decrypt the information.

The scenario also can be reversed. The entity can encrypt the message that it sends with its private key. Anyone can decrypt the message with the public key. This serves to prove the entity's identity. If it is the entity's public key that decrypts the message, it must be the same entity that encrypted in the first place.

Figure 5.3 illustrates asymmetric key encryption and decryption.

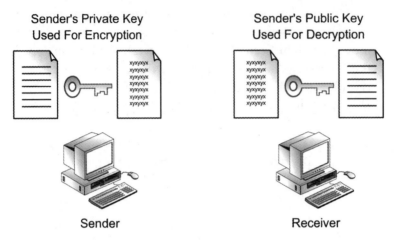

Sender's Private Key
Used For Encryption

Sender's Public Key
Used For Decryption

Sender

Receiver

FIGURE 5.3 *Asymmetric key encryption and decryption.*

Now that you've learned the various types of access control, take a look at another baseline measure—anti-virus.

Anti-Virus

The virus menace is not new to the computer world, and has always been a cause of disaster. Whereas the earlier viruses used to primarily spread through infected floppy disks, today's viruses are much more mobile, using networked environments and the Internet. A virus today can spread through to the other part of the world before it is diagnosed.

A *virus* is a program that breeds or replicates by attaching itself to another program, which thereby becomes infected. Viruses might bring down e-mail servers, corrupt systems and files, make operating systems inoperable, stop businesses, and lead to losses. In short, they are nothing short of impending disasters prowling around the globe. A special subset of viruses called *worms* are capable of causing even more havoc, and they spread at lightning speeds using the Internet as their vehicle.

Types of Viruses

Many types of viruses affect the computer resources in some way. They can primarily be classified into the following categories.

◆ **Boot sector viruses.** These viruses affect the Master Boot Records (MBRs) of the hard disk, whereby the virus loses or dislocates the partition table records. The virus substitutes its own code in place of the boot records in the boot sector. These viruses might lead to the operating system crashing completely.

Boot sector viruses are primarily spread through the use of infected floppy disks. These viruses were very prevalent in the early computing days. New boot sector viruses are seldom written today.

 TIP

To guard against boot sector viruses, administrators should disable the CMOS option to boot from floppy. This is recommended because users who boot from floppy disks can violate access control measures.

◆ **File viruses.** File viruses infect executable files. The virus inserts itself in the chain of command of the executable. Thus, whenever the legal program is executed, the virus code is executed as well. The virus code, in turn, can infect other memory resident programs. These viruses not only affect COM and EXE files, but they also can affect dlls, VxDs, screensavers, and font files. These viruses can then overlay or delete files. Even if a virus is seemingly harmless, it still troubles the system by using up memory, hard disk, and CPU cycles. Moreover, all viruses replicate.

◆ **Macro viruses.** Macro viruses are the rage today. They affect macro programming environments rather than specific operating systems. They are so dangerous because many applications support macros. Applications such as Microsoft Office (Word or Excel) become especially vulnerable because they allow code (macros) to exist in the same file as data. Thus, a simple Word document that a friend sends over the Internet can wreck havoc on your system if it's not scanned properly with appropriate anti-virus software. Melissa and Love Letter are notorious examples of e-mail-aware macro viruses.

◆ **Script viruses.** Script viruses are also increasingly being used in Windows environments. HTML scripts can contain VBScript or JavaScript programming. HTML-aware e-mail clients through the Windows Scripting Host can execute these. VBScript is especially used because of its many input/output capabilities, as opposed to the safer JavaScript.

◆ **Mimetic viruses.** Mimetic is an interesting class of viruses. They are not executable codes, but viruses of the mind. Often, unsuspecting employees get e-mail virus hoaxes, with the plea to forward them. There is no dearth of gullible believing these and adding to the load of the e-mail servers by circulating such warnings.

◆ **Worms.** Worms are a more dangerous subset of viruses that are especially prevalent on the Internet. Worms are self-replicating malware that rapidly spread across networks and systems. They can bring down e-mail servers if left to replicate unchecked.

Next let's look at anti-virus software.

Anti-Virus Software

Anti-virus software broadly comes in the following three categories:

◆ Generic software
◆ Virus-specific software
◆ Hybrid software

Generic software works by studying the environment of an infected object (such as a file) and looking for changes in it. It might look at file sizes and other integrity parameters, or it might look for a process that displays characteristic behaviors of a virus.

Virus-specific software checks suspected objects against a knowledge base of known virus definitions and reports the results. This software also might be able to remove the virus code from the infected object or recommend a replacement for the object. Virus-specific software can affect the scan on demand or can scan the objects transparently, as and when the user accesses them. You can commonly find products, such as Norton AntiVirus software, installed on computers that are connected to the Internet. You can put such software into an auto-scan mode so that it can scan material as and when it is downloaded.

Modern hybrid software is capable of both generic and specific techniques. Such software often uses a technique known as *heuristic analysis*, whereby the behavior of a virus is safely monitored under controlled conditions.

 TIP

Users in an organization should be educated about the threat of virus menace. They should be especially cautioned about downloading content from shady newsgroup sites and opening unsolicited mail attachments.

Everyone is aware of the fact that viruses are malicious computer programs that can damage computers. The confusion comes in deciding which type of anti-virus software to use out of the multitude that is available. Anti-virus programs indicate the possible presence of a known virus by looking for patterns in the files or memory of your computer. They know clearly what to look for through the use of virus profiles. Anti-virus software uses virus definition files, which contain the patterns and other signs associated with a virus.

New viruses pop up every day, and the anti-virus software that you have installed is effective as long as the virus definition files are the latest. These files are usually available on the Internet.

Installation of anti-virus software on your computer could have some undesirable side effects. Here are a few of them:

◆ **System slowdowns.** Virus protection software can sometimes slow your system. This is particularly true for older machines that have limited memory or other resources that can cause them to spend a good chunk of time scanning files. To prevent such slowdowns, turn off the auto-protect features and scan manually.

◆ **Problems with older systems.** On older systems, you might wish to disable all auto-protect features, especially those that run any time the computer is rebooted or scan all e-mail attachments. Be sure the program will work on your system before enabling those features. Remember, though, if you've turned off the auto-protect features, you must be vigilant about running regular scans and checking e-mail attachments.

◆ **Conflicts.** Two anti-viral programs are not better than one. In fact, two may be worse and may not work at all. Remove any other virus protection programs before installing your new software.

Firewalls

A *firewall* is a mechanism that enforces an access control policy for a network. Firewalls are designed to keep intruders out of your network. Some firewalls permit only e-mail traffic through them, thereby protecting the network against any attacks other than attacks against the e-mail service. Other firewalls provide less strict protections and block services that are known to be problems.

As might be evident to you by now, a firewall is a security system that is deployed on a network to prevent unauthorized access. The use of a firewall is not restricted to a network. You can even use a firewall to secure a personal computer that regularly accesses the Internet. A firewall can be a physical device or software. When you want to deploy a firewall on a physical device, you can use a router that connects the internal network to the Internet. Similarly, when you want to deploy a software-based firewall, you can use a proxy server. A proxy server has direct access to the Internet and processes all the requests from the other computers on the network.

Cheswick and Bellovin carried out research on Internet firewalls and concluded that a firewall has the following characteristics:

◆ A firewall is a single point of contact between two or more networks. All traffic must pass through this single point of contact.

◆ The traffic that passes through a firewall is logged.

◆ The traffic that passes through a firewall can be controlled and authenticated by the firewall.

Although the preceding definition of firewalls was provided in the early 1990s, it still holds true.

A firewall governs what comes in and goes out of the network. The bastion host model uses a single firewall to protect the network. All traffic that enters or leaves the network has to travel through the firewall. Small businesses that have an Internet presence can use this model.

Larger corporations use the more common screened subnet model. This model segregates all Internet-accessible resources—such as Web servers, e-mail servers, and FTP servers—from the rest of the network. The most common configuration involves an external firewall that is exposed to the Internet. Behind this are the Web and e-mail servers, which in turn are separated from the rest of the network by an Internal firewall. The area between the two firewalls is known as *screened subnet*, or more commonly as *Demilitarized Zone* (DMZ).

Functions of Firewalls

Regardless of the type of firewall, all firewalls perform some basic functions, such as authenticating users, securing a network from network scanning, performing Network Address Translation (NAT), and filtering services and packets. Let's look at these firewall functions.

Performing User Authentication

Users who place requests for data need to be authenticated before they are allowed to access the private network. A firewall can authenticate users to determine whether a request is genuine. The security policy of an organization determines the level of authentication that a firewall implements. If the policy states that only the users of the private network can access the Internet, then a firewall that validates the username and the password should be sufficient.

Sometimes users who are logged on to an external network should be allowed to access the private network of an organization. For example, the senior managers in an organization need to access their data using a laptop that is connected to the Internet. In such a case, the security policy would state that the users from a public network should be allowed to access the internal network. The threat perception of allowing external users to log on to the private network is high; therefore, the firewall might implement strong user authentication, as shown in Figure 5.4.

In strong user authentication, cryptographic techniques such as digital certificates are used to establish the authenticity of a user. Cryptographic techniques are much more reliable than authenticating users by a username and a password.

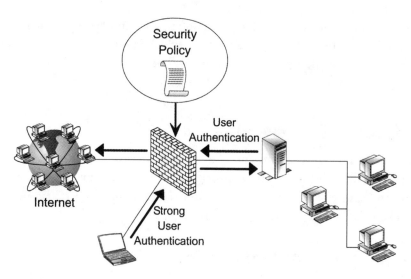

FIGURE 5.4   *Implementing user authentication on a firewall.*

Preventing Network Scanning

Network scanning is a technique employed by hackers to determine the hosts that are alive on a network and the services that are being run on these hosts. A hacker can then use this information to gain access to the network by using the services that are made available by the hosts.

To prevent network scanning, a firewall can block all IP-directed broadcasts at the router. You also can scan your own servers to determine the open ports that don't need to be open and can close these ports so that hackers are unable to access them.

Performing NAT

It is important to ensure that the IP addresses of the computers on your network are not exposed on the Internet. Exposing the IP addresses of internal computers to the Internet poses a security threat because hackers can use these IP addresses to gain access to your internal network.

NAT is a method that connects multiple computers to the Internet by using a single IP address. This enables home users and small businesses to cheaply and efficiently connect their network to the Internet. To avoid exposing the IP addresses of the computers in the internal network, you can implement NAT. NAT uses a set of public IP addresses to query all the data from the

Internet. When a computer in the internal network places a request for information, the following transaction takes place after the firewall has successfully authenticated the request:

1. The firewall receives the data packet from the client computer in the internal network.

2. At the firewall, NAT translates the IP address (in the request) to one of the public IP addresses that is available at the firewall.

3. The request is then forwarded to the destination.

If the destination sends a response, the following steps are followed to send the response to the client computer that had placed the request:

1. At the firewall, NAT translates the destination address on the data packet to the IP address of the client computer that had placed the request.

2. The response is sent to the client computer.

Figure 5.5 depicts the sequence of steps for making requests and receiving responses from a firewall that uses NAT.

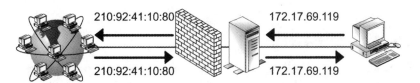

FIGURE 5.5   *Using NAT to hide the IP addresses of computers in a network.*

Filtering Services and Packets

Deploying a firewall ensures that the data that traverses the network conforms to the security specifications of the organization. For example, an organization might restrict users from downloading executable files from the Internet because they might damage the internal network. Similarly, an organization might restrict users from subscribing to and accessing newsgroups because they might cause undue load on the network.

A firewall enables you to impose such restrictions on the network. Service filtering and packet filtering impose these restrictions. These filters are described in the following list:

◆ **Service filtering.** Service filtering is used to grant access to selected services on a network. For example, if users are restricted from accessing newsgroups, the Network News Transfer Protocol (NNTP), which newsgroup services use, can be restricted. Similarly, the Simple Mail Transfer Protocol (SMTP) protocol can be restricted to ensure that users are not allowed to access e-mail services.

◆ **Packet filtering.** Data is transmitted on the Internet in the form of packets. Filtering the packets of data that are received from the Internet ensures that data that is not permitted to enter the private network is blocked at the firewall. For example, firewall administrators can specify a security policy that prohibits the firewall from receiving packets for executable files.

 NOTE

Instead of completely denying access to packets of data, a firewall also can send an error message to the sender of the data packet, send an alert message to a firewall administrator, or send the data but retain a copy of it that you can analyze later.

Types of Firewalls

Firewalls can be broadly classified into three categories: packet-filter–based firewalls, stateful packet-filter–based firewalls, and proxy firewalls.

Packet-Filter–Based Firewalls

These firewalls are typically implemented on routers and filter traffic based on the following parameters:

◆ Source and destination address

◆ Protocol

◆ Port

These firewalls are easy to configure and are widely used. Access Control Lists (ACLs) that are configured on a router form a packet-filtering firewall.

These firewalls, however, lack the ability to ward off advanced attacks that exploit TCP/IP anomalies such as distributed Denial of Service (DoS) attacks, SYN flooding, and attacks based on packet mangling. In addition, routers cannot keep track of session state information. Thus, administrators need to keep all ports above 1024 open to handle TCP session negotiations. Intruders can exploit this potential loophole.

Stateful Packet-Filter–Based Firewalls

These use the same concept as packet-filter–based firewalls, except that they can keep track of sessions. Internal state tables are used for this purpose.

These firewalls also give added protection for SMTP mail and are designed to protect against common forms of DoS attacks. Because these firewalls can track session states, administrators can keep ports above 1024 closed by default.

Proxy Firewalls

Although packet-filter–based firewalls check for source and destination IP addresses and ports, proxy firewalls inspect traffic at the application level on a protocol-by-protocol basis.

Thus, filtering occurs not only at the network and session layers, but also at the application level.

The application level proxy handles the request and then forwards packets to the internal network. Thus, an HTTP proxy handles Web requests, an FTP proxy handles FTP requests, and so on.

The only concerns with proxy-based firewalls are performance related because they are resource intensive.

Firewall Considerations

Most administrators tend to rely too heavily on firewalls and focus less on a comprehensive security policy. It would be appropriate to point out here that many network intrusions are internal as opposed to external. Firewalls need to be implemented as part of a larger security design.

> **NOTE**
>
> Simply installing a firewall is not enough. Misconfigured firewalls are the most common mode of intrusion into large networks. Always pilot test a firewall before deploying it.

In contrast, sometimes a firewall might be configured too stringently. Imagine this scenario. A company that provides e-commerce solutions decides to enhance security. The security expert moves the application servers to the firewall segment. A misconfiguration cuts these off from the database servers, resulting in considerable chaos.

Firewalls must be configured to balance the needs of security and functionality. You will learn about firewall products and deployment considerations in Appendix E.

The next section explains another baseline measure: Intrusion Detection Systems (IDSs).

IDSs

Hacking is a cool pastime for some teenagers, and Bob was one of them. The only son of a busy project manager, Bob began his hacking career by taking tips from the Internet and trying them out on the computer network at his school. He got his real break when his mother decided to work from home through a RAS connection to her office network.

Bob regularly snooped on his mothers' subordinates by reading the documents that were not password-protected. He then started hungering for more. Unfortunately for him, his first attempt proved to be unsuccessful. He had attempted to break into a machine, and an IDS installed at his mothers' office detected this attempt. Luckily for him, the matter was hushed up and he escaped being put in prison for a federal offense.

This is one of the few instances in which the intruder was successfully apprehended. Many companies often overlook this threat and end up losing valuable revenue clearing up the mess left behind by intruders. Intruders generally attempt to break into a system and misuse it. The misuse can range from stealing sensitive data to spamming. Whatever the case, intrusion is a threat that most networks face, and every network manager must take measures to ensure the security of his network.

As a system administrator, you have enough concerns on your mind. You have to ensure the day-to-day working of the network; you have to listen to people with silly problems; you have to ensure that everyone gets what he is entitled to; and you have to prohibit people from laying their hands on what they are not supposed to. On top of this, you must ensure that the mission-critical servers are always online, that they are never compromised, and that the backups are current and safe.

Wouldn't it be nice to have a helper around? Someone who can parse your logs, someone who can monitor your networks, someone who can raise alerts, and someone whom you can trust?

IDSs are based on this idea. They are meant to automate the process of detecting intrusions and safeguard your networks and systems. Most of these systems apply statistical analysis on audited data and analyze network packets to come to conclusions. They might in turn generate alerts or warnings about something being wrong. The idea is to have a sort of fire alarm installed that keeps watch around the clock. That way, you don't have to go around looking for smoke to detect the fire.

Think of these systems as fire or burglar alarms that alert you of an impending disaster, when there is still time left to act. Wouldn't it be wonderful to get alerts on an attempted breach of firewalls so that you can plug the loopholes in time? It also would be nice to get alerts on users who are trying to change their privileges or attempting to access restricted data. You might even be warned of an attempt to place Trojan code on one of your systems, or an attempt to compromise one of your servers. You might be warned of a user logging in at 2 a.m. on Christmas day!

However, before you start celebrating, you must be aware that these systems are not the panacea for all ills and do not relieve you of your duties. Even alert kits generate false alarms or might be fooled into snoozing while your house is being burgled.

 NOTE

IDS is still a technology that is in its infancy. It might take some time before the system really comes of age. Until then, you can only use them as helpers.

IDS Models

IDSs are based on various theoretical models. However, two of the most popular ones are misuse-based models and anomaly-based models.

Misuse-Based Models

These models are based on misuse detection. They rely on a built-in knowledge base of known attack patterns and signatures. They would monitor your system or network and constantly look for these patterns or signatures. They would then generate an alert if they smell anything fishy. The subsequent sections explain two categories of misuse-based models.

Network-Based IDSs

These are used to monitor a network segment for all traffic. They capture (sniff) all network packets and look for known attack patterns or signatures. For example, a DoS attack or a Trojan code might have its own signature. If this signature were in the list of known attack patterns of the NIDS, it would generate an alert. NIDS devices can be deployed passively (that is, without the need to install additional software on the network hosts).

Host-Based IDSs

These are used to monitor a particular system for possible intrusions or misuse. They normally monitor user logins and processes and check the system logs. Host-based systems require an active deployment. (That is, they require an agent software to be installed on the system that is to be monitored.)

Anomaly-Based Models

These models are based on the concept that anything out of the usual is suspect. An anomaly-based model would map the normal traffic and user patterns of the network over a period. It would then monitor the network for deviations from these normal patterns of behavior. For example, a user who logs in at 2 a.m. on Christmas Eve would appear suspicious to an anomaly-based model. These models, in theory, should be able to detect even those intrusions that are new and have unknown signature patterns.

NOTE

Most of the intrusion detection products on the market today are misuse based and not anomaly based. Ideal anomaly-based working models are the goal toward which we will eventually be moving.

Selecting an IDS

IDSs are an evolving technology; they aren't the ultimate security solution yet. IDSs can be useful for overworked administrators who just can't secure the network enough. Some network administrators use IDS to test the configuration of their firewalls. Some might use it to keep track of access violation attempts. Still others might use IDS to protect their servers from known trojans. IDS must be part of a broad security policy. IDS can be judiciously implemented in a multi-layered security policy.

The type of IDS that you need depends on the resources that you want to secure, the budget, and the manner in which the system fits into your current security setup. An organization won't accept an IDS unless it has deployed the basic security setup, such as firewalls, anti-virus, and system lockdown procedures.

One does not always need to look for features and the most dazzling user interface. For instance, if your requirement is to just parse the system logs on one of your servers, most Host Intrusion Detection Systems (HIDSs) do that. You don't need to purchase a state-of-the-art HIDS that is designed to look for deployment of Trojan code on the system. Also, the user interface for the system should be easy to use.

Keep in mind that the only thing static about the IDS technology is that it is continuously changing. Keep yourself abreast with the latest developments in the field. Product balances change quickly.

 TIP

Check the vendor you purchased your IDS from. An IDS needs to be continuously updated with the latest signatures and attack patterns or it becomes obsolete. The vendor must be willing to provide updates; otherwise, what is a gizmo today might turn out to be a legacy device tomorrow.

Analyzing IDSs

Each IDS has its own purpose, advantages, and disadvantages. A network intrusion detection system (NIDS) works by putting the network card in promiscuous mode, whereby it can sniff all packets on the network segment. One advantage of NIDS devices is that they are passive. Thus, they do not consume additional resource on the systems, and they are easy to deploy. A disadvantage with many products on the market is that they might struggle in high-bandwidth (100Mbps) environments. In addition, smart intruders can fool NIDS devices. Techniques such as packet fragmentation and resequencing of attacks can be used to evade NIDS detection.

Host intrusion detection systems (HIDSs) have their own advantages and disadvantages. These systems require the installation of agent software on the hosts. Therefore, they are an administrative burden, when hundreds of hosts need to be monitored. HIDS is useful in pointing out failed login attempts or access violations.

Some advanced systems can even detect attempts to install a Trojan code on a compromised system and can terminate the culprit process. HIDS have their share of problems, though. For instance, an HIDS cannot detect a hitherto unknown Trojan. Also, the HIDS agent software runs on the host machine and uses CPU cycles as well as memory. This might be a concern for overburdened systems.

A few products use the *anomaly detection model.* This is a concept that still has some way to go before it matures into a viable technology. The beauty of anomaly detection systems is they can even detect hitherto unknown attacks. The problem is that they also can generate a lot of false alarms because anything out of the ordinary might sound suspicious to them.

Data Backup

Even after placing all security plans in order, disasters do happen once in a while. People make mistakes, breaches happen, and hard disks crash. This is the time when backups are your only recovery solution. A sound backup policy and regular backups go a long way toward empowering you to face any eventuality.

Data is the most important thing that you need to back up. Data includes documents, spreadsheets, e-mails, address book records, accounting data, marketing data, and so on. You also might want to back up operating systems and applications. Most administrators tend to ignore these because they can be reinstalled. However, setting up another system with an identical configuration takes a lot of time and effort. The costs involved are simply too great to be ignored. Thus, even operating systems and applications need to be backed up.

 TIP

Back up your system before making major changes to it. This allows you the option to restore the system to its original state in case something goes wrong.

You need to decide on the frequency of backups when you're deciding on the backup policy. This period can be from a day to a month and varies from network to network. You also need to decide on the backup media. Tapes are the highly recommended media for storing backups. Other backup media options can be zip drives, CD-ROM drives, and removable hard drives.

 TIP

Small companies might consider backing up data on the Internet. This is useful if the data is not too critical and satisfactory encryption services are available.

Data backup is a critical measure that all companies must take, especially those that have an extensive network of computers. Restoring a few computers with simple configurations is a fairly easy process, but in large networks, several factors—such as configurations, shared resources, and applications—need to be reinstalled and reconfigured before you can return to normal operation. Even if you are well organized and have all the proper drivers, disks, manuals, and software for your equipment, this can be a very time consuming and expensive process during which you are unable to work.

You can prevent this costly downtime in several ways. One method is to have the proper backup system that executes a full systems backup on a daily basis. With large amounts of data, it is unrealistic to expect to complete a backup before leaving the office. A backup is best run overnight while the system is not in use and can be completed before arriving the next day. Another recommended safeguard backup is storing a mirror image of your data that allows you to keep working even if the main drive fails, thus allowing you to work through the day until a qualified technician can reach your office. This type of protection is known as *hard drive mirroring* and is typically a function of contemporary operating systems.

Data backup is big business these days, with service providers offering data storage and backup facilities known as hot sites. These facilities are more than just backup facilities. Hot sites are replicas of the clients' facility that provide business continuity in the event of a disaster. You will learn more about hot sites in Chapter 6, "The Recovery Plan."

It is important to secure data backup, both from intruders and natural disasters. Encrypting backed up data and placing it at a secure offsite location can achieve this.

You also need to decide how often you want to overwrite old backups. In other words, you need to decide on a backup rotation policy. This depends on the amount of resources available to you, such as the number of backup tapes you can afford. It is a good idea to keep old backups because they might prove invaluable in certain situations. Also ensure that the backed up data can be restored; otherwise, it will be like getting back to square one. You need to properly label and time stamp backed up data. Maintain backup media properly and periodically check it for integrity.

Backup servers provide load balancing and fault tolerance. You can promote a backup domain controller to a primary domain controller if the PDC crashes. It is important to keep the backup servers up to date with the information on the primary servers. The process that achieves this is known as *replication*. You might have two DNS servers sharing zone information through incremental backups. Multiple servers provide for load balancing.

 NOTE

Incremental backup involves backing up only the changes, as opposed to a full backup, which backs up everything. Only the modifications since the last backup need to be replicated.

Summary

In this chapter, we explored the various baseline measures that you can adopt to avert and cope with disasters. You learned about the methods used to implement access control, whereby different users have different rights to resources. Then we discussed viruses and anti-virus software. Firewalls are used to secure the network boundaries. You read about firewalls, their functions, and their types. This chapter also discussed the hottest disaster aversion technology on the market—IDSs. Finally, the chapter explained the need for backups and the considerations you should keep in mind while formulating a backup policy.

Check Your Understanding

Multiple Choice Questions

1. Which of the following characteristics of firewalls is not a direct consequence of the research conducted by Cheswick and Bellovin for Internet firewalls?

   a. Single point of contact.

   b. Controlled traffic.

   c. Logged traffic.

   d. Use for VPNs.

2. Identify the encryption technologies:

   a. Kerberos.

   b. Smart cards.

   c. VPNs.

   d. Digital certificates.

3. Identify the functions of firewalls:

   a. Performing user authentication.

   b. Filtering services and packets.

   c. Checking ACLs.

   d. Preventing network scanning.

4. What is the technique employed by hackers to determine the hosts that are alive on a network and the services that are being run on these hosts known as?

   a. NAT.

   b. Sniffing.

    c. Network scanning.

    d. Heuristic analysis.

Short Questions

1. Why should you back up your system before making major changes to it?

2. What types of organizations should consider backing up data on the Internet and why?

Answers

Multiple Choice Answers

1. d. The use of firewalls for VPNs was envisaged much after the research conducted by Cheswick and Bellovin on firewalls.

2. a. and d. Kerberos and digital certificates are encryption technologies. Smart cards are devices that provide security in authentication.

3. a., b., and d. The functions of firewalls include performing user authentication, filtering services and packets, and preventing network scanning.

4. c. Network scanning is the technique that hackers use to determine the hosts that are alive on a network and the services that are being run on these hosts.

Short Answers

1. It is a good practice to back up your system before making major changes to it. This enables you to restore the system to its original state in case something goes wrong.

2. Small companies might consider backing up data on the Internet. This is useful because their data is not voluminous, and satisfactory encryption services are available on the Internet.

Chapter 6

In Chapter 4, "Risk Analysis," you learned that the output of risk analysis helps you scope the efforts of disaster recovery planning. The report generated at the end of risk analysis aids management in creating a disaster recovery plan.

The September 11, 2001 incident caused unfathomable loss to property and lives. These were times when the disaster recovery plans that organizations had created were put to test. A case in point is that of Dow Jones and Co., publisher of *The Wall Street Journal*. With its main offices located near the WTC towers destroyed, the organization implemented its disaster recovery plan. It shifted its editors, reporters, and support personnel to alternate offices, installing 100 workstations and ordering additional network capacity. As a result, the organization was able to sustain its business operations and provide its readers the newspaper the next day.

The case of Dow Jones and Co. isn't a lone case. Many organizations implemented their plans, and those that didn't have a plan in place took up the task of creating a disaster recovery plan to prevent losses from future disasters.

This chapter focuses on the objectives of a disaster recovery plan. It also covers the steps involved in the creation and implementation of a disaster recovery plan.

Objectives of a Disaster Recovery Plan

In Chapter 1, "Disaster Recovery Planning: An Overview," you learned that a disaster recovery plan is a comprehensive set of statements created to address any disaster that is likely to damage an organization. Before embarking on the task of creating a disaster recovery plan, consider and list the objectives of the plan for your organization. Some of these objectives include the following:

◆ Safety and welfare of the people on the premises at the time of disaster

◆ Protection of critical information and records

◆ Protection of business sites and facilities

◆ Protection and availability of materials, supplies, and equipment for the safety and recovery of vital records

◆ Minimization of the occurrence and duration of disasters

◆ Reduction of the immediate damage and loss

◆ Preparation in advance for recovery from a major natural catastrophe

◆ Business continuity in the event of a disaster

◆ Recovery of damaged and lost records or information after a disaster

◆ Reduction of the complexity of the recovery effort

◆ Coordination of recovery tasks

The preceding list is not exhaustive. You might want to add or remove certain objectives based on the needs and nature of your organization. Regardless of the objectives, the main purpose of a disaster recovery plan is to respond to and recover from disasters. For this purpose, a disaster recovery plan includes disaster response and recovery procedures.

Disaster response procedures are developed to counter the threat or damage caused by a disaster to an organization's assets. These procedures are implemented as an immediate response to a disaster and are aimed at protecting people and property.

When a disaster affects an organization, the organization's normal business operations are disrupted. Long after the occurrence of a disaster, its aftermath continues to impact the organization until the situation becomes critical. Disaster recovery procedures are designed to reduce the aftermath of disasters and ensure recovery of the organization's business operations.

To achieve its purpose, a disaster recovery plan must have the following characteristics:

◆ **Authority.** Disasters often result in chaos when they're not adequately planned for. An important cause for the chaos is the lack of specification or communication of the flow of authority. A disaster recovery plan clearly states the flow of authority in times of catastrophe. This flow might not be the same as in normal circumstances. As a result, it is also necessary to specify the roles and responsibilities of individuals in each tier of authority. It should be clearly stated who makes key decisions when responding to and recovering from a disaster.

◆ **Process.** The response to and recovery from disasters involves a set of processes and procedures that need to be meticulously performed.

These processes and procedures should be clearly specified in a disaster recovery plan. This helps minimize the impact of the disaster on the organization.

◆ **Accessibility.** A disaster recovery plan is implemented during a disaster. However, if the plan cannot be found or implemented, it serves little purpose. A disaster recovery plan should, therefore, be accessible in times of need. To facilitate accessibility, the plan should be created in a format that is accessible during a disaster. For instance, you must not store a disaster recovery plan on a computer for which data backup has not been made. In the event of a system failure, the computer will be inaccessible and the plan will not be retrievable.

Now that we have examined the objectives of a disaster recovery plan, we will discuss the steps involved in the creation of a disaster recovery plan.

Steps to Create a Disaster Recovery Plan

The creation of a disaster recovery plan is a collective effort that involves individuals from all organizational departments. These individuals might perform different tasks in the creation process. For instance, whereas one individual might determine the order in which the systems will be restored after a disaster, another might oversee disaster recovery. In addition, the plan might be created and owned by the same individual or group or different individuals or groups.

Figure 6.1 displays data about the creation, ownership, and maintenance of a disaster recovery plan based on the survey conducted by Information-Week Research.

In Figure 6.1, the bars indicate the percentage of people who are involved in creation, ownership, and maintenance of the plan.

It is essential to include the personnel who will be involved in disaster recovery in the team that creates a disaster recovery plan. The creation of the plan by the employees of an organization ensures complete and dedicated effort.

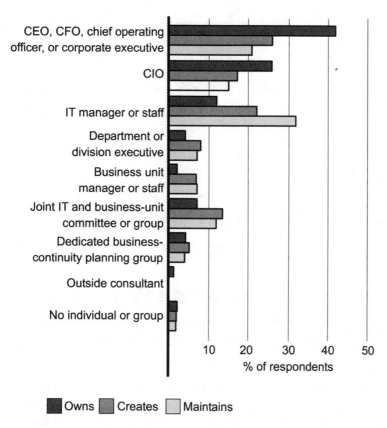

FIGURE 6.1   *Data about creation, ownership, and maintenance of a disaster recovery plan.*

However, if the organization does not have the expertise to create a disaster recovery plan, it can employ either of the following:

◆ **Consultants.** You can hire a consultant or an external specialist to tailor the plan to your specific needs. Such an individual helps meet the requirements of the various departments of the organization. The experience and expertise of a consultant in the field helps to make the plan better.

◆ **Specialized vendors.** You can also select a vendor that is specialized in disaster recovery to create a disaster recovery plan for your organization. However, based on the vendor's area of expertise, only specific areas of the planning task might be considered or emphasized at the expense of the other areas. As a result, all the needs of the organization might not be satisfactorily met.

With the preceding specialists providing only a limited support, many organizations opt for a combination that includes the expertise of the consultants or vendors and the dedication of the planning team composed of employees.

Now that you know about the individuals who are involved in the creation of a disaster recovery plan, you will learn about the steps involved in the creation of the plan. These include the following:

1. Identifying recovery strategies
2. Selecting recovery strategies
3. Creating the first draft of the disaster recovery plan
4. Creating the final draft of the disaster recovery plan

These steps are described in the subsequent subsections.

Identifying Recovery Strategies

All the plans and procedures that an organization follows to recover business and information within recovery objectives are known as *recovery strategies*. These strategies form an important part of the disaster recovery plan.

To identify recovery strategies, you should consider the short, intermediate, and long-term outages caused by the occurrence of a disaster. Strategies also differ on the basis of long-term and short-term recovery goals. For example, a short-term recovery strategy might be to implement a fix until a permanent solution is defined. The permanent solution is the long-term recovery strategy. You can adopt various strategies ranging from basic backup and recovery to moving critical records and operations to remote sites.

The strategies adopted to recover from disasters vary based on the resource for which strategies are being identified. In the subsequent sections, you will learn about the recovery strategies that you can implement for various resources, which include these:

◆ Computer center recovery strategies

◆ Department recovery strategies

◆ Telecommunications recovery strategies

◆ Data and documentation recovery strategies

Computer Center Recovery Strategies

The strategies to recover a computer center from disaster are aimed at recovering critical information, functions, and assets of the center in the shortest possible time. The critical functions of an organization can be recovered in a matter of hours or days. The strategies to recover a computer center from disasters include the following:

◆ Alternate sites

◆ Reciprocal agreements

The following sections discuss these strategies.

Alternate Sites

Consider a case in which the entire computer center is destroyed. In such a case, the information and assets stored at another site ensure successful recovery and resumption of business operations. In other words, to ensure the successful recovery from a disaster, you can store critical information at an offsite location. Such offsite locations that are selected to completely relocate a primary site are known as *alternate sites*. A *primary site* is the facility where an organization conducts its business operations under normal circumstances. Alternate sites are also known as *backup sites*. There are two types of alternate sites: cold sites and hot sites.

Cold Site

A *cold site* is a vacant facility with sufficient cabling and space so that it can be set up with equipment and personnel in a short time. Only the physical structure of the site is available; the equipment and other resources on which the business depends needs to be set up. As a result, the entire process of setting up the site might take a little longer than a site with the required equipment already installed.

Hot Site

To ensure that in the face of a disaster, an organization does not lose its customers, business, and profits, the organization can set up a remote site that includes all the resources required to successfully resume business. These sites are known as *hot sites*. Hot sites comprise all of the information and resources necessary to meet business requirements in the face of a disaster. The computer and network infrastructure are already installed. You only need to configure the infrastructure to suit your requirements. Hot sites are one of two types:

◆ **Internal hot sites.** If an organization owns the facility and the resources of a hot site, the facility is known as an *internal hot site*. Such an arrangement ensures that the hot site has all the resources required to ensure business continuity. In addition, the hardware and software at the hot site will be consistent with those in use at the primary site.

◆ **Outsourced hot sites.** Hot sites that service providers provide are known as *outsourced hot sites*. In such a case, the facility provided might either be fixed or mobile. A hot site that the service provider provides right at your doorstep is known as a *mobile hot site*. Hot sites might also be transported to the customer's facility and constructed upon delivery. Such sites are known as porta-sites.

Reciprocal Agreements

Often, organizations that share an excellent working relationship sign an agreement to store their data on each other's premises. Such organizations mutually reserve spaces to store their business-relevant data. However, because this strategy implies relying on the resources of another organization, it involves legal complexities.

Department Recovery Strategies

Each department in an organization performs critical activities and functions. When a disaster threatens a critical activity or function of a department, the department can follow any of the following strategies:

◆ **Deference.** In a *deference* strategy, the organization defers the business activity or function until the effect of the disaster passes. A function is deferred to a time when its restoration can be performed at the time of recovery. Departments that do not have urgent timing requirements, such as the audit department, often implement the strategy of deference.

◆ **Dispersal.** When a department distributes its business activities or functions among other departments to avoid the impact of the disaster on a single department, the strategy is known as *dispersal*.

◆ **Relocation.** Another strategy followed by departments is that of *relocation*. In this strategy, the department relocates the business operations during recovery.

Telecommunications Recovery Strategies

The recovery of telecommunications involves the recovery of voice communication and data communication. Only individuals such as recovery vendors and telephone carriers can perform telecommunications recovery because of the special knowledge involved.

The recovery of voice communication depends on the local and long-distance telephone carriers. The strategies employed for recovery rely on the local telephone organization. The local telephone organization intercepts calls with a recorded message or redirect calls to an alternate location.

The time required to implement these strategies depends on preplanning and the technological capabilities of the local phone organization. If an alternate site is available, switching communications to the alternate site is a matter of minutes or hours. However, the absence of an alternate site delays the entire switching process.

To recover data communications, you can use multiple strategies. Some of these include prearranged switch circuits and prepositioned dial backup, such as modem dial backup. You also can use redundant network paths and links.

Data and Documentation Recovery Strategies

An organization maintains two types of data: current data and historical data. It is essential to maintain both types of data for regulatory or legal purposes. Following are three recovery strategies for critical data:

◆ Offsite data backups

◆ Record dispersal

◆ Record re-creation

Offsite Data Backups

Data backup refers to the process of creating copies of data so that personnel can resume work after restoring files and applications. These backups are made backup sites.

Whereas a backup of the current data is made on a daily basis, backup of historical data is made only when the data is updated. To ensure backups of both types of data, you must assign the responsibility of backups to individuals. The document owner should be responsible for backups of paper or microfilm documents. Similarly, the responsibility for making backups of electronic data should be assigned to an individual.

You can perform offsite backups using the following methods:

◆ Backup with vaulting

◆ Replication

◆ Global clustering

Backup with Vaulting

In this strategy, an organization's data is transferred from the onsite location to a secure vault environment by using backup tapes. This is also referred to as the *pickup truck access method*. However, this strategy might result in recovery spanning days rather than hours. The two types of vaulting are as follows:

◆ **Physical offsite vaulting.** In physical offsite vaulting, data backups are transported every day from the primary site to an offsite location.

◆ **Electronic vaulting.** In electronic vaulting, data backups are transmitted electronically to backup tapes at a secure site.

Replication

In replication, you maintain an updated copy of critical data for immediate retrieval. This strategy allows you to maintain multiple copies of data at different locations. When data at a site is modified, the updated data is replicated across all locations. This strategy is employed to minimize the downtime of business operations and to recover mission-critical information within seconds or minutes. Data is replicated in two ways:

◆ **Synchronous.** In *synchronous replication*, the replication of data is committed across all the machines and nodes that are involved in the transaction. At any point in time, the data on the primary site and the other locations is the same.

◆ **Asynchronous.** In *asynchronous replication*, the replication of data is not committed. In addition, at any point in time, the data on the primary site and other locations might differ.

Global Clustering

Clustering is the grouping of two or more host machines, connected over the network, to share storage resources. Clustering ensures that if one host machine or node in the cluster fails, another node can resume a transaction. Consider a cluster with two nodes having the same applications and data available on shared disks. In this case, the failover from one node to another will be immediate and transparent to users and applications.

Record Dispersal

Another strategy for data and documentation recovery is to distribute copies of critical data across geographical boundaries. For this purpose, an organization maintains redundant data centers. If the original copy of the data is destroyed in a disaster, its copies can be used readily.

Record Re-Creation

You can re-create a document after it has been destroyed in a disaster. To achieve this, you can take input from customers and data users.

After identifying the different strategies that can be used to recover various resources from disaster, you need to select the appropriate strategy for implementation during a disaster.

Selecting Recovery Strategies

The selection of appropriate strategies helps you reduce the complexity of the disaster recovery procedures and enhance the efficacy and implementation of the disaster recovery plan. With so many business continuity strategies available, how do you select the appropriate one?

The following are some general guidelines for selecting recovery strategies:

◆ **Strategies should be flexible.** The strategies selected for implementation should not be rigid. These strategies should allow for the expansion of an organization and its resources. In addition, strategies should be able to adjust to the increase in the amount of data that the organization maintains. In other words, as the business grows, the disaster recovery plan should be able to change with the growing needs.

◆ **Strategies should be well planned.** All the strategies implemented in a disaster recovery plan should be well planned. In other words, all the resources, such as personnel, processes, and technology, that are required for response to and recovery from disasters should be identified when determining the recovery strategies.

◆ **Strategies should be comprehensive.** The strategies selected for implementation in the plan should address the most likely—if not all—types of disasters likely to impact an organization. In addition, the strategies must ensure recovery from minor disasters as well as the disasters likely to cause the maximum damage.

◆ **Strategies should meet the recovery objectives.** The selection of recovery strategies is driven by their ability to meet RPO and RTO values. Based on these values, the strategy deployed might vary from tape backup to electronic vaulting or mirroring.

◆ **Strategies should be cost effective.** When you're selecting strategies, consider the reduction in the cost of recovery and the increase in ROI achieved by implementing the strategy. The organization's budget plays a significant role in the selection of the strategy. When you're evaluating the costs of the strategies, include the purchase of equipment required for recovery, such as data processing emergency support and backup equipment. In addition to these one-time costs, you also must consider the ongoing costs, such as the rent and maintenance contracts for alternate sites.

In addition to these general guidelines, specific considerations need to be kept in mind based on the resource being recovered. The importance of each consideration might vary from one organization to another, but the most important issues remain those on which the survival of the organization is dependent. The subsequent sections detail the considerations for selection of the following recovery strategies identified in the earlier section "Identifying Recovery Strategies."

◆ Computer center recovery

◆ Department recovery

◆ Telecommunications recovery

◆ Data and documentation recovery

Selecting Computer Center Recovery Strategies

The selection of computer center recovery strategies requires the evaluation of the locations to be implemented as disaster recovery sites. These sites are also known as disaster recovery centers. The factors to be considered while evaluating strategies are as follows:

◆ **Site location.** The site to be selected as a disaster recovery center ideally should not be located in the same geographical area as the primary site. This ensures that if the primary site is destroyed in a disaster, critical data and resources of the organization are safe at the remote location. To reduce the likelihood of the disaster recovery center being damaged by the same disaster, the site should be located five or more miles from the primary site. However, if the region is prone to disasters, a location outside the primary site should be considered.

◆ **Site accessibility.** All the information stored in a disaster recovery center should be accessible on short notice. In addition, the site should be accessible from the primary site to ensure a smooth transfer of material to the site. This is of significance particularly when a disaster strikes and the routes to the disaster recovery center might be blocked. You must also consider the time required to acquire, activate, or prepare a disaster recovery center for use.

◆ **Site security.** Because disaster recovery centers store confidential and critical information and documentation, you should spare no efforts to secure the site. It is advisable that you implement the same access control and security measures for the backup data at the disaster recovery center as in use at the primary site. To ensure security, procedures to identify the personnel allowed access to the disaster recovery centers should be implemented. These procedures should be reviewed and improvised on a regular basis. Additionally, all environmentally controlled factors that affect equipment and media should be kept in mind.

◆ **Automatic failover.** To ensure an automatic failover, the disaster recovery center should be ready to assume the workload in the event that the primary site is destroyed. Clustering of the disaster recovery center and the primary site should be considered to achieve true automatic failover.

◆ **Availability of trained personnel.** It is important to ensure that at the time of disaster, when the disaster recovery site comes in use, trained personnel are available to ensure primary takeover. During *primary takeover*, the disaster recovery center assumes the role of the primary site. If the takeover is dependent on vendor support, you must also ensure vendor support. However, while considering the vendor support, you must assess the reliability and commitment of the vendors.

Selecting Department Recovery Strategies

When you're selecting the recovery strategy for the functions of a department, you should consider the impact of the interruption of the function. In addition, you should consider the impact of any resultant loss of information.

Selecting Telecommunications Recovery Strategies

When you're selecting a telecommunications recovery strategy, you must consider the ongoing costs incurred due to a disaster. In addition, you must assess and evaluate how many phones and terminals need to be restored and when. Finally, you must consider what recovery plans exist for communication recovery if centralized computing is being used.

Selecting Data and Documentation Recovery Strategies

The selection of the recovery strategy for data depends on the needs of the organization and the budget allocated by the management for disaster recovery. For instance, you can make backups of data from the primary site to the disaster recovery center or use recovery software.

For the selection of data and documentation recovery strategies, you must consider the following:

- ◆ **Data integrity.** Consider the accuracy of the data when you're selecting a recovery strategy.
- ◆ **Data currency.** Consider how often backups are performed to determine how current the data is.
- ◆ **Performance.** Assess the performance of a recovery strategy. To do this, evaluate the time taken to recover data and the time within which data recovery can be implemented.
- ◆ **Distance.** Evaluate the distance across which data backup and recovery can occur.

By assessing the business continuity needs of the organization, prioritizing, and combining strategies in different ways, you can find the best strategies to meet your needs.

After you select the appropriate disaster recovery strategies, you need to document all the disaster recovery procedures in a disaster recovery plan.

Creating the First Draft

All the strategies decided earlier are placed together in the form of a draft known as the *disaster recovery plan*. A disaster recovery plan should include all aspects of recovery. For instance, you should even document the procedures of how to cooperate with police, medics, firefighters, and other emergency workers and ensure the safety of employees. Therefore, a disaster recovery plan comprises extensive information that can be used during a disaster. The main purpose behind providing extensive information is to ensure that the occurrence of a disaster does not lead to chaos. To this effect, the plan includes the following information:

◆ Description of how, when, and by whom the disaster recovery plan is activated

◆ Description of the roles and responsibilities of the individuals involved in disaster recovery

◆ Coordination of the organization with local agencies

◆ Procedures for notification of disasters to external authorities

◆ Procedures for notification of personnel when disaster response measures are initiated

◆ Specification of information about disasters, such as severity levels

◆ Management of scheduling, modification, and discontinuation of services

◆ Management of staff activities and staff or family-support activities

◆ Management of logistics of critical supplies

◆ Management of security

◆ Evacuation of the facility of the organization

◆ Movement of critical information from the organization facility to a secure site

- Tracking the movement of critical information and resources
- Protocols for including agencies in disaster recovery procedures
- Communication with other corporate offices and local government agencies
- Specification of conditions where assistance from local government agencies and corporate offices is required
- Names, telephone numbers, and other contact numbers of key recovery personnel
- Criteria for determining when restoration should be attempted and when it should not
- Lines of succession of key personnel and procedures for movement to alternate headquarters
- Procedures for training, implementing, testing, and maintaining the disaster recovery plan
- Implementation of changes to user procedures, upgrading existing data processing operating procedures to support selected recovery strategies and alternatives
- List of resources—such as personnel, equipment, and tools—that are required to perform a recovery task
- Vendor documentation for standard methods of performing a task
- Vendor contract negotiations and the definition of recovery teams
- Communication with customers, suppliers, business partners, and investors
- Communication between the main facility and the disaster recovery site

 NOTE

Store all vendor documentation at the alternate sites for retrieval in the event of a disaster.

The preceding list is not a complete listing of the information that needs to be documented in a disaster recovery plan. Several more details go into creating the first draft of a disaster recovery plan.

As you can see from the preceding list, responsibilities, policies, procedures, agreements, and understanding for internal and external resources should be documented in a disaster recovery plan. It is also essential to document all the actions and processes required to resume the normal functioning of the organization. This ensures that the recovery is quick, efficient, and cost effective. A disaster recovery plan also includes maps, building plans, and location of emergency equipment, supplies, and utilities in a facility. In addition, an organizational chart and notification hierarchy of key personnel is documented.

A disaster recovery plan is a blueprint for the successful recovery of an organization. Figure 6.2 traces the steps involved in the recovery from a disaster.

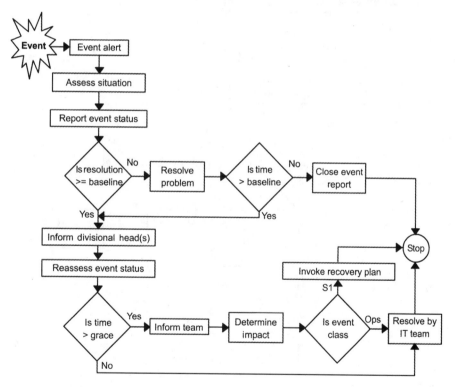

FIGURE 6.2   *Flowchart for the recovery from disasters.*

After you determine that the occurrence of a disaster occurs beyond a grace time period, notify the planning team. Report information related to the disaster, such as type, cause of occurrence, and extent of damage caused. The planning team determines the impact and identifies the severity level of the disaster. This information is used to decide whether to invoke the disaster recovery plan. When the plan is invoked, the recovery personnel activates the disaster recovery procedures.

An important consideration in a disaster recovery plan is the resumption of activities in the primary site after a disaster. How can these be accomplished, and what are the steps involved? Figure 6.3 displays a flowchart that traces the steps for the restoration of the primary site.

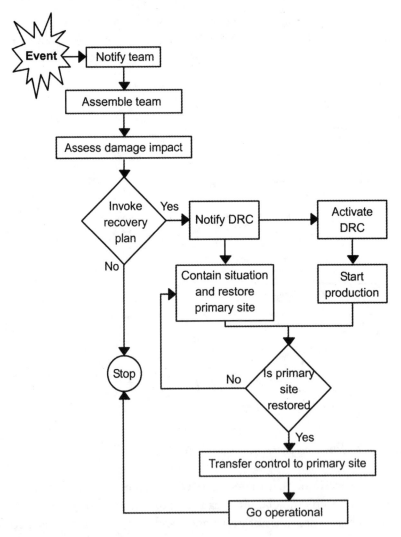

FIGURE 6.3 *Flowchart for the restoration of the primary site.*

After a disaster has occurred, the initial response team composed of the planning coordinator and the disaster recovery coordinator assesses the damage. Based on the assessment, the team decides whether to implement the disaster recovery plan. If the situation demands the implementation of the disaster recovery plan, the disaster recovery center is notified and activated. Before activation, ensure that the system configuration and the network requirements are accurate. This is performed as part of testing of the alternate sites.

All business operations are moved to and performed from the disaster recovery center until the primary site is restored. To restore the primary site, the critical function and assets are restored. The critical applications are restored to the most current data available in backups. In addition, network connectivity is established. After restoration of the primary site, business operations are moved from the disaster recovery center to the primary site.

In addition to the preceding information, a disaster recovery plan emphasizes the following issues, which you need to keep in mind while recovering from disasters:

◆ Creating administrative policies

◆ Taking charge of the situation

◆ Ensuring communication

◆ Protecting lives

◆ Protecting property

◆ Seeking assistance

◆ Performing administrative and logistical tasks

Creating Administrative Policies

Disasters lead to situations that are quite different from normal circumstances. As a result, new policies need to come in effect during a disaster. Such policies should be created to prevent an outbreak and ensure a smooth recovery process. Administrative policies for the following should be considered:

◆ **Tracking expenditure.** In the days after a disaster, an organization experiences panic expenditure. In other words, there is a loss of control over expenditure in the period immediately following the occurrence of a disaster. Therefore, you need to create policies to track all recovery-related expenses.

◆ **Reporting recovery status.** Due to the potential of disasters to cause loss of personnel and property, it is essential to report the status of recovery. Reporting should be done at regular and preplanned intervals. Whenever a recovery milestone is reached or an exceptional recovery has happened, it should be reported. The task of reporting recovery status helps to eliminate misunderstanding and its resultant problems and channel funds in the appropriate direction.

◆ **Bypassing normal policies.** In disaster recovery, the main aim of an organization is to recover in the shortest possible time. As a result, many existing policies are overridden to achieve recovery. A common and obvious example is the bypassing of signatures for purchasing recovery resources.

Taking Charge of the Situation

During a disaster, individuals must be placed in charge of managing resources, analyzing information, and making decisions. Such tasks might lead to the creation of teams that depend on the size of the organization. For instance, large organizations have their own fire and hazardous material team.

The disaster recovery plan must define the roles of personnel and establish procedures for each role. For instance, all the procedures and responsibilities for firefighting, medical attention, and engineering should be defined. One important task is determining lines of succession for continuous leadership and authority. It is likely that the individual who makes important decisions can become either injured or killed in a disaster. In such a situation, the next in command who will assume the roles and duties of the injured or deceased should be specified.

Account for tasks such as notifying suppliers where to deliver and notifying customers about what has happened. All the equipment and supplies required for each critical function must be specified and planned for. Specify the responsibilities for the recognition and reporting of disasters, implementation of security and safety measures, and evacuation.

 ## Ensuring Communication

Do not overlook the significance of communication during disaster. As stated earlier, disasters are times of chaos. In the ensuing chaos, the practices that an organization follows to perform normal operations are likely to change. Further, the unavailability of documentation of practices followed in an organization stating who does what and when aggravates the situation. Communication is essential to report disasters, warn personnel, keep the next of kin informed about the situation and circumstances, and retain contact with customers and suppliers. With communication being hampered following a disaster, confusion and miscommunication between employees is likely to occur.

To ensure communication during disaster, you need to set up a communication center. In addition to ensuring communication, this center acts as a centralized point for coordinating support activities. The communication infrastructure comprises telephones, fax machines, interoffice mail, e-mail, and face-to-face communication.

For communication purposes, you must allocate two centers—offsite and onsite centers.

◆ **Onsite centers.** Onsite centers are used for common disaster management, such as power or communications failure.

◆ **Offsite centers.** Offsite centers are used when the primary site is unavailable. Such a center should be located at least 500 ft and preferably 1 or 2 miles away from the primary site.

While creating the plan, plan for partial to total communications failure. For this purpose, consider the role of communication in everyday life and the impact of a lack of communication. Establish the procedures for restoration of communication systems. Also consider communication with government agencies.

Protecting Lives

After a disaster strikes a facility, the first thing to ensure is the evacuation of all the people in the building. For this purpose, you must develop an evacuation policy and procedure and determine the conditions under which evacuation is necessary. You must also establish a clear chain of command to authorize evacuation and identify the personnel to assist in evacuation. In addition, lay down procedures for assisting disabled individuals during evacuation. Assign personnel the responsibility to shut down the premises of the organization after evacuation.

Protecting Property

While ensuring the protection of property, you must consider the facilities, equipment, and vital records of the organization. You must, therefore, outline procedures for shutting down equipment and moving the equipment to a safe location. Further, you must specify which systems need to be installed to protect the premises from disasters, such as fire protection systems and water overflow detection systems.

Seeking Assistance

The protection of an organization's personnel and property is often influenced by its relationship with the community and the assistance of vendors. Maintain contact with community leaders, government agencies, and other agencies that might be of assistance during a disaster. In addition, you should establish mutual agreements with local agencies and businesses.

You must sign agreements and contracts with vendors for post-disaster services, such as records preservation, equipment repair, and so on. In addition, you should discuss property and business resumption policies with insurance carriers.

Performing Administrative and Logistical Tasks

During a disaster, you must maintain complete and accurate records at all times. This might be essential and required for regulatory purposes, insurance coverage, or legal matters. You must also plan for training, drills, exercises, and involvement of local disaster response organizations. Other administrative tasks include notifying family members, issuing press releases, managing finances, and documenting recovery procedures.

The logistics prior to a disaster might include the acquisition of equipment and establishment of training facilities. Also included in logistics are movement of backup equipment to its correct place, repair of equipment parts, and arrangement of medical support, food, transportation, shelter facilities, backup power, and backup communication.

After examining the information that is documented in a disaster recovery plan and the issues that need to be considered while preparing the documentation, you will now learn about the components of a disaster recovery plan.

Components of a Disaster Recovery Plan

The scope of a disaster recovery plan is based on the requirements of the organization. Although the contents of a disaster recovery plan might vary from one organization to another, the main components of a disaster recovery plan remain the same and include these:

◆ Executive summary

◆ Disaster recovery procedures

◆ Support documents

The components of the plans might be based on the discretion of the organization and its personnel.

Executive Summary

The executive summary gives an overview of the purpose of a disaster recovery plan in the organization. This section of the plan also states the organization's disaster management policy. The disaster management policy includes information related to the coordination with the local bodies. This policy forms the basis of the disaster recovery and resumption procedures. In addition, the summary defines the roles and responsibilities of key disaster recovery personnel and lists the different types of disasters that are likely to impact the organization. The policy also specifies the locations where the response operations will be managed.

Disaster Recovery Procedures

The disaster recovery procedures section of the disaster recovery plan includes measures about how the facility will respond to a disaster. While developing these procedures, consider the actions to assess the disaster situation and protect employees and assets on the premises of the facility. Also consider the procedures required to restore business operations. In addition, you might require specific procedures for purposes such as shutting down operations, evacuating premises, and warning employees and customers.

Support Documents

The support documents section of a disaster recovery plan includes information required during a disaster and the documents that might be required during a disaster. Such information includes a list of resources—such as equipment, supplies, and services—that might be needed in a disaster and a list of personnel involved in responding to disasters with their roles, responsibilities, and telephone numbers. The design of the building and site maps indicating details such as exits, escape routes, floor plans, and the location of fire extinguishers are also included. Further, all the agreements with other companies and government agencies are included.

The manner in which the disaster recovery plan is organized is based on the size of the organization and the scope of the disaster recovery effort. For instance, for an organization dispersed around the world, a disaster recovery plan might be organized based on regions or departments.

The documented plan should not be more than 15–20 pages. A lengthy plan will not receive due attention from the personnel in charge of implementing it. It is likely that a lengthy plan might not be read or used.

After the first draft of the disaster recovery plan is created, it is reviewed. The suggested changes are incorporated to create the final draft.

Creating the Final Draft

After the first draft is created, it is distributed among the members of the planning team for review. The review tests the reasonableness of the plan in the organization environment. You can also conduct discussion sessions to review procedures specified in the disaster recovery plan. In addition, you can conduct a tabletop exercise that involves the management and personnel with disaster management responsibilities. A disaster scenario is identified in this exercise. The participants discuss their roles and responsibilities in the identified scenario. Based on the discussion, you identify areas of overlap and confusion as well as areas that the plan ignores. You then update the plan accordingly.

After you make the appropriate changes, you send the plan for a written approval to the CEO and senior management. After approval, the plan is distributed to the CEO, senior management, key personnel involved in disaster recovery, and organization headquarters as hard copies. In addition, sections of the plan are shared with the community disaster response agencies. Finally, the disaster recovery plan is distributed among the employees. The purpose of the task is to make the employees aware that a plan for disasters is in place. The plan can either be posted on an intranet Web site or circulated as a hard copy or through e-mail for this purpose. The plan should be communicated to business partners, service providers, and investors.

Now that you know the steps to create a disaster recovery plan, you will learn about the steps to implement the plan.

Steps to Implement the Plan

After you have created a disaster recovery plan, you need to implement the plan in the organization. To implement the plan in the organization, you need to incorporate it into the organizational policies. Communicate with the individuals mentioned in the disaster recovery plan about their respective roles and responsibilities. Make all newly recruited employees aware of the disaster recovery plan. Also specify the roles and responsibilities found in the disaster recovery plan in the documentation of the procedures for specific departments. Communicate any modifications in the plan to the employees as and when the plan is updated.

A disaster recovery plan is meticulously designed for implementation in situations with the least potential to damage and those with the maximum impact. Depending on the situation and the damage caused, the recovery team might implement selected portions of the disaster recovery plan.

The implementation of the plan involves spreading awareness among the employees of the organization and conducting exercises to assess the disaster preparedness of the organization. The following steps are involved in the implementation of a disaster recovery plan:

- ◆ Conducting training
- ◆ Conducting drills and exercises

Conducting Training

After the disaster recovery plan is created, all the personnel who are required to implement the plan are trained. The importance of training cannot be overlooked. Consider a scenario in which the employees of the organization do not know how to use a fire extinguisher or even where the extinguishers are located. Such a situation demands training. The training, although motivated to familiarize the employees with the basic use of equipment in the event of a disaster, does not need to be extensive.

The main purpose of training is to ensure awareness among the employees about disaster recovery policies and procedures. To ensure this, a training program is designed. This training program aims to ensure the following:

- ◆ Key personnel who are involved in disaster recovery understand the policies and procedures laid out in the plan.
- ◆ Employees know the procedure to follow when a disaster occurs.
- ◆ Employees know how to use disaster management equipment in disaster recovery.
- ◆ Personnel understand their roles and responsibilities in disaster recovery.

The employees should be trained on the recovery procedures on a regular basis. You can adopt various methodologies to conduct the training program. For instance, the training modules can be conducted over the Web or in a classroom mode. You also can use a combination of these methodologies. No matter which methodology is employed, it is important that training be conducted to spread awareness of the disaster recovery process. It is essential to train employees as an ongoing process with every change in the plan.

To develop an effective training program, you need to follow a structured and phased approach. The phases involved in the creation of a training program for disaster recovery are displayed in Figure 6.4.

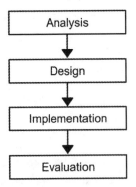

FIGURE 6.4 *The phases in the creation of a training program.*

These phases are described in the following list:

1. **Analysis.** In the analysis phase, you analyze the requirements of the training program. You identify the most effective means of communicating with the target audience.

2. **Design.** The second phase is the design phase, in which you identify the tasks that the employees need to perform to effectively carry out all aspects of the plan.

3. **Development.** Based on these tasks, you develop the various components of the training program, such as the lesson plan slides, presentations, and so on. This is the development phase.

4. **Implementation.** In the next phase, the implementation phase, you conduct the training and assess its effectiveness.

5. **Evaluation.** Finally, you evaluate the training program and make the appropriate changes to it.

Consider the training and information needs of employees, contractors, visitors, managers, and individuals who have a role in the disaster recovery plan. For an employee training on disaster recovery, you must include information about the following:

◆ Threats, hazards, and protective actions

◆ Notification, warning, and communications procedures

◆ Emergency response procedures

◆ Evacuation, shelter, and accountability procedures

◆ Location and use of common emergency equipment

◆ Emergency shutdown procedures

In addition, you must involve community responders in training activities.

Conducting Drills and Exercises

In addition to conducting training, you also can conduct evacuation drills and full-scale exercises. This ensures that the entire organization is confident and competent about the plan. Some drills that you can perform to ensure disaster preparedness of employees are the walkthrough drill, the functional drill, and the evacuation drill. To learn more about these drills, refer to Appendix B, "FAQs."

Summary

In this chapter, you learned that to respond to and recover from disasters, your disaster recovery plan must include disaster response and recovery procedures. Whereas disaster response procedures are implemented in immediate response to a disaster, disaster recovery procedures are designed to reduce the aftermath of disaster and ensure recovery.

You learned that authority, process, and accessibility characterize a disaster recovery plan. The steps involved in the creation of the disaster recovery plan are as follows:

1. Identifying recovery strategies
2. Selecting recovery strategies
3. Creating the first draft
4. Creating the final draft

While implementing a disaster recovery plan, you conduct training of those who are directly involved in the execution of the plan. In addition, you conduct drills and exercises.

Check Your Understanding

Multiple Choice Questions

1. Identify the characteristics of a disaster recovery plan.
   a. Authority.
   b. Process.
   c. Specialization.
   d. Accessibility.

2. What is the purpose of disaster recovery procedures?
   a. Reduce the aftermath of disasters and ensure recovery of the business operations of the organization.
   b. Provide a task list that can be implemented in immediate response to a disaster.

   c. Provide a rule for the organization to follow to recover business and information technologies within the recovery objectives.

   d. Define support documents for the disaster recovery plan.

3. Identify the components of a disaster recovery plan.

   a. Executive summary.

   b. Support documents.

   c. Disaster recovery procedures.

   d. Disaster response procedures.

4. Which of the following is the correct definition of a cold site?

   a. Site provided by the service provider right at your doorstep.

   b. Remote site that consists of all the resources required to successfully resume business.

   c. Reserve space with other organization to store relevant business data.

   d. Vacant facility with sufficient cabling and space so that it can be set up with equipment and personnel in a short time.

5. Identify the purpose of drills and exercises.

   a. Ensure that the entire organization is confident and competent about the disaster recovery plan.

   b. Assume the workload in the event that the primary site is destroyed in a calamity.

   c. Spread awareness among the employees of an organization.

   d. Make key decisions when responding to and recovering from a disaster.

Short Questions

1. What are the factors to consider when selecting a computer center recovery strategy?

2. What are department recovery strategies?

3. Elaborate on the significance of communication in disaster recovery.

4. List the general guidelines to select recovery strategies.

Answers

Multiple Choice Answers

1. a., b., and d. Authority, process, and accessibility are the three characteristics of a disaster recovery plan.

2. a. Disaster recovery procedures are designed to reduce the aftermath of disasters and ensure recovery of an organization's business operations.

3. a., b., and c. The components of a disaster recovery plan are executive summary, disaster recovery procedures, and support documents.

4. d. A cold site is defined as a vacant facility with sufficient cabling and space so that it can be set up with equipment and personnel in a short time.

5. a. and c. Drills and exercises are performed to ensure that the entire organization is confident and competent about the plan. In addition, they help to spread awareness among the employees of the organization.

Short Answers

1. Following are the factors to consider when selecting a computer center recovery strategy:

   ◆ **Site location.** The site to be selected as a disaster recovery site ideally should not be located in the same geographical area as the primary site. To reduce the likelihood of the disaster recovery site being damaged by the same disaster, the site should be located five or more miles from the primary site. However, if the region is prone to disasters, a location outside the same location should be considered.

   ◆ **Site accessibility.** All the information stored in a disaster recovery site should be accessible on short notice. In addition, the site should be accessible from the primary site to ensure a smooth transfer of material to the site.

   ◆ **Site security.** Because disaster recovery sites store confidential and critical information and documentation, you should implement the same access control and security measures for the backup data at the disaster recovery site as in use at the primary site. To ensure security, it's important to implement the procedures to identify the personnel who is allowed access to the sites.

◆ **Automatic failover.** To ensure an automatic failover, the disaster recovery site should be ready to assume the workload in the event that the primary site is destroyed in a calamity. Clustering of the disaster recovery site and the primary site should be considered to achieve true automatic failover.

◆ **Availability of trained personnel.** When the disaster recovery site comes in use at the time of a disaster, trained personnel must be available to ensure primary takeover. If the takeover is dependant on vendor support, this must also be ensured.

2. To ensure recovery from disasters, department can implement the following recovery strategies:

◆ Defer activity until the effect of the disaster passes.

◆ Distribute activity among other departments to avoid the impact of the disaster on a single department.

◆ Relocate the business operations to another area.

3. The significance of communication during disaster cannot be overlooked. Communication is essential to report disasters, warn personnel, keep the next of kin informed about the situation and circumstances, and retain contact with customers and suppliers. With communication being hampered following a disaster, confusion and miscommunication between employees are likely to occur.

4. Following are the general guidelines to select recovery strategies:

◆ **Strategies should be flexible.** The strategies on which a disaster recovery plan is created should not be rigid. These strategies should allow the expansion of the organization and its resources. As the business of the organization grows, the plan should be able to change with the growing needs.

◆ **Strategies should be well planned.** All the strategies that are implemented in a disaster recovery plan should be well planned. In other words, all the resources—such as personnel, processes, and technology—that are required for response to and recovery from disasters should be identified when determining the recovery strategies.

◆ **Strategies should be comprehensive.** The strategies selected for implementation in the plan should address maximum, if not all, types of disasters that are likely to impact an organization. In addition, the strategies must ensure recovery from minor disasters as well as the disasters likely to cause the maximum damage.

◆ **Strategies should meet the recovery objectives.** The selection of recovery strategies is driven by their ability to meet RPO and RTO values.

◆ **Strategies should be cost effective.** When selecting strategies, you must consider the reduction of the cost of recovery and the increase in ROI achieved by implementing the strategy. The budget of the organization also plays a significant role in the selection. In addition to these one-time costs, consider the ongoing costs, such as the rental and maintenance contracts for alternate sites.

Chapter 7

Testing and Maintaining the Recovery Plan

In Chapter 6, "The Recovery Plan," you learned how to create a disaster recovery plan. Consider a situation in which a disaster recovery plan has been made; the plan documents have been prepared; the teams have been formed; alternative solutions have been decided upon; and recovery strategies for data, systems, network, and users have been finalized. Is the disaster recovery planning complete in this situation? The answer to this question is "No." Unfortunately, many planners and management teams leave the plan at this.

Sadly, this is the reason many disaster recovery plans fail miserably in the event of an actual contingency. You cannot ignore the need for testing and maintenance. Testing and maintenance of a disaster recovery plan is essential to ensure that the plan has no gaps. In Chapter 1, "Disaster Recovery Planning: An Overview," you learned that testing and maintenance of the plan are two phases of the disaster recovery plan. The disaster recovery plan is not a project for you to complete and forget. It is a living process, and testing and maintenance are the ways to keep it alive.

In this chapter, you will learn how to test and maintain a disaster recovery plan. You also will learn about various types of tests and the issues that you should consider while testing and maintaining a disaster recovery plan. To start, let's discuss why we need to test and maintain a disaster recovery plan.

Need for Plan Testing and Maintenance

After you have formulated a disaster recovery plan, you need to test for its efficacy. You need to test in an actual crisis scenario the recovery alternatives you planned and decided upon so that you can bring out the shortcomings, make the necessary modifications, and design alternative strategies. It is also a test of the disaster recovery team—to find out whether its members are able to work together as a group in a crisis situation. In fact, a proper testing of a disaster recovery plan can answer many questions, such as whether the members are aware of their roles, whether they are able to meet the demands made of them, and whether the team needs any restructuring. You should carry out the testing periodically. This helps identify whether you need to upgrade or modify the plan.

Maintenance is also an integral part of the disaster recovery plan. It prevents the plan from getting rusted. Organizations are constantly developing, and so are their business processes. Therefore, changes in processes, hardware, applications, vendors, and employees warrant necessary changes in the plan; otherwise, the plan becomes outdated.

 TIP

Do not expect everything to automatically fall into place when a crisis strikes. Plans cannot be simply taken out of shelves and executed. Testing and maintenance are the only ways in which you can ensure that a plan works as desired.

Testing and maintenance also becomes necessary because a lot of people associated with the company demand that their interests are looked after. These people include customers, shareholders, employees, government agencies, and suppliers. These people will not allow their interests to be compromised because of an incomplete and inadequate disaster recovery plan. Organizations do not like to be dragged into litigations because this results in loss of credibility with a consequent adverse impact on their businesses.

Having covered the need for testing and maintenance of a disaster recovery plan, let us look at testing of disaster recovery plans in detail.

Plan Testing

The *Disaster Recovery Journal*, in an online poll conducted between May and June 2001, reported that 65.5 percent of 2,223 respondents had not exercised their disaster recovery plan during the past 10 years, and a further 26.32% had exercised it only one to three times. These figures are alarming and give you a clear idea of how people neglect testing. The figures become even more telling when you consider that the concerned period included the Y2K issues.

Awareness has certainly increased after the terrible attacks of September 11, 2001. Most of the organizations are slowly but surely realizing that if they want their disaster recovery plans to work in the event of an actual disaster, they need to keep their plans updated.

Objectives of Plan Testing

Although the need for testing should be obvious by now, let us see what testing provides. The following list discusses some of the reasons to test a plan:

◆ **Ensure plan effectiveness.** The primary reason for testing is to ascertain whether the disaster recovery plan works as intended. Testing also checks whether the recovery solutions are feasible in a real contingency scenario, whether any flaws need to be eliminated, and whether the planning team is able to achieve its objectives and implement the plan.

Therefore, testing helps to determine the state of readiness to cope with and respond to the disaster. It also helps ascertain whether the recovery alternatives at an alternate site are adequate to restore computer processing. It assists in checking whether the vendor solutions are workable.

Testing also aids in determining whether the state of the plan is current—that is, whether it has been properly maintained and upgraded to meet the current recovery needs of the organization.

◆ **Auditing.** Testing can be used to audit the disaster recovery plans. Tests can assure the auditors that the organization has a working disaster recovery plan. Moreover, it helps emphasize the fact that the organization is making a sincere effort to keep the disaster recovery plans in workable order. In fact, you should encourage auditors to take an active part in the testing efforts so that they can have a first-hand account of the quality control that the organization is implementing.

◆ **Benchmarking.** Testing helps to collect important data about the working of the recovery alternatives. You can use this data for an objective analysis of the alternatives, which is not possible without the testing.

Testing checks whether the estimated timeframes for the recovery alternatives are actually matched by the test results. This might necessitate a revision in the timeframes or enhancement of the recovery procedures. In addition, testing provides an estimate of the efficiency levels of the alternate solutions. For example, you can ascertain the levels of performance for the alternate network and telecommunication facilities.

◆ **Dry run.** Testing helps provide a dry run for the disaster recovery plan. This is where the team members actually get to implement their roles. The team gets a first-hand feel of working in a crisis situation. The team members become more familiar with the tasks and procedures.

The interteam coordination also is tested during the test. It's crucial for the teams to coordinate their efforts to be successful in recovery. The tests also aid in bringing about unity and camaraderie between team members. A dry run can bring out issues that the disaster recovery plan coordinator might have missed. These issues normally come out to the fore during the team debriefings after the tests.

The following section explains what you should do prior to testing.

Preliminaries to Plan Testing

You must ensure two things before proceeding with plan testing: getting management support and training the team.

Management Support

As discussed in Chapter 1, it is important to get management support before even starting the disaster recovery planning. The same is applicable for plan testing. Understanding, commitment, and funding are required to successfully carry out the testing.

A *Disaster Recovery Journal* survey taken in 2001 queried respondents about the biggest challenge that they face in their planning efforts. More than 38 percent of the respondents quoted funding as the biggest challenge. The next highest percentage (33 percent) rated staff shortage as the biggest challenge. Both these challenges point toward management's reluctance to provide financial support for faithful implementation of a disaster recovery plan. Therefore, it is critical to get management's approval before starting with the testing of the plan.

Training the Team

Getting the recovery team prepared is essential both for mock and actual implementation of the disaster recovery plan. The team not only needs to be educated and briefed, but also motivated for the job.

Different training modes are available, and you can employ a combination of these. Some of these modes include formal training sessions, meetings, distance learning, and handouts. The plan coordinator must get the team members to realize the seriousness of the job at hand and then proceed with the training. The members must not see the training sessions as interference from their normal jobs; they must participate actively.

The plan coordinator needs to keep certain points in mind while conducting or organizing training sessions:

◆ Use of multimedia presentations makes the training interesting and easier to grasp. Use of software such as PowerPoint has become common. In addition, you can use video and audio clips.

◆ The plan coordinator must be brief in his discussions. In addition, he should avoid going into details unless they're asked for. He needs to keep the level of the trainees in mind while framing the discussions.

◆ The plan coordinator must keep the target group in mind while making the presentation. For example, he doesn't need to explain Ethernet and firewalls to a group of network professionals.

◆ Each training session must have a predefined agenda and objectives. The coordinator needs to predetermine the timeframes. The overall look should be professional and formal. This gives the trainees an idea about the seriousness of the project.

◆ The coordinator needs to answers queries satisfactorily. If the coordinator is unsure about some fact, he should make a note of it and make it a point to clarify it during the next session.

◆ The coordinator should begin and conclude the session on time. Any unfinished agenda should be rescheduled for subsequent sessions.

◆ The trainees must understand that their managers will evaluate their performances during the plan test.

◆ The coordinator should hand out copies that contain clear-cut instructions to the team members. The coordinator should ask team members to review these instructions and report any comments, queries, or suggestions by a specified date.

In addition to the preceding preliminaries, the coordinator should answer many other questions before proceeding with the plan testing. Following are the two most important questions:

◆ What needs to be tested?

◆ How often should the testing be conducted?

What Needs to Be Tested?

This is an important and pertinent question. The answer for this is simple: Most critical business processes need to be tested. Processes with high risks and high probability of occurrence are natural candidates for testing. The processes with high Risk Probability (RP) but low business impact values (calculated using business impact analysis) are the ones where the management needs to decide whether testing should be carried out. The plan coordinator can devise a ranking system to classify the processes to make it easier for management to make decisions in a more objective manner.

You can use several methodologies to devise a ranking system for identifying critical processes. Following is one such methodology that employs a step-by-step approach:

1. The processes that need to be tested are identified and isolated by using the Business Impact Analysis (BIA).

2. The BIA value for each testable process is reassessed and ranked from 0 to 5 based on the severity of impact.

3. The RP for each testable process is reassessed and ranked from 0 to 5 based on increasing risk.

4. A matrix of the BIA and RP is constructed to help management decide on the threshold of testing.

The reassessment of the BIA and RP is essential to ensure that the information is based on current analysis. An example of a ranking matrix is illustrated in Figure 7.1. The shading denotes the threshold limit of testing—that is, the values of BIA and RP of the business processes for which testing would not be carried out.

BIA

BIA is a process that identifies which business processes and assets need the highest level of protection. It also includes recommendations on possible recovery strategies and alternatives and provides financial data to help organizations select the appropriate levels of investment for business protection.

		RP Values					
		0	**1**	**2**	**3**	**4**	**5**
BIA Values	**0**	1	2	3	3	4	5
	1	1	1	2	3	4	5
	2	2	2	2	3	4	5
	3	3	3	3	3	4	5
	4	4	4	4	4	4	5
	5	5	5	5	5	5	5

FIGURE 7.1   _BIA versus RP values matrix._

According to Figure 7.1, management has decided that a BIA value of 3 and an RP value of 2 is just above threshold limit—that is, this process would be tested. Similarly, a process with a BIA value of only 1 but an RP value of 5 would be tested. Any cell in the gray area indicates that the process would not be tested. Therefore, a process with a BIA value of 2 and an RP value of 2 would not be tested.

How Often Should the Testing Be Conducted?

There are no strict rules for how often testing should be conducted. The guiding principle is to test as often as it is required or as often as it is feasible. It all depends on how often the changes take place in the organization. Any change in business process, hardware configuration, software acquisitions, and the like warrant a re-evaluation of the plan.

It is recommended that the structured tests be held at least annually. This ensures that the plan stays current and prevents the recovery team from rusting.

Next, we'll look at the different types of tests that are available.

Types of Tests

You can carry out and further customize many types of tests according to the needs of the organization. Some planners prefer to carry out surprise tests to simulate the environment of a real disaster and give first-hand exposure to the disaster recovery team. For example, you might conduct a surprise test to recover computer processing at an alternate facility. This way, production processing can continue in parallel and is not affected much. These tests normally involve only a small part of the operations, and only a subset of the recovery team is required at a time. An alternative is to conduct a planned test and evaluate the results in a controlled environment. The advantage of the former method is the surprise element, whereas the advantage of the latter is better data collection and less disruption.

You can carry out the tests as separate units or test the whole plan at once. Normally, it is much more practical to carry out the former. This is because it involves less intervention in the day-to-day working of the organization. It might not be feasible to shut down critical systems at the same time and disrupt business functions to carry out the tests.

The following guidelines are useful when you're deciding on the types of tests to be carried out:

◆ You should test the plan to the fullest extent possible. In other words, the system shutdowns and recovery operations should be as real as they can be.

◆ The costs associated with the test type should not be prohibitively steep; if they are, management might decline to sanction the funds for testing.

◆ The tests should not lead to major business and service disruptions. If these disruptions are inevitable, try to keep them to a minimum.

◆ The tests should be reliable in their assessment of the recovery solutions. If the test is flawed, you cannot rely on the results.

◆ The test result analyses should produce credible input required for disaster plan maintenance.

The following section discusses the most commonly used testing model: the cycle testing model.

Cycle Testing Model

The cycle testing model is a common model that can classify various types of tests. It is a useful, comprehensive, and rigorous model of testing that involves repeated testing of the plan using different test methods in each cycle.

The test methods increase in their complexity after each cycle. After each testing, the plan is re-evaluated, and the corrections suggested by the test are implemented before moving on to the next cycle.

This model ensures comprehensive testing of the plan. Each plan facet is tested, evaluated, and documented multiple times through different modes of testing. The end of each cycle is marked by debriefing of the team, audit of the test results, and result analysis. The iterative nature of the test cycle ensures continuous evaluation of the disaster recovery plan. This leads to constant updating of the plan in response to business processes and configuration changes in the organization.

Figure 7.2 illustrates a disaster recovery planning cycle testing scenario in which different types of tests are carried out in increasing order of complexity.

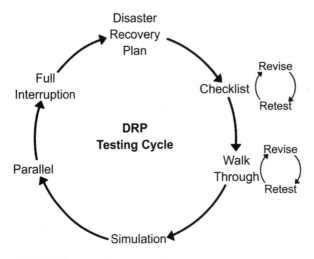

FIGURE 7.2 *A cycle test scenario.*

> ### NOTE
>
> The test types illustrated in Figure 7.2 are compiled from the *Disaster Recovery Journal* DR Glossary and *Testing Methods* by Geoffrey H. Wold and Robert F. Shriver, 1994.

Let us now look at some of the testing methods that are employed at various stages of the cycle testing model.

Checklist Tests

Checklists are an inexpensive, simple, and effective means of testing. A list of objectives or tasks is set for each team, and checklists are used to track whether a task is completed successfully. Checklists test multiple components of the plan. For example, a checklist can verify the following:

- ◆ The recovery plan and operational manuals
- ◆ The key procedures in a disaster recovery plan
- ◆ The hardware and software configuration documents' comprehensiveness and currentness
- ◆ The tape backup libraries' currentness and completeness
- ◆ The process-specific resources that are available during the implementation of the plan

Structured Walkthrough Tests

A walkthrough test involves verbally "walking through" the recovery plans. This requires a test scenario in advance. Team members discuss the plan step by step, which helps to confirm the effectiveness of the plan and points out any loopholes.

The presence of at least the team leaders and alternates is required for the test to go through. Walkthroughs are often conducted in conjunction with checklist tests. Walkthroughs are useful in the sense that a larger group of people sitting together can review the plan. Thus, there is a greater scope of discovering hitches.

Simulation Tests

As the name suggests, these tests are performed by simulating the disaster. The areas that might require testing in a contingency situation are alternate site processing, communications, network, hardware, software, personnel, documentation, utilities, supplies, and forms.

However, all simulation tests might not be practical or economically feasible to conduct. For example, cutting off all communication links or transporting heavy equipment might not be feasible. You can use validated checklists for these areas.

You should carry out simulation tests only after the simpler tests, such as checklists and walkthroughs, have been conducted. In addition, you must ensure that the results of these tests have been analyzed and their recommendations implemented before performing the simulation tests.

Parallel Tests

Parallel tests are conducted in parallel to checklist or simulation tests. These tests involve testing for data integrity at the alternate processing site or hot site. The previous day's or week's business transactions at the original site are compared with the backup copies at the alternate site. The two figures must be in agreement for the tests to be considered successful.

Full-Interruption Tests

As the name suggests, this is a full-blown test of the disaster recovery plan. This might lead to the normal business getting disrupted and could entail considerable economic costs. Hence, you must carry out the test with caution.

It is important to ensure that the earlier test recommendations be implemented before going in for a complex full-interruption test.

Next, we'll look at another important aspect of the testing cycle: auditing.

Auditing Test Cycle

Each phase of the test cycle is audited and analyzed for shortcomings and improvements. The cycle as a whole is also audited. The audit consists of the following components:

◆ Training and awareness aspects
◆ Organizational and administrative aspects
◆ Security of important records
◆ Structure, layout, and implementation of the test cycle as a whole
◆ Disaster recovery plan maintenance procedures
◆ Contracts and other agreements
◆ Supplier responses
◆ Flow of logistics
◆ Success/failure of individual test phases

Last but not least is the rounding off of the test cycle. The next section explains this.

Rounding Off the Test Cycle

Before rounding off the test cycle, it is imperative for the plan coordinator to ensure that the recommendations from each phase of the testing cycle have been duly implemented in the disaster recovery plan.

You should conduct an analysis of the test cycle as a whole, especially with focus on the flow and comprehensiveness of the cycle. Doing so provides valuable input for the next disaster recovery plan cycle.

You need to present an assessment document for the test cycle to the management. This would contain the details of the changes made to the disaster recovery plan as a result of the test cycle. Highlight any shortcomings that could have been catastrophic in a real contingency situation but that have been eliminated as a result of testing.

Include costs that were incurred in the test cycle as a line item in the budget for the next fiscal year. It is best to secure funds for the next testing cycle when you're presenting the reports for the current cycle. The testing cycle provides a high level of assurance to the management and the business stakeholders alike about the workability of the disaster recovery plans and their ability to recover mission-critical services within a specified timeframe.

Disaster recovery plan tests allow the plan coordinator to maintain a disaster recovery plan that is always functional. Disaster recovery plan documents are highly dynamic, and tests help to keep them up-to-date. A cyclic testing process provides exhaustive and cost-effective assessment of all input variables. It also minimizes service disruption.

Now that you understand the testing cycle, let's look at the key steps in plan testing.

Key Steps in Plan Testing

Plan testing involves several steps, but following are the primary ones:

1. **Planning the test.** As the name suggests, this step involves planning for the test of the disaster recovery plan. This step involves the following activities:

   ◆ Setting goals for the test plan

   ◆ Setting guidelines for the testing team

   ◆ Scoping the test to a level that can be realistically achieved

2. **Developing the test.** This step includes the following activities:

  ◆ Designing the test

  ◆ Developing exercises with defined objectives and realistic scenarios

3. **Evaluating and documenting the test.** This step includes the following activities:

  ◆ Developing methods that you can use to evaluate the test

  ◆ Setting targets for the test results and documenting them

4. **Conducting the test.** This step includes the following activities:

  ◆ Facilitating the test

  ◆ Recording the outcome of each exercise

5. **Analyzing the test results.** This step includes the following activities:

  ◆ Identifying the areas of the plan that worked fine and those that did not

  ◆ Summarizing the results

  ◆ Recommending modifications to the disaster recovery plan

Now let's look at some guidelines to follow to ensure successful execution of the plan testing:

◆ **Clearly define a test scenario.** The test is always carried out with few goals in mind. You either need to test specific subsystems or the entire plan. The scenario helps to clearly specify the boundaries of the disaster. For example, a test scenario could relate to a fire in the data center. Another scenario might envisage destruction of the entire facility.

The scenario must clearly define the assumptions that have been made. Every disaster scenario is based on an assumption. For example, it might be assumed that recovery personnel are available during the contingency.

The plan coordinator might specify additional details in the test scenario that are specific to the test. For example, a test might specifically try to ascertain if the accounting subsystem can be recovered during the contingency.

Some other considerations to keep in mind while developing the test scenario are as follows:

  ◆ The test scenario could include a retest for the plan segments that were found to be lacking in the earlier tests.

◆ The test scenario would normally include critical applications that have not been tested for a while and those that have never been tested.

◆ Those disaster recovery team members whose tasks need previous experience should be included on a priority basis.

◆ To ensure the adequacy of offsite inventory, the test scenario should use only offsite inventory items.

◆ **Clearly define test objectives.** Precise objectives that are stated in clear figures make the test more meaningful. For example, a clearly stated objective might be this: How long does it take to restore processing activities at a hot site facility in the event of a disaster? Another test might aim to measure the time required for database restoration in case a day's transactions have been lost.

 TIP

Clearly defined and specific objectives help you conduct the tests in a more scientific and objective manner.

◆ **Clearly define the rules for the tests.** The tests are carried out under a set of rules or guidelines. For example, one of the rules could be to stick to the instructions in the disaster recovery plan. The team members must strictly abide by the instructions in the disaster recovery plan to bring about the recovery. If they are unable to do so, you need to modify the plan.

◆ **List members and observers.** Clearly document the list of team members who are participating in the test and the list of observers. The observers might be auditors and members of management.

The members and observers must be made aware of their duties and roles. Tell the members the rules and require them to execute instructions. The observers must make observations.

◆ **Put test results on paper.** You need to document the test results for analyses and future records. The output might be in the form of system performance data, transaction logs, or the like, depending on the nature of the tests. Documented test results are analyzed so that you can come to conclusions. The plan is then modified accordingly, if needed.

Other test documents might include reports prepared by the test team members. The test participants might be required to collectively formulate a test assessment report. The steering committee and the test team members evaluate whether the tests were successful. All this forms a part of the test documentation. Test documents are also important for the auditors because they require the auditors to assess the effectiveness of the disaster recovery plan.

Now we'll look at what you can include in plan testing documents.

Plan Testing Documents

A plan testing document can include the following details:

- Introduction, including preface, scope, recovery site, primary test objectives, secondary test objectives, and test assumptions
- Test team participant details, including their roles and responsibilities
- Pre-test planning details, including the activities, issues, and concerns
- Testing timelines, including the planned and actual schedule of each activity
- Critical test checkpoints, including the activity and the responsible party
- Problem log, including the problems encountered during testing and the deviations

In addition to the preceding plan testing document, it is a good practice to prepare a post-test review document. This document lists the problem areas and recommends the improvements required in the plan testing. Following are some areas that can be included in this document:

- Test objectives
- Highlights of the plan testing
- Problem log listing the problems encountered during the test
- Follow-up on pretest problems
- Summary and observations
- Recommendations for the next test

That winds up the discussion on plan testing. Now, let us look at plan maintenance in detail.

Plan Maintenance

Maintaining a plan is as important as creating one. After you have created and tested a plan, you need to maintain it to ensure that it stays current and effective. This is something like maintaining a piece of machinery or an automobile. You need to oil and service it regularly to keep it in good running condition.

It is the same with the disaster recovery plan. You need to keep the plan updated with changes in the organization's business processes or with changes in the IT infrastructure that supports these processes.

There are two primary ways that you can ensure that the plan is current. One way is periodic testing, which has already been discussed. Testing helps to bring out inadequacies in the plan. It is especially useful to spot those inadequacies that have been brought about by a change in the way the organization conducts its business, thus rendering the old plan ineffective. Testing emphasizes the need for plan maintenance. Another way of ensuring that the plan remains current is through change management.

Change Management

Change management is the process of tracking and managing all changes in the organization so that the disaster recovery plan can be kept current. The plan changes with changes in the organizational processes and infrastructure.

No organization would want a disaster to occur to point out deficiencies or inadequacies in its disaster recovery plan. Consider a scenario. An organization has a hot site solution agreement in place. As discussed in Chapter 6, a hot site is one of the computer center recovery strategies. An unexpected disaster suddenly wipes out the main facility, and the organization decides to utilize the services of its hot site vendor. However, the agreement with the vendor is a couple of years old. The hot site can no longer support the significantly higher processing requirements of the organization. The situation arose because the organization failed to implement proper change management.

Even if you do not take the worst-case scenario, a non-existent plan management program is analogous to a non-existent disaster recovery program. This can lead to unpleasant audit reports, which reflect poorly on the plan coordinator and senior management. It is worse if the media highlights the fact and the shareholders and customers hear about it.

Change management begins by identifying those dynamic entities that are responsible for changes in the business process of the organization. The IT infrastructure of an organization normally changes due to adjustments in the following:

- Personnel
- Data and applications
- Building or infrastructure
- Systems and equipment
- Hardware
- Communication links

Let us look at these changes and the change management process that is associated with them.

Data

This element probably changes the most often, so it requires the greatest amount of attention. Company data requirements change often and databases are upgraded regularly. The size of the databases always grows, and these assets become more valuable.

The need is for the backup and storage techniques to be continually updated along with changes in the data needs of the organization. The plan coordinator needs to be aware of the updated procedures for archiving and restoring data. As new databases are installed and new servers and workstations come up, the coordinator must update his data backup/storage requirements and procedures.

The plan coordinator can coordinate with the IT department to keep track of new computer equipment that is installed and update the data needs accordingly. If the purchases are not made via the IT department, the coordinator can make arrangements with management and have department heads inform him about new purchases in their departments as and when they are effected.

With the growing data needs of a company, the necessity for storage media also grows. Some examples of storage devices are tapes, hard disks, arrays, and Network-Attached Storage (NAS). The plan coordinator must update the inventory stocks in the disaster recovery plan. Moreover, he must reflect these needs in any agreements that the company has with external suppliers, such as vendors providing hot site services. It is important to update these agreements with the current requirements for the recovery plan to remain effective.

Software

Software changes almost always affect the disaster recovery plan in some way or the other. Even if it is a minor application change that does not warrant a change in recovery procedures, it needs to be properly documented in the plan, normally as a function of IT development operations.

Major software changes might involve application overhauls or operating system upgrades or replacements. These changes might entail a lot of issues other than updating the documentation. For instance, newer applications might demand significantly increased processing and memory requirements. The recovery resources also need to be updated accordingly, if the solutions are still to be effective. Thus, an application upgrade might require a hardware resource upgrade in the recovery plan. Also, if agreements exist with external hot site vendors, these have to be revised upward to accommodate the increased processing requirements.

Software changes can similarly affect the network requirements of the organization. In addition, end user recovery is affected. Changes in software inventory and processes can be indicative of changing business processes for the organization. The plan coordinator is required to keep track of this. He can do so by distributing questionnaires among the department heads asking them to update the information provided during plan creation.

Documentation

With changes or upgrades in software, the associated documents also change. This affects the offsite storage plans in the disaster recovery plan. The offsite storage team leader should ensure that the documents at the offsite storage are current and purge any obsolete documents. He must maintain a proper inventory for this.

With changes in business processes, you also need to change accessories, such as preprinted forms. Thus, you need to update the corresponding offsite inventory of these accessories. You must replace old inventory with new inventory and then properly document the change.

You also need to review the supplier documentation periodically. Some of the questions might be whether any new suppliers need to be added, whether some of the suppliers have gone out of business, and whether the contact information for any supplier has changed.

Hardware

Hardware changes also might have far-reaching impacts, and the changes must be reflected in the plan inventory. Major hardware changes could invalidate the current hot site solution because the vendor might not be able to support the increased backup requirements any longer. Thus, a new contract needs to be established with the increased requirements. It might also be necessary to look for another vendor.

Hardware changes also can include changes to the network infrastructure or communication systems hardware. These might have their own implications in the sense that the current network backup solution might no longer work. Even traffic rerouting strategies, enumerated in the plan, might have to be revised.

Personnel

A change of personnel requires that the new personnel be trained in the disaster recovery process. Also, you need to assign roles to and brief the new personnel on the disaster recovery team.

It's important to update the disaster recovery emergency contact directory with the contact information for the new personnel. The human resources department can manage this job at the organization level. At the team level, the team leader should update the member list with information from the new personnel.

Now that you understand change management, let's look at the ways to implement it.

Means of Change Management

The logical question to ask here is this: Are there software products in the market that help perform change management? Before we consider this question, it is important to understand that the change management processes of any two organizations can differ greatly, depending on the plan requirements.

Some vendors provide tools for disaster resource planning, where you can feed data into tables and then edit it when necessary. This methodology is highly unsatisfactory and inadequate for plan maintenance. First, not all co-ordinators would want to use the plan template provided by the vendor. Companies have their own specific needs and priorities.

Moreover, even if plan software is used, only the data elements in tables can be edited. Let us take an example. An application upgrade in the organization calls for change management. As mentioned in the previous section, software changes entail several issues besides changing the application executable name in the plan.

The key to change management is proper communication regarding all changes taking place in the organization. For this, the plan coordinator needs to be in constant touch with the team leaders, department heads, senior managers, and inline managers.

You need to work out a system for reporting changes between the plan coordinator, senior management, and the team leaders. Scheduled reporting requires team leaders to report after fixed periods of time about the changes in their respective areas. Team leaders normally submit these reports quarterly. You need to create a standardized format for such reports.

The other form of reporting is event-based reporting. The concerned team leader reports to the coordinator when any major change that affects the IT infrastructure and the business function takes place in his department. Communication channels that the plan coordinator can use include e-mails, team meetings, and questionnaires (paper or online).

After the reporting mechanism is fixed and the communication channels have been decided upon, it ultimately depends on the analytical skills of the plan coordinator to implement change management. The changes need to be evaluated and their impact on the organization needs to be judged. Consultations and brainstorming help the plan coordinator in coming up with conclusions.

Thus, you can say that change management plays an important part in the plan maintenance phase and serves to keep the disaster recovery plan current.

Scheduled and Unscheduled Maintenance

Scheduled maintenance is a result of scheduled plan reviews. Companies usually conduct scheduled plan reviews on a quarterly basis. All team leaders attend these reviews, and it is here that the maintenance needs are discussed.

The review discusses changes that have occurred in each team's area of operation and concludes whether maintenance changes are required. The steering committee or the plan coordinator who is also responsible for subsequent updates to the plan initiates scheduled reviews.

Maintenance changes that are unpredictable and cannot be scheduled come under unscheduled maintenance. Following are some events that might trigger unscheduled maintenance:

◆ Changes in operating system or application software programs

◆ Changes in the production database design

◆ Changes in communication network design, such as the addition of a new router and route

◆ Changes in offsite storage facilities and procedures for cycling items

◆ Changes to the data center structure

◆ Discarding of an application system that is no longer used for processing

◆ Development of a new application system

◆ Changes in the disaster recovery team because of transfer of personnel or promotions

Maintenance Cycle Checkpoints

Maintenance cycle checkpoints are recurring checkpoints that are built into the plan to keep it current. Let's look at some of these checkpoints:

◆ **Change control checkpoint.** This checkpoint looks for any change in hardware, software, communication network, or environment and checks the change for effects on the disaster recovery plan.

◆ **Production turnover checkpoint.** This checkpoint looks for any change to the production environment and reviews it for effects on the disaster recovery plan. The plan coordinator accomplishes the production turnover checkpoint through the following actions:

1. He reviews the project document for any impact on the disaster recovery plan.

2. If he finds a relation, then he exchanges the information with his team and activates the administrative machinery.

3. He activates inventory update procedures. This is done to accurately and timely reflect any changes in the inventory.

4. He updates the disaster recovery plan to ensure that it reflects the current environment.

Summary

This chapter explored the need for testing and maintaining the disaster recovery plan, as well as the objectives and needs of testing. It discussed the types of tests and the testing cycle model. From there, it covered other issues related to testing, such as test team training, tips for effective testing, and the frequency of testing that is required. Then, the chapter moved on to the issue of plan maintenance. Finally, the chapter discussed scheduled and unscheduled maintenance, as well as maintenance cycle checkpoints.

Check Your Understanding

Multiple Choice Questions

1. Identify the objectives of plan testing.
   a. Auditing.
   b. Training the recovery team.
   c. Benchmarking.
   d. Ensuring plan effectiveness.

2. Which of the following is the most common and inexpensive type of plan testing?
   a. Full-interruption.
   b. Simulations.

      c. Checklists.

      d. Parallel.

3. Identify the key steps in plan testing.

      a. Planning the test.

      b. Evaluating the test results.

      c. Developing the test.

      d. Auditing the test.

4. Identify the primary ways of ensuring that a plan is current.

      a. Periodic testing.

      b. Test auditing.

      c. Change management.

      d. Plan checkpoints.

Short Questions

1. What are the guidelines for effective plan testing?

2. List some events that might trigger unscheduled maintenance.

Answers

Multiple Choice Answers

1. a., c., and d. Auditing, benchmarking, and ensuring plan effectiveness are the objectives of plan testing.

2. c. Checklists are the most common and inexpensive type of plan testing.

3. a., b., and c. Planning the test, evaluating the test results, and developing the test are the key steps in plan testing.

4. a. and c. Periodic testing and change management are the primary ways of ensuring that a plan is current.

Short Answers

1. Some guidelines for effective plan testing include the following:
   - Create a clear test scenario.
   - Define the test objectives.
   - Define the rules for the tests.
   - List members and observers.
   - Record test results on paper.
2. Following are some events that might trigger unscheduled maintenance:
   - Changes in operating system or application software programs
   - Changes in communication network design, such as the addition of a new router and route
   - Changes in offsite storage facilities and procedures for cycling items
   - Discarding of an application system that is no longer used for processing
   - Development of a new application system

Chapter 8

Centralized computing traditionally refers to mainframe-centered computing. In this type of computing, high-capability computers that are the central sources for data processing are used. Traditional disaster recovery planning concentrated only on the restoration or replacement of the mainframe computer. The restoration procedures involved setting up compatible hardware, reloading the operating system, restoring applications needed to continue the business operations, restoring backup data to direct access storage devices, restoring network and terminal server connections, and completing other tasks to get the mainframe computer back into operations.

With the advent of personal computers, distributed computing, and the *n*-tier client server architecture in the 1990s, times have changed. With the duo of Windows and Intel taking the market by storm, many companies have moved away from mainframe-centered computing. Even IBM, the mainframe giant, released its OS/390 operating system for the open systems environment.

This decentralization of operations has had a significant impact on the disaster recovery planning process. The planning methodology has become more complex with the emergence of multiple data centers in the organization. Many new requirements for disaster recovery have been introduced.

With the increasing complexity of managing distributed systems, the number of physical platforms for the distributed servers is being reduced, and attempts are being made to centralize the distributed servers within the boundaries of the data center. An increasing number of applications for thin clients in the market are indicative of attempts to recentralize applications and data onto "application servers."

The traditional strategies of mainframe recovery are still valid for these centralized systems. In this chapter, you will learn about the recovery plan for centralized systems. This comprises planning for recovery of data, system, building, communication link, and personnel.

Disaster recovery planning for mainframes does not involve the mainframe unit alone. You must restore the critical business functions that are supported by the mainframe as well. Restoring the critical business functions implies that you consider the IT infrastructure that supports these business processes. This includes the hardware, software (operating system and applications), data, documentation, network, and end users.

Planning for Data Recovery

Data recovery is the primary element in any recovery plan, especially in a centralized system recovery plan. The primary goal of a centralized system recovery plan is to restore the centrally stored data and restart database operations.

Data recovery involves complete and reliable restoration of systems in the event of a contingency, whether it is lost files, corrupted databases, a virus outbreak, or an absolute catastrophe that destroys all assets, both intangible and tangible.

Besides reliability, another important element of data recovery is *time to data*. This refers to the time required for the restoration of data and the resumption of critical business processes as a result. Lost time implies loss of revenues, loss of business, loss of credibility, and perhaps even litigation. Therefore, the restoration time must be within the allowed outage times for the critical processes; otherwise, the recovery plan collapses.

You can purchase systems on-the-fly and reconfigure networks, but without a proper data restoration mechanism, the entire recovery plan will fail because there are no alternatives to quick data restoration. Data recovery planning primarily involves the following tasks:

◆ Analyzing and classifying data based on criticality
◆ Reviewing existing backup policies
◆ Selecting and evaluating a backup strategy
◆ Implementing the backup strategy

Analyzing and Classifying Information

The first task in disaster recovery planning is identifying and classifying information. It is important to ascertain the location of data in an organization. After you determine the location, you must identify the critical data, which is the data required for critical business functions. You need to back up this data on a priority basis.

The task of locating data is easier in a centralized system than in a decentralized system because data in a centralized system is stored in a central location. In a decentralized system, locating data can be a tedious task that merits special attention. This will be discussed in Chapter 9, "Recovery Plan for Decentralized Systems."

To gauge the enormity of the data location task, let us look at some statistics. In large corporations, databases double their size every year. Database sizes measuring in terabytes are not uncommon any more. In addition, most organizations do not employ standards and policies for proper classification of data. According to the 1998 Information Week/PricewaterhouseCoopers Global Information Security survey, 43 percent of companies surveyed around the world do not use any means to classify data. 14 percent of the companies classify their records only once—annually.

Reviewing Existing Backup Strategies

An organization might already have backup strategies in place. You need to evaluate these strategies against the current needs for their effectiveness and reliability.

For example, an organization might be making routine backups remotely on a tape device by using backup and restore software. However, some organizations store their backups onsite where it is liable to be damaged along with the facility. Such a practice is strongly discouraged.

Even if the backups are being stored remotely, they need to be evaluated for reliability. You must determine if the backup mechanism is valid for the redefined business processes and applications. You also must determine if the restore mechanism ensures recovery within the allowed time limits. All these requirements are considered while reviewing the existing backup strategy.

When you review the existing backup strategy, consider issues such as the backup media, the transportation of media to the remote site, and site security. You need to evaluate the backup strategy against potential threats. For example, keep in mind the impact that a flood or earthquake can have on your data when you're evaluating the backup strategy. The backup data could become corrupted while it is being restored, or data tapes that are stored at the site could be stolen. Therefore, it is important that you construct test scenarios to evaluate the data recovery strategy against these perceived threats.

Selecting and Evaluating a Backup Strategy

You need to analyze the perceived threats and the current business process requirements before determining a backup strategy. The methods chosen and their corresponding timeframes must be compatible with the critical business process requirements. The critical data for backup includes not only the working data for the organization but also user account information, system and equipment configurations, e-mail communications with customers and suppliers, and financial and accounting documents. In addition, it might include legal documents, proposals, and research material.

A backup strategy for the critical data must address the following issues:

♦ How frequently should the backups be made?

♦ Which backup media should be used?

♦ When will the backups be made?

♦ Will the backups be manual, semi-automated, or automated?

♦ How will it be verified that the backups have been made successfully?

♦ How long should the backups be stored?

♦ Where will the backups be stored?

♦ How long will the restoration process take?

♦ Who will be assigned the responsibility for completing the scheduled backups and who will verify them?

♦ Who will take the responsibility of backing up data if the person who is assigned the responsibility is unavailable?

Before you select a backup strategy, determine the backup software available.

Backup Software

Traditional backup strategies involved making backups after office hours when networks and systems were free and databases were not in use. However, with the advent of the Internet, businesses and organizations are working 24 × 7. Therefore, vendors are increasingly equipping their software with Application Programming Interfaces (APIs) that can be used for *hot* backups, which are made when the database is still in use. This new software is more efficient in backing up databases of enormous sizes, which can be to the magnitude of a few terabytes.

NOTE

1 terabyte = 10^{12} bytes.

Improvements in technology, such as advances in tape technology, which include improved interface speed, parallel multiplexing capability, and so on, have made the process of backup and restoration faster. The backup software chosen must provide reliable and efficient backups and should be determined based on the needs of the company. For example, a company that does not require *no-window* (a backup solution that does not have specific time slots associated with it) terabyte backups can opt for a more cost-effective backup solution.

Methods of Data Backup and Restoration

As a business decision maker, you must select an appropriate method of data backup and restoration for the organization. Several methods are available for data backup and restoration. This section discusses three such methods: the routine and traditional method, electronic vaulting, and remote mirroring.

Routine and Traditional Method

The routine and traditional method involves the following steps:

1. Backing up the data on tapes.
2. Transporting backed up data to an offsite storage site for safe storage.
3. Transporting the backed up data from the storage site facility to the recovery facility or hot site in the event of a contingency.
4. Restoring the data back from the tapes at the recovery site.

The advantage of this method is that it is reliable and cost effective. However, the same cannot be said about the recovery times. When you need to recover mission-critical applications in few timeframes, the efficiency of this method is questionable.

Electronic Vaulting

Electronic vaulting reduces the time losses involved in the transportation of tapes to and from the offsite storage location. This type of backup method is implemented by using WAN links. A WAN link between the organizational data center and the remote storage site helps transfer the backup data to the tapes at the remote site. For transporting data to the remote site, you can use high-bandwidth technologies, such as the channel extension technology.

Backups also might be required onsite for restoring business processes quickly. Intelligent tape controllers allow simultaneous backup on local and remote tape devices. For these purposes, shadowing or multiplexing technologies are used.

The only drawback with electronic vaulting is that WAN links can sometimes introduce latency into the backup process because of their limited bandwidth.

Remote Mirroring

Remote mirroring is the fastest means of achieving data recovery. It eliminates the process of making tape backups. Remote mirroring involves duplicating the data that is on one disk array to another disk array stored at a remote location. The remote location is ideally the recovery location. No restore operation would be required at the recovery site, and restoration of business processes could theoretically begin immediately after the disaster.

Remote mirroring is an extension of the Redundant Array of Inexpensive Disks (RAID) technology in which data is mirrored for fault tolerance. Whereas RAID involves mirroring data within the disks inside an array, remote mirroring involves mirroring of information across two disk arrays. The second array is located at a remote location so that it is not affected by the disaster that affects the organizational facility.

Data streams are sent from the organization's site to the remote site across a WAN link. The remote site can be a self-owned site of the organization, and the WAN link could be part of the internal network. However, the backup solution also could involve the services of a hot site vendor, in which the remote location would be the hot site facility that the vendor provides.

Many remote mirroring solutions are available in the market today. These solutions advertise different features and come in all cost tags. One remote mirroring solution that has become popular with hot site vendors is the EMC Corporation's Symmetrix Remote Data Facility (SRDF).

The mirror imaging technology might appear attractive to disaster recovery planners. However, this is not the ultimate solution to backing up and restoring data because the technology is still evolving and is not perfect.

In addition to the latency brought about by WAN links, other problems, such as data gaps, exist in the mirrored images. These problems lead to a difference in the state of the original and mirrored data. Improper array maintenance and disk swapping can cause reference points for data in the mirror configuration to be lost, rendering the mirror array unusable. Therefore, organizations should not rely only on mirror imaging. Other conventional means, such as tape backups, should remain a part of data recovery planning.

Storage Options

Several storage options are available for keeping data backups safe so that they are easily and reliably retrievable in times of a disaster. Deciding on the data storage options is an important part of data recovery planning. The disaster recovery plan might require the use of more than one of these options for different assets. Let us discuss some of the storage options available.

Onsite Storage in Fire-Proof Cabinets and Safes

A variety of fire-resistant safes and cabinets are available for safe storage. These come in various tags and are rated by Underwriters Laboratories (UL) for their effectiveness.

 TIP

Preferably, data should be stored away from the area of operation, even if it is stored onsite. In other words, data must be stored away from the data center so that any disaster that affects the data center is unlikely to affect the backup copies.

Shell Game Strategy

You can use the shell game strategy if an organization is spread across a large area or several buildings. In this strategy, a replica of the data from one location is stored in another location and vice-versa. This strategy enables protection of data in the event of a contingency that affects a particular location.

The shell game strategy might be expensive for some organizations because it has to provide for safe storage facilities at all centers. Safety measures employed at a data storage site should relate closely to those employed at a data center. Following are some of these measures:

- Adequate fire protection
- Intrusion protection
- Humidity control
- Temperature control
- Voltage fluctuation alarm
- Circuit breakers
- Generator failure alarm
- UPS failure alarm
- Water detection
- Leak detection

Shared Storage Arrangements

Two organizations can share a common storage facility to meet their storage requirements. However, both organizations have to mutually agree on access to the facility. Also, each organization needs to trust the other for the security of their data assets. For this arrangement to be effective, the two organizations should have a documented agreement.

Commercial Offsite Storage

A commercial offsite storage facility involves the use of services of a third-party service provider, who assures safe storage for a payment. These providers could be banks or other storehouses and professional storage site providers.

 TIP

A professional service provider is preferable to a bank for data storage because these organizations specialize in data storage. These organizations meet the necessary environmental and security guidelines for safe data storage that might not be available in a bank.

Service providers cost less than the cost an organization would incur in building a storage facility of the same standards. They are also a better option than the shared agreements because there is no access control issue involved—a team of trained professionals manages the storage facility.

Before the plan coordinator can finalize offsite storage as a data storage option, he must convince the management about the need for offsite storage. The plan coordinator then needs to justify the costs that would be incurred for it. The following hints might help the plan coordinator in justifying offsite storage to management:

- Offsite storage entails the security of important contracts, accounts, and agreements besides facilitating data recovery.
- All departments of an organization can share the costs for offsite storage.
- Expenses for offsite storage, in many cases, are tax deductible.
- The vendor competition and incentives reduce the expenses that the organization incurs.

Implementing the Backup Strategy

After deciding on the backup strategies, an organization can implement the strategies. First, you should decide the schedules for the movement of the data records to offsite locations. You must maintain a log to keep track of all media that is transported to the vendor site. The log is also useful in billing and assessing vendor compliance to the schedule.

The strategy implementation involves reviewing the offsite storage program periodically and making regular checks about required changes in the organization's storage requirements. Reviews should include the following:

- **Check for classification criteria being met.** Ensure that the plan guidelines for classification of organizational data are being met. Data must be classified in accordance with criticality so that the offsite requirements are judged correctly.
- **Evaluate vendor performance.** Check for a vendor's compliance to storage agreements, adherence to schedule, correct billing, and meeting of emergency needs. Checks might include inspections, reviewing of vendor contracts, and reviewing of schedule logs.
- **Check for new disaster recovery requirements.** Review offsite inventory for any obsolete and irrelevant records. Such records can be

removed after due consultations. Ask the vendor to revise the charges if there is a reduction in the data being stored.

♦ **Organize awareness programs.** Carry out diligently the training and awareness programs that are recommended in the plan and document the successful completion of these programs. These programs are more important in a decentralized system.

Planning for System Recovery

In the previous section, you learned about planning for data recovery. Although data recovery forms a primary part of the recovery plan for centralized systems, another crucial part of such a recovery plan is planning for system recovery.

In this world of rapid technological developments, operating systems provide some backup and recovery options in case of a disaster. For example, DOS and Microsoft Windows provide options to recover lost data. Besides, it is also possible to recover data from Microsoft Windows NT systems, regardless of the FAT or NTFS partition being used. As a result, access to information stored on the server can also be restored.

However, to prepare for total system failure resulting from a disaster, such as a flood or earthquake, the system recovery planning process starts by identifying the critical applications and critical hardware required to run them. This section describes the steps to identify the critical applications and hardware and examines the strategies for system recovery.

Identifying Critical Applications and Hardware

Certain applications are critical to the running of organizational processes. These applications are categorized as critical applications of the organization. Such applications are of great significance for centralized systems because the entire working of the organization depends on them. After you have identified critical applications, you need to identify the hardware required to run them. This section describes the process of identifying the critical applications and hardware.

Critical Applications

Critical applications are the applications required to directly or indirectly support the business functions that have been identified as critical. In the event of a disaster, you need to restore these applications on a priority basis.

While you're making a list of the critical applications, consider application interdependencies. For example, the back-end transaction processing application that works on a mainframe might be utilized for the front-end Enterprise Resource Planning (ERP) application that runs on a distributed platform. The ERP application has been identified as critical in the plan document. Furthermore, the transaction processing application also becomes a critical application by default because of its dependability on ERP applications.

Critical Hardware

As mentioned earlier, after you have identified the critical applications, you need to identify the critical hardware required to run them. The hardware required is usually of a lower configuration than the hardware used in production. This is because the production hardware also supports a lot of other applications that do not necessarily support the critical applications of the organization. Therefore, the CPU cycles, memory, and other resources that these applications use do not qualify in the critical hardware requirements.

You often can replace a high-end CPU with a lower-end one for restoring critical applications. In other words, the centralized platform doesn't need to match the production system on a one-to-one basis.

Let us now look at some of the strategies to effect centralized system recovery.

Next Box Off the Line Strategy

The next box off the line strategy involves replacing the mainframe processes with manual alternatives until a new compatible system is installed and the network installation of peripherals is completed. While the manual processes start, a new facility is searched or the same facility is renovated. The backup of the operating system and applications is also retrieved for installation on the new systems.

The next box off the line strategy is a traditional strategy that can rarely be employed in today's competitive environment because it is not normally feasible to replace critical business functions manually. In addition, the time of outage is not known. Therefore, considerable time could elapse before the system would be restored. A significant loss of time also could occur because an alternate facility does not exist beforehand and must be searched and prepared for the restoration of operations.

Reciprocal Backup Strategy

Reciprocal backup strategy involves agreements between two organizations to mutually support each other in times of crisis. Therefore, if one organization faces a disaster, the other provides system restoration facilities to it and vice-versa.

This strategy is difficult to implement because both organizations must have compatible hardware and spare processing facilities to accommodate mutual requirements. In addition, both the organizations must be inclined for such an agreement. This is not likely because the organizations are located at the same place in most cases; otherwise, both organizations might be affected by the same disaster at the same time.

Even if two organizations go for such an agreement, implementing it can be difficult. For example, the supporting organization might have put some of its spare resources into other uses and might find it difficult to free them at a time when these resources are required. The estimated recovery requirements of the first organization might turn out to be greater than expected. Such a scenario might put additional burden on the second organization to support the first. It might even affect the operations of the second organization. Finally, with the second organization having to declare a disaster, two organizations might be looking for help!

Cold Sites

As you know, cold sites are an alternative means of systems recovery. They are preprepared facilities that you can use in the event of a disaster. However, even with cold sites, an organization must find the replacement hardware required to support the critical business processes.

Cold sites can be owned by an organization or procured commercially. The latter are significantly inexpensive because many customers share them. Companies such as Hewlett-Packard, IBM, and SunGard are into the business of providing cold sites.

The rationale behind cold sites is that the organization facility is already pre-pared. Because cold sites provide the workspace and the basic utilities, such as power, air conditioning, heating, and maybe even network cabling, they pro-vide better alternatives as compared to manual operations or reciprocal backup strategy. However, the organization should be able to support its business-critical functions until you can procure and install the alternative systems; otherwise, it would stand incurring losses.

The disadvantage with cold sites is that if system procurement and installa-tion cannot be done in the estimated timeframe, there could be difficulty in the organization sustaining its business processes.

To overcome this disadvantage, cold sites have been moved into a new role today. Presently, they are primarily used to continue business operations after the contract for a hot site has expired. It is a common practice for hot site vendors to provide contracts for limited periods of time. The organization can recover its business operations at the hot site while it continues to prepare its own systems at the cold site. When the contract for the hot site expires, the organization can shift its operations to the cold site, which would be prepared by then.

The concept of mobile and porta-cold sites has also been introduced. These sites are used to set up cold sites and begin temporary operations at the setup location. Mobile sites can be driven to the client location. However, this is more useful for distributed systems recovery and user recovery.

Hot Sites

Hot sites are facilities that are fully equipped with the IT infrastructure and are ready for a customer to occupy. These facilities have become the most reliable solution for mainframe backups in the recent past.

In the event of a disaster, an organization only needs the recovery personnel to carry its backup media to the hot site, which might not be required if the organization uses remote mirroring to mirror its database to a hot site. At the hot site, the backup media is used to restore operations and reactivate the critical business applications. Users are provided access to the site from their workplaces, or they can move to the hot site.

Most hot site vendors also allow customers to test the system recovery opera-tions on their hardware. The only features that the customer has to look for in a hot site are compatible hardware and competitive costs. Hot site vendors also might allow customer-specific equipment to be installed at the site for additional costs. For example, a vendor might allow the customer to install backup equipment for its backup needs at the hot site. Therefore, the hot site also enables data backup while it is being used for system recovery.

The only disadvantage of the hot sites might be their cost factor, but with proven reliability and effectiveness, most organizations are willing to pay for critical business recovery in the event of a major contingency.

Service Bureaus

A service bureau provides application-processing services in the event of a disaster. Software vendors often provide these services. These services are highly specific to applications, and the client must be working on that particular application to make use of the service. In this setup, the users submit their requests from their organizational offices and a data link connects them to the bureau. The systems at the bureau perform the processing.

A new class of service bureaus is evolving in the form of application hosting facilities on the Internet. The companies that provide these services also might provide services for database applications and ERP applications.

The disadvantage of service bureaus is that they are highly specific to applications. In addition, the organization requires a facility where remote access to users can be provided so that they can access the service bureau facility. The organization also must ensure that the application is updated with the latest updates from the vendor; otherwise, the application processing solution might not work.

Redundant Systems Strategy

The redundant systems strategy involves maintaining an identical data center as a backup alternative. In the event of a disaster, the organization simply needs to shift operations to the alternate data center and resume operations. Therefore, the recovery timeframe is extremely short. This is the most reliable means of centralized systems recovery.

You need to locate the alternative data center far away from the original data center to prevent its chances of being affected by the disaster. You can either move users to the new data center or provide them with remote access to the new data center.

Although this strategy is reliable and fast, it is the most expensive systems recovery strategy. Few organizations can afford to maintain a fully equipped duplicate data center. However, this strategy is highly effective when the recovery times for the business functions are extremely low.

Planning for Building Recovery

A disaster might affect the building in which the operations of the organization are carried on. The extent of this effect might vary depending on the density and the type of disaster. For example, the building can be affected by a fire or by an earthquake.

If minor damages to the building result, repair work needs to be carried out. However, you need to ensure that the repairs of the building do not create an unsafe environment for the employees who are working there. Moreover, trained workers should carry out the repair work. Apart from these repairs, it might also be necessary to restore the communication links and power supplies.

On the other hand, if the building is completely destroyed in a disaster, the operations of the organization need to be shifted to another location. Either the organization or a third-party vendor can own this location. Hot sites are examples of such locations that vendors own.

Such relocation of business operations might be temporary or permanent depending on the extent of damage to the building. Therefore, there should be an organized way to transfer the restored items and equipment to the new location. You also need to take care of the transportation needs of the employees.

Following are some important considerations to keep in mind before choosing the new building:

- ◆ The floor capacity of the building should be able to easily accommodate the employees who need to work there. There should be enough space for all the employees and their equipment.
- ◆ The building should be clean and free from insects or mice.
- ◆ The air conditioning, heating, and humidity control systems should be working properly.

◆ Fire protection and extinguishing systems should be readily available and in proper working condition.

◆ All the security systems and emergency exits should conform to the standards.

◆ All communication links should be working properly.

◆ The construction of the building should not be substandard.

◆ If the building is located in a skyscraper, it should meet all the specified security standards.

If the relocation is temporary, then appropriate measures and plans need to be implemented to reconstruct the original building. This reconstruction should take into account all the necessary safety standards and the basic facilities that need to be provided in the building. After the reconstruction or repair of the building, the building should be certified for occupation before it is actually reoccupied.

Planning for Communication Link Recovery

Communication link recovery is an integral part of the disaster recovery plan. This includes recovery of network and telecommunication links. Without restoring the network, the critical business processes cannot be brought online because most of the processes today make use of the network in one way or the other. Network and telecommunication recovery planning also involves the same steps and methodologies as the disaster recovery plan.

You need to design recovery strategies for the following:

◆ **Internal enterprise networks.** These include the departmental LANs interconnected through switches or a routed backbone network. The telephony networks, local loops, and WANs are also included in internal enterprise networks. Therefore, recovery strategy for internal enterprise networks needs to include the recovery of computer peripherals and the servers to which they are attached.

◆ **Network relocation.** These include mission-critical internal network services. These services need to be rebuilt and WANs and telephony services need to be rerouted to alternate sites in the event of a disaster.

The following sections examine the recovery strategies in these two areas, which are important in the context of centralized systems recovery.

Recovery of Computer Peripherals and Terminal Network

Device networks are common in the centralized mainframe-computing environment. A system's management software can detect the failure of peripheral devices and access failures. This software can be part of the server operating system, or you can purchase it from a third-party vendor. Hardware failures can be corrected promptly with alternate hardware replacements. Moreover, you need to ensure the recovery of network devices and equipment because they support the availability of the network and telecommunication links.

Restoring WAN and Data Network Links

A contingency might necessitate that the data center or the employees of the organization be relocated to another site. This would require the network recovery plans to be put to practice even if the network infrastructure of the organization were still intact. Relocation would force network rerouting and new links.

Whereas the LAN links would ensure that the users have access to the applications they require, the WAN links would connect them to the recovery facility for their data and voice communication needs. Users here include employees of the company and also suppliers, partners, government agencies, and other entities that must connect to the organizational network.

Some of the factors that govern efficient and expeditious recovery of the network are as follows:

◆ Interdependency with the systems and user recovery plans affects the network recovery plan. For example, if the system's recovery site is unknown, the network planner has to wait before he can reroute links and establish new WAN links.

◆ The plan must take into account the worst-case scenario. Plans often go awry because the assumptions made did not envisage a disaster of the actual magnitude. For example, a hurricane might be much worse than predicted by weather forecasts. The plan might have assumed for cellular and phone services to be available, but they might not be in a real scenario. This could lead to panic and confusion, thereby affecting the recovery process adversely.

◆ The network recovery plans must be generalized to work in all situations. The organization's systems and user requirements are constantly changing, leading to changes in network requirements. It is difficult to keep up with all these changes all the time. Network recovery should, therefore, be based on generalizations so that the plan works in all situations. For example, a recovery planner would not accept restoring each user account when recovering the network. The planner might be well advised to base recovery on roles rather than on an individual basis.

◆ The planner must be aware of the minimum network requirements of business recoverability and try to achieve them first. This prevents unnecessary panic and stress. Just as the application and user requirements in a crisis situation are much less than the normal requirements, so are network requirements. The network does not need to be brought to its peak performance. It just needs to be restored so that the critical business processes can be supported with a minimum number of users.

◆ It helps if the network recovery processes have been tested and tried before. You can use the experience gained from this in a real contingency situation. Of course, the network planner can come out with new ideas and plans to improve network performance, but the basics must have been tested before to effect expeditious recovery.

Planning for Personnel Recovery

Traditional recovery plans often completely ignore the issue of personnel recovery. The focus is solely on data center recovery. The employees are assumed to be independent of the data center and require a simple connection to the data center facilities.

However, modern-day planners have emphasized the need for personnel recovery plans, even in a centralized system environment. It's not guaranteed that the disaster would affect the data center only and leave the employee facilities untouched. Evacuation of personnel is the first and the most important task in the event of a disaster. Moreover, the employees might need to be relocated in such a scenario. They might need to be provided with shelters and supplies. If a major disaster occurs, personnel might also require counseling services and guidance.

Depending on the intensity of the disaster, personnel might be relocated to another building or site. In such a case, transportation facilities need to be provided. In addition, for proper functioning of the organization, the employees need to be provided access to the recovery facility besides access to communication links. No recovered system or network can work without interaction with the employee.

Therefore, even centralized recovery plans must include the following considerations:

◆ Are evacuation procedures for employees in place in the event of a potentially life-threatening situation?

◆ Are backup facilities available for user relocation?

◆ Is a process defined to notify the recovery staff?

◆ Are transportation facilities for recovery personnel to the alternate site catered for?

◆ Is a provision in place to arrange for contingency staff?

◆ Is there a provision to redirect mails and calls to the alternate site?

◆ Can supplies be acquired at the alternate site?

The actual implementation of the user recovery plan depends on the nature of the disaster. If the disaster affects only the organization's data center, then user relocation is not required; users can continue to work from their original work areas. Users would, however, need access to the restored network and remote access services at the alternate data center for data processing activities. Users also might be required to substitute certain automated operations with manual operations as a temporary measure.

If the disaster affects the user facility as well, the plans for user relocation come into force. An alternate site needs to be implemented, transport facilities to the site need to be provided, and users need to be equipped with forms, stationery, PCs, and communication links at the alternate site.

The emergency procedures included in the plan can be useful when immediate evacuation is required as a result of some life-threatening situation, such as fire or earthquake. These procedures help contain panic and systemize the procedures of evacuation and rescue.

Chapter 9 will discuss in greater detail the personnel recovery plan for decentralized systems.

Summary

This chapter described the issues and strategies related to disaster recovery in centralized systems. It started with the description of centralized systems and the issues that are pertinent to it and proceeded to the recovery of the data center, which is the most important component of centralized systems recovery. It discussed in detail the planning methodology and strategies related to it.

Next, this chapter discussed systems recovery and described the traditional as well as the modern means to achieve it. After that, the chapter provided a discussion regarding planning for building recovery.

From there, this chapter discussed communication links recovery, which is a part of centralized system recovery. In communication services recovery, you need to re-establish terminal services and reroute the WAN and data links to the alternate recovery site. Users need to be able to perform data processing tasks from their offices.

Finally, this chapter discussed the user recovery plan, which is often the most neglected area of centralized systems recovery. User recovery plans depend on the nature of the disaster and are implemented accordingly.

Check Your Understanding

Multiple Choice Questions

1. Which of the following issues does a backup strategy not need to address?

   a. Which backup media will be used.

   b. Who will verify the backup.

   c. What the maximum backup size will be.

   d. Where the backups will be stored.

2. Which of the following backup strategies involves two locations that store each other's data?

   a. Shared storage arrangements.

   b. Shell game strategy.

   c. Reciprocal backup strategy.

   d. Commercial offsite storage.

Short Questions

1. Describe the strategies used to plan for system recovery.

Answers

Multiple Choice Answers

1. c. A backup strategy does not need to address the maximum size of a backup.

2. b. The shell game strategy involves two locations that store each other's data.

Short Answers

1. You need to consider the following factors when selecting a computer center recovery strategy:

   ◆ **Next box off the line strategy.** This strategy involves replacing the mainframe processes with manual alternatives until a new compatible system is installed and the network installation of peripherals is completed. While the manual processes start, a new facility is searched or the same facility is renovated.

   ◆ **Cold sites.** Cold sites are an alternative means of systems recovery. Cold sites are pre-prepared facilities that you can use in the event of a disaster. However, even in the case of cold sites, an organization must find the replacement hardware required to support the critical business processes.

◆ **Reciprocal backup strategy.** Reciprocal backup strategy involves agreements between two organizations to mutually support each other in times of crisis. Therefore, if the first company faces a disaster, the second would provide system restoration facilities to it and vice-versa.

◆ **Service bureaus.** A service bureau provides application-processing services in the event of a disaster. The software vendors often provide these services. They are highly specific to applications.

◆ **Hot sites.** Hot sites are facilities that are fully equipped with the IT infrastructure and are ready for a customer to occupy. In the event of a disaster, an organization only needs the recovery personnel to carry its backup media to the hot site and restore operations.

Chapter 9

Recovery Plan for Decentralized Systems

Decentralized systems involve distributed computing and an *n*-tier client/ server architecture. This is different from the centralized nature of traditional mainframe computing. These systems have specific requirements and add new dimensions to the disaster recovery plan.

The fact that the data center is spread across user workplaces and not segregated safely in a glass house raises several concerns. For instance, servers are spread all over the office across various floors and workstations. No boundaries separate the data center from the user work areas. Therefore, data protection and unified administration become difficult. The distributed nature of data also makes the backup and restoration operations more complex.

However, segregating data does offer some advantages. Sometimes, a disaster might affect only a part of the facility and data and processors located in other parts might remain intact. In that case, segregating data makes it easier to resume operations because the scale of the disaster is contained. However, data segregation has some disadvantages, such as data inconsistencies. The planner needs to ensure that data is up-to-date and is easily accessible whenever required.

Distributed systems also involve a myriad of platforms and operating systems. The functioning of many of the critical business applications depends on the interfaces, gateways, and bridges used to make these systems work together. Therefore, in a decentralized system, recovery operations must make these systems work together.

In the recent past, many experienced planners have neglected the need to recognize the nuances of decentralized systems planning. Many of them have chosen to ignore the issue completely and focus only on mainframe recovery because it normally hosts a greater proportion of the critical business functions.

However, distributed processing is a reality, and the planner needs to understand the particular needs of distributed system recovery planning. As you read this chapter, you will realize that the disaster recovery planning process for decentralized systems is to disassemble the framework developed for centralized systems recovery. We only need to account for the nuances brought about by distributed systems in our plan.

The basic three-step approach to the plan doesn't alter at all:

1. Identify critical business functions.
2. Identify the minimum resources that are required to support these.
3. Design a recovery plan for making available these resources in the event of a disaster.

Much of our disaster recovery discussions from Chapter 8, "Recovery Plan for Centralized Systems," hold true in this chapter as well. We won't restate the planning process again here. The steps involved in data recovery for centralized systems are the same for decentralized systems. This chapter focuses on the peculiarities brought to the process with decentralized systems.

Planning for Data Recovery

Distributed systems came into being in the 1970s and 1980s. The PCs were aimed at providing greater flexibility to business professionals than that provided by the mainframe. It also meant fewer costs and more independence.

However, this trend gave rise to decentralization distribution and management of resources. Data moved out from data centers to workgroup servers scattered around the company offices. PCs began to be procured like office items, and the tight administration of the data center became distributed.

All this necessitates adding new dimensions to the data recovery plan discussed in Chapter 8. Let us recapitulate the broad steps involved in data recovery planning:

1. Locate and analyze the data based on criticality.
2. Review existing backup policies.
3. Select and evaluate the backup strategy.
4. Implement the strategy.

Because we already covered these steps in Chapter 8, this section focuses only on the additional considerations brought about by distributed data or information resources.

The first step attains new dimensions and becomes more challenging in the context of distributed systems. The network planner must search for critical information throughout the organization setup and come up with a comprehensive list.

The first task of the planner is to discover the locations of files stored on PCs, storage arrays, Network-Attached Storage (NAS) devices, and Storage Area Networks (SANs). The planner can take the help of autodiscover software in this regard. This software helps to locate volumes' databases and files on the network.

Next, the planner needs to determine the usage characteristics and criticality of data. The usage characteristics relate to how often someone accesses the data and details, such as where and in what form the organization requires the data. The criticality relates to the role of the concerned data in supporting critical business applications. If the data is critical, it must be available at all times.

Identifying data from various departments requires a planned and methodical approach. Department heads need to furnish reports about the data in their departments. They also might be required to fill out questionnaires and answer queries. The planners should collect and analyze the data from all departments to reach a conclusion. They should seek clarifications from department heads whenever required.

In addition to computer files and other machine-related data, data also includes paper and microform data. It's important to document data interdependencies that might exist between paper and electronic data. For example, you might have duplicate or complementary paper and electronic data.

When a planner documents paper data that needs to be included in the data recovery plans, he might want to seek the help of the record managers. The company needs to have a proper document management system where data is neatly classified and stored.

It is of immense help if the organization has an electronic document management system. The planner might want to recommend the adoption of such a system to assist future planning efforts.

Sorting Data

After you have collected a comprehensive set of data locations and descriptions, you must sort data according to its criticality in relation to the business processes that are to be recovered. You can use the following steps to sort the data.

Identify Critical Input and Output Data

A planner needs to first identify the critical input and output data for business functions. This data is required to restore the critical business processes to a workable condition. Input data might include coded source documents that are machine readable, software required to run the processes, and the like. Output documents might include important reports and other data that you can use for the purposes of audit or analysis. The planner should prepare an inventory of all these documents and the media on which they are stored.

When you include system and application software in the inventory of data, be sure to include corresponding license agreements and software keys. The keys are required to reinstall the software during the recovery process.

Identify Documents That Are Required to Effect Business Recovery

The system software and application software are required to restore the business applications directly. However, the planner also needs to include several other pieces of documentation. For example, don't forget to include insurance documentation along with the other data. Other subsidiary requirements might include data forms, user manuals, and so on.

Identify Documents That Are Required to Satisfy Legal Needs

Documents that pertain to legal obligations are not related to the recovery of the business processes. However, they are important from the organization's point of view.

For example, legal documents might include important contracts, drafts of intellectual property rights, and so on.

Examples of important contact information might be list of clients, suppliers, customers, and e-mail addresses. Business processes can continue without these lists, but rebuilding them requires significant effort.

Policy-Based Administration of Data

We have just seen the importance of data identification and classification in a decentralized system environment. This is not a one-time exercise; it is dynamic, as are the recovery plans. The planner needs to design a policy for proper data identification and classification. The policy helps in continuous evaluation of the data and processes. Any changes are then reflected in the data recovery plans. The planner might need to modify the plan slightly as a result. The policy generally includes the following:

◆ **An owner-wise classification of information.** It is important to assign ownership to all data to fix responsibility. The owners might be department heads or workgroup managers. These people are required to look for any changes in the data that they own and report these changes to the plan coordinator. This helps establish accountability in the process of data identification and classification.

◆ **A rating system for data criticality.** The planner should grade data according to its criticality to the business operations that are to be recovered. It's essential that the grading system be objective. The auditor can help in this regard. The same tools that were used for business impact analysis, and you can use risk analysis to rate data for criticality. The grade levels might include the following:

1. **Critical data.** This is data deemed to be imperative for the restoration of critical business processes or important data such as business legal documents.

2. **Vital data.** This is other data used in the critical business processes. It includes data that is not required for restoring business processes but is necessary to sustain them. For example, client information databases that have taken years to build are included under this category.

3. **Sensitive data.** This is other data that is important to the business processes but can be reconstructed at a cost to the company. For example, large e-mail lists might require considerable efforts to be rebuilt.

4. **Non-critical data.** This includes data that does not affect the functioning of the critical business functions and data that can be reconstructed at minimal costs.

◆ **Software-based management of electronic data.** Many software packages can assist in the process of identifying network-wide data, classifying it, and backing it up. The use of these packages can be a part of the organization data recovery policy. Computer Associate's ARCServeIT and Legato System's NetWorker are examples of software that manages electronic data. Considering the large volume of data that needs to be backed up and the multiplicity of systems that are involved, the use of management software is prudent.

◆ **Data replication.** Various techniques are available to facilitate data replication. Data replication involves copying data to different locations to ensure the availability of data if the original data is corrupted. The servers where the data is replicated are known as *replica origin servers*. You should ensure regular updates of data on the replica servers.

◆ **Data consolidation.** Data consolidation displays data from different locations. Various data consolidation software, such as DataFix, is available. Data consolidation software combines data from different data sources and displays it in a formatted form.

Planning for System Recovery

When a planner plans for system recovery in decentralized systems, several concerns other than those involved in a centralized system come into the picture. A thorough understanding of the client/server architecture and distributed computing is essential for the disaster recovery planner. He must devise strategies and plans.

Basic 2-tier client/server models entail putting the client part of the software on one set of machines and the server part on another set. Both parts interact through the network. Today, 3-tier and n-tier applications are also common. 3-tier applications involve another component besides the client and the server. This is called the *middleware* and is used to handle communication between the client and the server. The clients communicate with the middleware, which is loaded on the application servers. The middleware, in turn, forwards the requests from all clients to the database servers in a systematic manner. The replies are forwarded back to the clients.

n-tier applications facilitate Web access and e-commerce. Figure 9.1 shows an n-tier client/server model. These models often involve a combination of technologies because they have been developed over the years by adding tiers and applications.

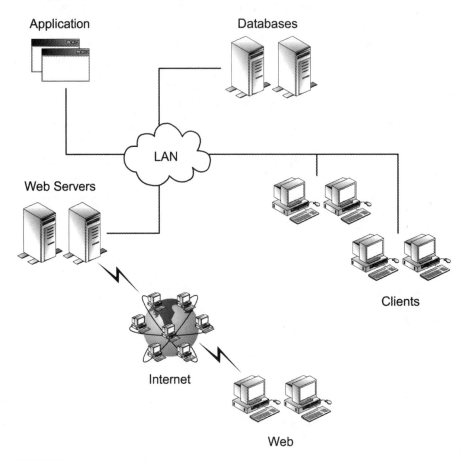

FIGURE 9.1   *An n–tier client/server configuration.*

Most vendors compete in adding more features to their products to achieve greater marketability and to stay ahead of the competition. Therefore, vendors rarely focus on disaster recovery considerations when coming up with client/server products. Many times, the only option available for the planner is a complete replacement of the software and hardware in the event of a disaster.

Replacement is not the most cost-effective solution. Let us examine other strategies that the disaster recovery planner can adopt to minimize the need for replacing the complete system.

Employ Replication

The idea is to have replicated servers for replacement and use in the event of a disaster. However, the drawback of employing redundant systems is that it might prove to be a costly proposition in distributed systems as it is in centralized systems.

Therefore, in a decentralized system, a planner often comes across backup domain controllers that take the place of primary domain controllers in the event of a disaster. Similarly, multiple DNS or Web servers provide fault tolerance.

Another advantage of replication is that it helps improve application performance besides guarding against disasters. For example, cluster servers are often employed to reduce the loads on individual servers. You can employ backup domain controllers to provide network services in place of primary domain controllers, simply because they might be easier to access from a particular site.

Choose Middleware Judiciously

The disaster recovery planner needs to sensitize the application developers with the need to choose middleware judiciously. The planner must sensitize them of disaster recovery considerations when choosing a middleware product for their application design.

Certain middleware products are flexible in the sense that they do not require hard-coded server and client addresses. For example, if a certain database server fails, the middleware products can use broadcast messages to locate an alternate server on the network and update their configuration to use the new server. Other middleware products require the server addresses and names to be hard-coded; therefore, they are more difficult to reconfigure in the event of a disaster.

The final decision of the middleware ultimately resides with the application developers because middleware considerations also involve several other factors, such as application performance and compatibility issues. The disaster recovery planner can make them aware, however, about the need to consider recovery issues.

The application developers should also choose the middleware consistently and should not go for a different product after every upgrade. An application solution that involves a myriad of products from different vendors often requires a complete redo in the event of a disaster.

Encourage a Clearly Defined Partitioned Design for Applications

Applications that are most easily recoverable are the ones for whom the individual processes comprising the application are clearly defined along with their data sets. Such a partitioned design facilitates speedy, process-wise recovery, as opposed to the design in which a clearly partitioned structure is non-existent.

Encourage Fault-Tolerant Configurations

Client/server platforms sometimes crash because of equipment failures and hacker/virus attacks. This is where fault-tolerant technologies can provide the necessary backup in the event of a disaster. Examples of a fault tolerant technology are employing RAID disks, array controllers with failover capabilities, redundant power supply means, and redundant network cards.

Encourage Web-Enabled Applications

Web-enabled applications are accessible from a simple browser interface to locations anywhere in the world. You can utilize this advantage in a disaster scenario to provide the employees access to the applications that are recovered at an alternate site. You can provide access to partners, suppliers, and customers in a similar way.

To plan for this opportunity, the planner can work toward Web-enabling the client/server applications that the organization uses. That way, it is easy to employ them in a disaster scenario.

 NOTE

Exposing your applications on the Web also entails security issues that you have to consider separately.

Planning for Building Recovery

The organization must decide on the recovery policy to be employed and design the recovery plans accordingly. An organization might choose from a number of alternative strategies. Some of these have been already discussed in detail in Chapter 8. Let us briefly examine all the recovery strategies available for decentralized systems.

Next Box Off the Line Strategy

We discussed the next box off the line strategy in Chapter 8. In this strategy, the organization keeps all the systems and application backups ready and procures hardware on an emergency basis in the event of a disaster.

Hot Sites and Redundant Systems

Hot sites and redundant systems are the only solutions available when the organization's applications have not been chosen with disaster recovery in mind. A combination of haphazardly chosen technologies and applications from numerous vendors can jeopardize a recovery plan. In such cases, the only solution is an entire replicated system or a hot site solution that a vendor can provide.

Service Bureaus

Service bureaus are increasingly emerging as one of the available solutions, especially with the rise of Internet-based Application Service Providers (ASPs). However, these solutions are mostly application specific and cannot work for all business operations.

Application Consolidation

Application consolidation refers to employing distributed applications that lend themselves more easily to disaster recovery techniques. Proper application partitioning, replication, and thoughtful middleware design are part of application consolidation strategies. This solution is much more cost effective than redundant systems. This recovery solution requires only a minimal workable configuration with the requisite number of users to sustain critical business processes.

Centralization

The centralization strategy tries to build some order into the anarchic distributed environment. The scattered servers are pooled in a data center environment resembling that of a centralized system. This leads to better management, easier data backups, and improved network productivity.

The concept of *thin client computing* has also come into being. This is an attempt to center most of the processing operations on the server and limit the capabilities of the client. The application servers serve as the central repository for software and data as opposed to the PC. This helps to bring about greater order and control besides reducing the number of data centers in the organization.

The recovery planner also can use a combination of the preceding solutions to design a system recovery solution. For instance, you can use both the next box off the line and application consolidation strategies together.

Planning for Communication Link Recovery

We discussed some of the issues related to network and communication link recovery in Chapter 8. Let us now discuss some of the other issues related to decentralized systems.

LAN Recovery

LANs are used in decentralized systems to facilitate the client/server model. LANs are an important means of communication between the client and server, and ensuring their workability is an important part of the network recovery process.

The disaster recovery planner must be aware of the LAN concepts, such as the OSI networking model and its application to the organization network. The planner must be aware of the products that are being used in the organization because different vendors implement the networking model in different ways. Moreover, the planner must be familiar with the network topology and have a good working knowledge of the network. All this aids the planner in analyzing requirements with network administrators and effecting network recovery.

A familiarity with the OSI networking model helps the planner better understand the networking concepts involved. With knowledge of the seven layers and their usage and interaction, the planner can then go on to analyze the application of the model to the organizational LAN.

Following are the seven layers of the OSI model:

- ◆ **Layer 7: Application layer.** Applications use this layer to interact with each other. Protocols such as HTTP and FTP belong to this layer.

- ◆ **Layer 6: Presentation layer.** This layer is utilized to decide upon the format of data that is to be used. Encryption and compression are normally performed at this layer.

- ◆ **Layer 5: Session layer.** This layer handles sessions between the clients and servers.

- ◆ **Layer 4: Transport layer.** This layer includes protocols that ensure safe and correct delivery of data packets. The TCP protocol belongs to this layer.

- ◆ **Layer 3: Network layer.** This layer handles network addressing. The IP protocol belongs to this layer.

- ◆ **Layer 2: Data link layer.** This layer handles packaging of data and marking it on the network.

- ◆ **Layer 1: Physical layer.** This is the lowest layer. It decides the data flows across the media and physical devices.

A thorough familiarity with the preceding protocol stack (stack of layers) and an understanding of how data flows down and up these stacks is important to understanding the networking model.

A study of the organization network can help the planner decide recovery parameters. For instance, knowing whether nodes are identified by name or address can help planning of the recovery of workstations and servers accordingly. It is more difficult to replace hard-coded addresses than flexible names.

Depending on the operations of the lower layers, the planner also can contemplate solutions like deploying a wireless LAN in an emergency until the original infrastructure is restored.

The planner can study the network layers for the security measures being employed in the network. For example, an encryption protocol might be working at the presentation layer. The planner needs to decide how alternative communications would take place in the event of a disaster and how these security standards would be maintained. Is it okay to compromise encryption security in the event of a disaster? The planner needs to answer such important questions when choosing a recovery solution.

An idea of the organization's network topology gives the planner better insights into single points of failure in the network, cabling issues, and the case for using redundant hardware. Sometimes it is also possible to effect recovery of distributed systems on a centralized platform. It might be possible to replace distributed servers with a single server and restore operations. Again, the planner must keep network parameters in mind before contemplating such a solution.

An important point that cannot be understated here is the importance of working in conjunction with the network administrators. Network administrators are possessive about their networks and have a complete knowledge of how the network ticks. A successful network can be achieved only with the active cooperation of the network administrators. Network administrators can help with the following:

◆ Network administrators have a workable knowledge of the service-level requirements of networked applications.

◆ Network administrators are thorough with the design of the network and can suggest innovative changes in the event of a disaster.

◆ Network administrators can help determine the minimum network requirements—such as bandwidth requirements in the event of a disaster—so that the critical applications can be sustained.

◆ Network administrators also have a first-class knowledge of the traffic patterns in the network that can help in load-management tasks.

◆ Security is the prime concern of the network administrators. They can help in determining the security standards that must be in place while recovery is carried out.

◆ Network administrators are adept at using network management software like the network monitors that can help provide valuable input for the planning process.

Internal Voice Communication

We discussed relocating WAN and data links in the event of a disaster in Chapter 8. Let us take a look at internal voice communications now. Modern voice communications are normally based on PBX networks. Failures in these systems might involve a particular operational area or the entire PBX system.

When a failure is caused due to a station failure or media failure in a particular line, it often leads to a partial disruption of communication lines. The need of the hour is to quickly localize the problem and solve it. Planning for such failures might entail the use of the following:

◆ Redundant media to provide fault tolerance.

◆ Network fault detection software to expedite the recovery process. Technicians must be trained in the use of such software to make optimum use of them.

Internal voice communication failure might be caused due to the failure of the PBX switch. The following measures are helpful to guard against such failures:

◆ Most modern-day PBX systems are programmable. PBX programs for call forwarding, call pickup, and other such services should be backed up properly to restore operations in case the PBX program is misplaced.

◆ Make an uninterruptible power supply (UPS) and fire-detection mechanisms available to the PBX system.

◆ In the event of a PBX failure, you can use leased dedicated lines to temporarily restore operations in critical areas until the PBX comes back online.

◆ A redundant PBX switch is also an option. The redundant switch must be located separately from the original switch so it will be immune from the disaster affecting the original equipment.

Planning for Personnel Recovery

Chapter 8 discussed the importance of a user recovery plan. A disaster recovery plan is not complete without a plan for user recovery and relocation. Centralized system plans have long ignored this aspect of disaster recovery. Planning for data center recovery alone is not enough because users are required to perform the mission-critical processing tasks.

The issue of user recovery becomes even more pronounced in a distributed system because of obvious reasons. The data centers are spread across the organization and any disruptions affect the users as well. Users might be required to be relocated. Also, users need more than a terminal server access in a distributed system. They need functional LAN, WAN, and data links to carry out their data processing jobs.

A planner can use the usual recovery planning techniques and analyses methods, such as Data Flow Diagrams (DFDs), to decide on the user requirements in relation to the following:

◆ Facility

◆ System requirements

◆ Supply and logistics

◆ Application requirements

◆ Network requirements

You have many considerations when you're deciding on a strategy for the preceding requirements. For example, when you're choosing a facility, you have to decide whether a company-owned facility or a contracted facility is more feasible. Issues such as transport to the facility, personal hygiene, work environment, and security at the alternate facility become concerns. The users might be able to work from home as well. In that case, you need to provide suitable dial-up access to the organization network.

The timeframe of the strategy also plays a part in its acceptance or rejection, besides the costs involved. The strategy must provide user recovery within acceptable timeframes and costs. A strategy should also be testable before it is implemented in a disaster scenario.

Many recovery solutions are available, and the ones that the organization should choose depend on organization-specific requirements and priorities.

Let us discuss some of these solutions.

"On-the-Fly" Approach

As the name suggests, this approach postpones the decision to look for facilities until the disaster actually happens. The inherent assumption is that you can obtain leased office space easily at short notice. You also can use alternate locations such as hotel conference rooms or warehouse facilities if needed.

The distinct advantage of this method is that the organization is absolved of any costs until a disaster occurs (that is, no predisaster charges are involved).

On the other hand, the disadvantage is the timeframe for recovery. You must equip an alternate facility with all the necessary systems, telecommunication and network connections, and so on. You need to notify the users of the alternate facility and arrange transport there. In addition, you need to look into issues such as user comfort and hygiene.

Another disadvantage of this method is that it is unpredictable, and sometimes the assumptions can go awry. This normally happens in a disaster of a regional scale. The supposed recovery facilities are not unaffected by the disaster, and it might be hard to find an alternative facility. A facility that is further from the disaster scene might be the only option in such a scenario. However, this will also entail transportation issues of user and equipment.

The Alternative Approach

An alternative to the "on-the-fly" approach is having a dual strategy in place. The first strategy relates to localized disasters and is the same as the "on-the-fly" strategy. You can apply the alternative approach in cases of regional disasters. You can use a predefined remote facility of the company to effect disaster recovery.

The thinking behind this approach is that the "on-the-fly" approach becomes too uncertain in cases of regional and large-scale disasters. On the other hand, the strategy might be feasible for small-scale disasters in which it is easier to notify users, find vendors for equipment and telecommunication restoration, and locate alternate facilities.

The alternate company facility is equipped with all the necessary infrastructure to be used in case of a regional emergency. The employees must be relocated to this previously defined site in such a scenario.

The advantage of this method is that it is less of a risk proposition than the "on-the-fly" approach. However, the uncertainties still remain for localized disasters simply because this plan is never tested until an actual disaster.

Another concern with this approach is justifying the cost issues involved in maintaining a fully equipped alternate recovery site simply for user recovery operations. However, the company might intelligently handle this by using one of its remote branch offices or storage sites as a temporary recovery center.

When planners use an alternative company site as an option, they must evaluate the costs involved in providing the necessary infrastructure, such as telecommunication links, WAN links, systems, and transportation facilities.

Commercial Recovery Facilities

Hot site and offsite storage vendors provide commercial recovery facilities. The organization can subscribe to them for a reasonable monthly fee. In the event of a disaster, the vendor provides the user recovery facility.

The advantage of this method is that it is cost effective when compared to the expenses involved in maintaining recovery sites of the company. Many customers share these facilities at different times, which is why they are cost effective. Also, this approach is more reliable than the haphazard "on-the-fly" approach.

Mobile and portal sites are increasingly being used as effective alternate facilities provided by the vendors. The advantages of these sites are multifold. They can be constructed in little time and can be moved close to the original user worksites. You can even set up a mobile site in a parking lot, if needed.

The possible disadvantage of using such a solution is that the vendor facilities are also vulnerable in regional scale disasters. Moreover, the simultaneous contingency in many companies can provide a lot of pressure on the vendor to serve each of them satisfactorily.

Remote Access

User recovery might not always require relocation or alternative user facilities. Remote access solutions can provide users with the option to work from their original sites through remote connections to the recovery site. Also, it might be possible for users to work from their homes through a dial-up connection to the recovery site.

Companies are increasingly using remote access technology for providing connectivity to mobile salespersons and executives, who need to access the company network from various places. Employees who are working from home also use remote access increasingly.

You can put these technologies to good use in a disaster scenario, too. You can use dial-up connections from home to connect to the company network and access applications as if they were on the user desktop at home. Of course, security considerations come into the picture. You need to encrypt and secure the communications in other ways to avoid compromise of important information.

If the organization uses a Remote Access Server (RAS), it can manage all remote connections of employees, suppliers, and partners. You can configure security policies on the RAS server to manage access levels to the organization's internal network. Figure 9.2 shows a remote access configuration.

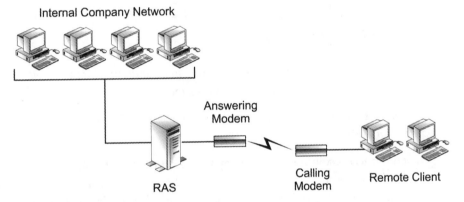

FIGURE 9.2 *A remote access configuration*

Virtual Private Networks (VPNs) also are emerging as an increasingly popular method of accessing the company network. VPNs use a public network, such as the Internet, to connect two private networks. The advantage here is that the infrastructure of the Internet Service Provider (ISP) is being used in this case and the company does not need to invest in it.

Moreover, the company does not have to pay long-distance call charges. The only call charges are the ones that are required to connect to the local ISP.

Another advantage of VPNs is that they provide security by implementing tunneling technologies, whereby data is encrypted and tunneled through a public network. The use of VPNs would not have been feasible without the use of encryption and tunneling technologies because data flows through unprotected, public networks. Figure 9.3 illustrates the concept of a VPN.

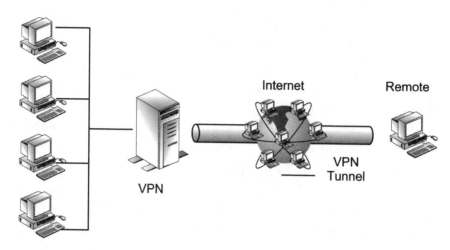

Internal Network

FIGURE 9.3 *Concept of a VPN.*

You also can use remote access solutions in conjunction with the other solutions discussed before this to effect user recovery.

There are a few concerns with remote access solutions as well that you should address.

Remote access solutions must be capable of supporting the increasing workload in a disaster situation. Users who might be working from office in normal situations would require using remote access solutions in a disaster situation.

You also need to ponder the security aspects of the remote access solutions and look into at consultation with the network administrator. Is it safe to transmit sensitive information over public networks? Are the encryption algorithms reliable? These are just a few of the questions that you need to answer.

Another concern is the bandwidth. Not all applications can perform well on a limited bandwidth connection. The remote access solution might not be feasible for many applications thus.

The organization can plan for thin client applications, which you can easily use in conjunction with remote access. In these applications, much of the processing is done at the server end, which is faster. The remote access solution might be rendered incapable if the disaster destroys the telecommunication infrastructure as well. VPNs are more robust to such destruction because the organization might be able to reroute its connections through a different ISP, who is unaffected by the disaster.

Summary

In this chapter, we discussed the disaster recovery plan for decentralized systems. We discussed the elementary concepts in Chapter 8. This chapter sought to emphasize the differences between centralized and decentralized recovery.

Next, you learned about the nuances that are added to the plan in a decentralized system recovery. Although the basic plan remains the same, certain other considerations that are peculiar to distributed systems come into the fray. You learned about data recovery for decentralized systems. The issue of data identification and classification attains prime importance in a decentralized system. This chapter dealt with this issue at length.

From there, you learned about system recovery and the various strategies available for it. We discussed the strategies for client/server models and discussed building the plan and choosing one of the predetermined strategies.

Network and communication recovery plays a big part in decentralized system recovery. Users do not simply need a terminal connection to the server, such as in a centralized system. This chapter discussed the issue of LAN recovery at length, as well as restoring the PBX system.

User recovery has been the neglected aspect of disaster recovery planning. However, no recovery can be affected without the users. The issue of user recovery planning was discussed in detail, and we came up with strategies for user recovery in a distributed environment.

Check Your Understanding

Short Questions

1. Briefly discuss the personnel recovery plan.
2. Briefly discuss failure in internal voice communication.

Answers

Short Answers

1. The personnel recovery plan assumes more importance in a decentralized system because the data centers are spread across the organization, and any disruptions might affect a large section of users. The recovery solutions that are available for personnel recovery are given next:

   ◆ **"On-the-fly" approach.** In this approach, the organization decides to pursue disaster recovery only after disaster strikes the organization. This plan has cost-saving advantages associated with it.

   ◆ **Dual strategy.** In this approach, the "on-the-fly" strategy is applied, but only to regional disasters on the presumption that disasters are regionally centered.

   ◆ **Commercial recovery facilities.** In this strategy, commercial facilities that are provided by hot site vendors are subscribed to for disaster recovery planning.

   ◆ **Remote access.** In this strategy, facilities are created for users to log on to the recovery site remotely and perform their tasks.

2. Modern voice communications are normally based on PBX networks. Failures in these systems might involve a particular operational area or the entire PBX system. When a failure is caused due to a station failure or media failure in a particular line, it often leads to a partial disruption of communication lines. The need of the hour is to quickly localize the problem and solve it by using measures such as redundant media and network fault detection.

   Internal voice communication failure might also be a result of the failure of the PBX switch. To prevent such failures, you can program backup call forwarding, call pickup, and other such services on PBX systems to restore operations in case the PBX program is misplaced.

Chapter 10

Implementing a Disaster Recovery Plan

In the previous chapters, you learned about how to plan for disaster recovery. You learned about the steps and intricacies involved in the planning process and the tasks to perform prior to the occurrence of a disaster. What happens when a disaster strikes an organization? How and when is the disaster recovery plan implemented? How does an organization recover from a disaster?

This chapter seeks to answer your queries related to the recovery of an organization by implementing a disaster recovery plan. To aid your understanding of the process, this chapter illustrates an organization's recovery through a fictitious case study. The case study has been created to give you a better understanding of the disaster recovery planning concepts in a real-world scenario.

This chapter traces the steps involved in the organization's recovery. In addition, it discusses the factors that contributed to the organization's successful recovery.

Case Study

Mucarz, Inc. is an online trading organization that sells goods and provides services to customers over the Internet. The Web site of the organization allows customers to buy and sell goods through auctions and fixed price trading. On a typical day, the organization trades millions of items with profits running into thousands of dollars. Customers buy and sell a wide range of items, including automobiles, sports goods, and computers. Among the many services that the organization offers is the online bill payment service that allows payment by credit cards. In all its transactions, the organization promises and maintains trust, safety, and privacy.

The manual force of the organization is composed of 800 employees. The employees are distributed across these various departments:

- ◆ Financial department
- ◆ Legal department
- ◆ Personnel department
- ◆ IT department

◆ Public relations department

◆ Security department

The market presence of the organization depends on the availability and reliability of its IT infrastructure. The IT infrastructure includes communication links and IT operational processes, such as backups. The organization uses diverse storage platforms ranging from Server-Attached Storage (SAS), Network-Attached Storage (NAS), and Storage Area Networks (SANs) to perform its various business operations. The organization has a distributed system setup with branch offices located across the country. The distributed system setup ensures that if one data center is impacted, the other data centers can distribute the workload among themselves.

The main data center of the organization is in California. The organization's branch offices are spread across the country in Florida, Pennsylvania, and Texas. Each office of the organization relies on critical assets—such as a backup system, a Web server, a data server, communication links, and personnel—for its business.

The main data center forms a critical asset of the organization because of the following reasons:

◆ It hosts mainframe computers and major server support to the organization's applications and data. All critical operations of the organization, such as payment and transaction processing, are performed at the main data center.

◆ It acts as a payment gateway where connections are made with merchant banks for authentication of the payments made. All critical data, such as the credit card details and buying patterns of customers, is stored in the client database at the main center.

◆ It acts as the dealer network for the distribution of information between the other data centers.

Therefore, the continuity and the reliability of the main center are imperative to the business continuity of the entire organization. Further, the operations that the main center performs cannot be distributed among other data centers. The criticality of the main data center and the complexity involved in dispersing the operations of the data center to other data centers stipulate the presence of the main center activities at a single location. In addition, low Recovery Point Objective (RPO) and Recovery Time Objective (RTO) values require the recovery of the critical activities of the main center in the shortest possible time. Figure 10.1 displays the organization's RPO and RTO values.

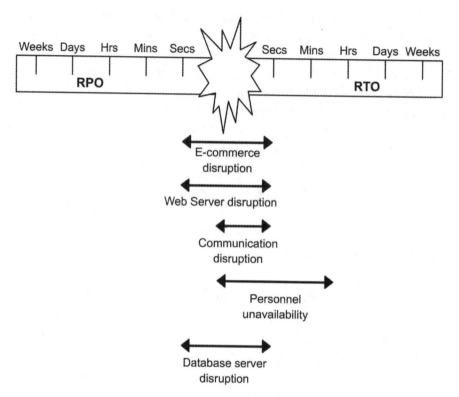

FIGURE 10.1 *The RPO and RTO values for Mucarz, Inc.*

The main center of the organization is in an earthquake zone. In the past two years, the main data center has withstood the impact of two earthquakes. This prompted management to create a disaster recovery plan. Based on the spread of the organization across the country, each branch of the organization has a disaster recovery plan of its own. The disaster recovery plan for the organization, therefore, is a compilation of the individual disaster recovery plans of the various branch offices.

In the disaster recovery plan, the organization made adequate arrangements to ensure successful recovery of the organization from any disaster that is likely to occur and impact the organization and its business operations. The plan focused on the major disasters that each of the facilities was prone to and their subsequent repercussions.

Based on the requirements of low RPO and RTO values, the organization selected a hot site as a recovery strategy. The organization contracted a recovery vendor, Alarmag, Inc., for recovery purposes. According to the contract, Alarmag, Inc. would provide the hot site facility. This hot site facility is located in Nebraska.

To ensure that skilled personnel performed all the logistics-related activities, Alarmag, Inc. promised the assistance of its recovery personnel. The recovery personnel would ensure IT setup, logistics, and other recovery-related tasks in the disaster recovery center. In other words, the recovery personnel would ensure that the systems at the disaster recovery site were functional before the employees of the organization moved to the recovery site.

Disaster Recovery Plan Activation

The media had been flashing warnings about an impending earthquake since the beginning of the new year. At 11:00 p.m. on the second weekend of February, the security personnel at the main data center of Mucarz, Inc. felt the earth beneath their feet tremble. It was the earthquake that the meteorological department had been sounding alarms about. The earthquake measuring 7.2 on the Richter scale reduced the main data center to a mass of debris. It also cut off all power and communication links.

The security personnel followed the notification procedure as specified in the disaster recovery plan and informed the planning team representative using the special distress line reserved for emergency. The security personnel specified details related to the extent of damage, the time at which the earthquake occurred, and so on. By 12:00 p.m., the representative had informed the planning coordinator, Ruben Huxley, about the earthquake and its impact on the data center.

In the early hours of the next day, Ruben Huxley, the security manager at Mucarz, Inc., arrived at the site with an assessment team to evaluate the extent of damage that the earthquake caused. Simultaneously, the recovery team coordinated with the local authorities, such as the fire department, to rescue and salvage the equipment at the damaged site. The team also ensured the continuance of security controls for protection of the assets at the disaster site.

For the evaluation, the assessment team used the parameters as specified in the disaster recovery plan. The assessment team performed the following activities:

◆ Documented the data about the damage that the earthquake caused to the critical assets

◆ Salvaged the equipment that was relatively undamaged and capable of being used or that which had critical information

The salvage team shipped the equipment with critical data to the hot site; the remaining equipment was stored at a temporary storage in California.

Based on the results of the assessment, Ruben activated the plan. Next, Ruben informed the contact person from Alarmag, Inc. that the employees would be reaching the hot site. The vendor activated the hot site accordingly and configured the workstations and the WAN links. In addition, the recovery personnel that the vendor provided performed the following activities:

◆ Provided Internet access

◆ Routed all incoming phone calls to the offsite location

◆ Met the requirements for the resumption of all critical activities at the earliest possible time

◆ Got the employees acclimatized to the new work environment

To ensure that the employees could acclimate to the new work environment, the recovery personnel provided the employees with the same desktop as that at the primary site, plans of the building, and evacuation routes.

The recovery personnel provided information related to the location to which the employees needed to report to work and furnished answers to specific inquiries at the emergency phone number with the voicemail capability. They also made special arrangements for the transportation of the employees to the hot site facility. Meanwhile, the public relations person who was in charge provided the media and the public with details related to the earthquake damage and the corresponding recovery efforts.

During the time of recovery from the impact of the disaster, the organization controlled and tracked the funds related to recovery activities. All the legal- and insurance-related tasks to the recovery of the business activities were initiated.

At the hot site, employees resumed their work. All critical activities including transaction processing for customer accounts could be performed as under normal circumstances. The movement of the employees and the subsequent resumption of business operations of Mucarz, Inc. happened in a couple of hours from the time of notification. For the customers and the branch offices of Mucarz, Inc., this meant a disruption of only a few minutes of business. As a result, the currentness of the data was maintained without missing a single transaction.

The employees continued to work from the disaster recovery center at the hot site for four months after the main data center was destroyed. All this time, the audit team at Mucarz, Inc. audited the recovery procedures and the plan to maintain the standards and policies of the organization. In the meantime, the main center was reconstructed. The organization replaced the damaged equipment and made the required network and communications links functional.

Therefore, all the recovery plans and procedures that the organization had developed and regularly tested ensured the recovery of business in the shortest possible time and with minimal disruptions.

Factors That Lead to a Successful Recovery

The successful recovery of the main data center can be attributed to several factors. To aid understanding, we will discuss these factors in the following stages:

- ◆ Predisaster stage
- ◆ Planning stage
- ◆ Post disaster stage

Predisaster Stage

The decision of Mucarz, Inc. to plan for disaster recovery was the first step in the right direction. The realization that an organization can be affected by a disaster and then planning to ensure business continuity was the primary reason for the successful recovery of the main center. In the absence of planning for disaster recovery, the organization would have incurred immense financial loss. It is also likely that without planning for disaster recovery, the organization might have faced closure.

However, closure and financial loss didn't come to Mucarz, Inc. Management of Mucarz, Inc. realized that as an organization, it was vulnerable to disasters and, as a consequence, its business was susceptible to closure. With this perspective in mind, management created a panel of key personnel to head the disaster recovery planning process. This panel prepared an outline of the tasks and the accomplishments promised at the end of the planning exercise. In addition, the team outlined the course of the planning project, the cost, and the deadline details.

Planning Stage

The planning stage contributed the most to the success of the recovery process. Members from all departments were involved in the planning process. The planning team followed the steps involved in the creation of recovery plans and procedures.

During risk analysis, the team created an inventory to include information related to all the assets. This inventory was a detailed and accurate list of all the physical assets in the organization. All critical assets, such as mainframe computers, bridges, routers, and gateways, were listed as critical.

In addition to the physical inventory, the team created an equipment inventory for all the applications and software installed on the computers in the organization. The equipment inventory consisted of the following:

◆ List of all the equipment by type and model number

◆ Software packages with their version numbers

◆ Date of purchase and cost of the equipment

The team also created a software inventory. This inventory listed information related to the software required by the organization, such as its purpose, cost, license number, and version number. In addition, the team performed the following activities:

◆ Identified personnel who had specialized skills

◆ Assessed the premises of the organization and its surrounding buildings

◆ Identified the critical activities and assets

◆ Identified values for critical assets

◆ Prioritized critical activities and assets

◆ Ensured that management approved critical activities and assets

For asset valuation, the team conducted workshops and brainstorming sessions. All through the creation of the plan, management extended its support to the planning task.

As the next step, the risk analysis team conducted face-to-face interviews of the role holders in the organization. In addition, the team circulated questionnaires among the employees. This helped the team to acquire an extensive list of all the risks that the organization was likely to face. In addition, they employed a consultant to identify the risks to the organization and used his expertise to create the disaster recovery plan.

Management ensured that the backup procedures and other such security measures were in place. Mucarz, Inc. underwent extensive automation as a means to reduce dependency on personnel. The planning team clearly defined the scope of the disaster recovery plan while documenting it. In other words, the team identified the events that classified as a disaster.

The team planned strategies for short-term recovery and long-term recovery. Resuming work from an alternate site was the short-term recovery strategy that the team decided on. A long-term recovery strategy included ways to resume business operations at the primary site. The team evaluated the need for an alternate site and chose to have one. For this purpose, the team decided on the vendor, the type of alternate site, and the resources required at this site.

To assess and select an alternate site, the team considered issues, such as the distance of the site from the primary site and the resources at the site. Keeping these considerations in mind, the team decided on a site located away from all the company offices. This was done to ensure that the alternate site would not be affected by the same disaster that affected a branch office. While considering the vendor for the recovery services, management conducted extensive research.

The organization implemented data mirroring as a solution to meet the low RPO and RTO values. To ensure data mirroring, the organization invested in high-speed fiber-optic circuits between the target and the source data centers. Mirroring eliminated the need to retrieve backup tapes from their offsite storage and reload the data. In other words, the recovery was instantaneous.

The team identified all the resources that were likely to be required during a disaster prior to the occurrence of the disaster. For instance, the organization identified assistance from the local fire department and ambulance services. The team also wrote down all the contact information required to contact the vendor and resources at the time of a disaster.

After the team documented the plan, employees were trained in the recovery tasks as documented in the disaster recovery plan. Finally, the plan was put through tests that simulated a real-life scenario. The test exercise involved the participation of local disaster response bodies.

 NOTE

In the Appendix of the plan, the team included the following details:

- ◆ Technical details required to set up the network infrastructure. For instance, the team recorded the manner in which a particular router was to be set up.

- ◆ All the documentation available in the organization. The team performed this process for each department and tracked and recorded all the documents that had a direct bearing on the organization.

- ◆ The internal and external connectivity details. This included the details required to establish connectivity within the time frame and documentation of the ISP contact information.

- ◆ The screenshots of the settings of the server configurations for each department. They captured the details about the DHCP, DNS, and WINS settings.

- ◆ The pictures, diagrams, and directions to specify the location of the disaster recovery equipment.

- ◆ Information such as an emergency call list of recovery teams, the vendors, and personnel in the notification list.

The team put the plan through multiple rounds of testing. They then incorporated the results of each test before performing the next test. To begin testing, the team conducted the checklist test to validate the components of the disaster recovery plan. Next, the team performed a walkthrough of the steps in the plan. For simulation testing of the plan, Ronald Green, the LAN administrator, went on a long vacation without informing anyone in the organization except the members of the testing team. In a LAN, the administrator is responsible for all the activities that ensure that the LAN is working at all times. The purpose of this entire exercise was to acclimate the employees to a situation without the LAN administrator and identify their response in the situation. The team also simulated a fire situation. After performing parallel testing as stated in Chapter 7, "Testing and Maintaining the Recovery Plan," the team performed a full interruption test. In the full interruption test, the team tested the entire plan.

The testing team prepared a document for management detailing the results of all the tests conducted for the disaster recovery plan. They also documented all the changes made to the plan.

Post Disaster Stage

Times of disaster are often times of chaos. But Mucarz, Inc., resumed critical business activities within hours without chaos. This is because all the personnel involved in the recovery tasks knew what to do. This was made possible through the extensive documentation in the disaster recovery plan about the roles and responsibilities of all personnel involved in the task of recovery. A prior notification and extensive drills and exercises that the organization conducted ensured the communication and knowledge of the respective roles and responsibilities. Take, for instance, the notification procedure. The security personnel knew the name and the contact number of the person to notify when a disaster struck. There was also no confusion related to the flow of authority.

The recovery personnel from the vendor, Alarmag, Inc., also participated in the tests that Mucarz, Inc. performed. Therefore, communication was clear about the tasks that the vendor personnel needed to perform. Additionally, Alarmag, Inc. ensured the security and communication of the disaster recovery site.

The team decided to store the information of the contacts at the offsite location. In addition, all the papers related to information such as banking and corporate registrations were moved to an offsite location. This proved helpful because the salvage team did not have to search the contact numbers from the rubble of the main center.

All the electronic equipment was restored, software was reloaded, and power, UPS, and other common building systems were restored. In addition, fire suppression systems were replaced, the building was rewired, and LAN and WAN connections were restored.

Summary

In this chapter, you traced the steps involved in the recovery of Mucarz, Inc. In addition, you learned about the steps involved in the activation of the disaster recovery plan. Finally, you learned about the factors that contributed to the organization's successful recovery.

Appendix A

Best Practices

You already have a fairly good idea about how to recover from a disaster and have learned to create a disaster recovery plan. Now is a good time to look at some of the established practices to follow to ensure the success of disaster recovery plans:

- Identify the top 10 disasters that can most severely cripple the organization prior to drafting the disaster recovery plan. Carefully analyze the possible impact of each disaster on the organization. Some examples of possible disasters are fire, earthquake, storm, flood, terrorist attack, plane crash, and chemical accident.

- Always assess the impact of a disaster on your organization from both the financial and physical perspectives. To accomplish this, you might begin by asking the following questions:

  - What are the resources that could be lost?

  - What would be the total cost of the lost resources?

  - What efforts would be required to recover these resources?

  - How much time and money would be required to recover these resources?

  - How much revenue would be lost due to curtailment or halting of production?

  - What would be the impact on the overall organization?

  - What would be the impact on the customers?

  - What would be the impact on the share price and market reputation of the organization?

- Use the following list as a guideline for building a successful disaster recovery plan:

  1. Establish a planning group.

  2. Carry out risk assessments and audits.

  3. Prioritize resources.

4. Develop recovery strategies.

5. Create up-to-date documentation.

6. Define verification criteria and procedures.

7. Implement the plan.

8. Analyze the gaps, if any.

◆ Store the support documents at the disaster recovery center.

◆ Store procedures that are related to security and reconstruction of records on different media, such as optical disk or magnetic media. In addition, make sure these media are adequately protected.

◆ Include performance indicators in a disaster recovery plan. These performance indicators help in assessing the performance of a disaster recovery plan as a whole. Some performance parameters include regular testing, periodic report to management, and analysis of the gaps found in actual implementation of a disaster recovery plan.

◆ Ensure that management is involved in all phases of a disaster recovery plan. Make management well aware and conscious of the serious consequences of not having a disaster recovery plan and the positive benefits of having one. With this awareness, it becomes easy to get funds and other resources to implement a disaster recovery plan.

◆ Include copies of contracts and agreements with all the support agencies (such as reconstruction consultants), suppliers of essential equipments, and vendors in the disaster recovery plan document.

◆ Assess the resilience of the organization's network. Keep in mind the levels of network availability. These levels could be reliable networks, high-availability networks, and nonstop networks. This, in turn, helps to prioritize risks and identify the mission-critical resources of the network.

◆ To assess the resilience of your organization's network, evaluate the following areas:

◆ Network links

◆ Hardware

◆ Network design

◆ Network services

◆ Include a backup services strategy for the disaster recovery plan. This strategy should be consistent throughout the whole organization. For example, frame relay services can use ISDN as a backup.

◆ When selecting a vendor, look out for answers to the following questions regarding vendor support:

  ◆ Does the vendor have enough resources to support the disaster recovery plan?

  ◆ Are the contracts in place?

  ◆ Was the vendor involved while planning for the disaster recovery plan?

 NOTE

Most of the disaster recovery vendors have enough experience in handling disaster situations. Cisco is one such vendor that offers a wide range of services and support solutions.

◆ While documenting a disaster recovery plan, follow a standard format for writing the detailed procedures (before, after, and during a disaster) and other information. This ensures ongoing maintenance of the documentation.

◆ Base the disaster recovery plan on team approach. Assign specific responsibilities to the appropriate contingency team for each functional area of the company. For example, teams should be available who are responsible for administrative functions, facilities, user support, computer backup, logistics, restoration, and other important areas in the organization.

◆ Know the organization's goals, methods, procedures, and desired results. Doing so helps you prepare the best disaster recovery plan documentation.

◆ Understand what needs to be documented. Ideally, you should only use disaster recovery plan documentation for disaster recovery and disaster recovery training. For other stakeholders, use separate documents. For example, you can modify the same document you used for marketing employees to reflect the sales perspective. It is equally important to know your audience before documenting. For example, a highly technical organization will have its own jargon and preferred format. If the audience is comfortable with this jargon, then use it. If your organization is less technically oriented, avoid jargon. To make things easier, listen to the way members of your audience talk. This will help you develop the tone of the document.

◆ Determine who will need to read the disaster recovery document and have access to it. This is another way to define your audience.

◆ Document the plan after taking into account that it will be several weeks or months before the plan is published. Considering all the things that will be in place by the time the document is published helps reduce the updating cost and effort later on.

◆ Make the plan document easy to read and have it follow these guidelines for improving the appearance and readability of the document:

◆ Use short sentences to convey information.

◆ Use bullet lists for complex ideas.

◆ Use graphics to support the text.

◆ Use a large point-size typeface for the text.

◆ Develop a comprehensive index.

In short, keep it simple.

◆ Always keep in mind that a disaster plan is not a fixed and finished document; it evolves and gets better with the passage of time. The disaster plan doesn't need to be perfect the first time you create it. It's more important to get started on it.

◆ Be systematic in your plan. Don't outguess nature and plan for a fire, a hurricane, or a flood. Instead, look at the common elements in any disaster, such as loss of information, access to information and facilities, and people.

◆ Make sure the plan coordinator has a second-in-command to take over his duties and responsibilities in case he can't do it himself. If you don't plan for this backup, then the plan becomes inherently highly vulnerable.

◆ Assign individual responsibilities ahead of time by assigning specific people to each task. Some examples of such tasks include informing your suppliers, board members, and important customers about the disaster.

- Protect critical paper records. This is applicable even for a fully computerized organization because even in those organizations, some records are vulnerable. Examples of such records are pending contracts, research, or loan applications, which generally exist only on paper.

- Prioritize your activities. In other words, after a disaster, you cannot return everything to normal at the same time. Decide beforehand the maximum time to devote to each activity.

- Ensure that employees can exit without a key. In many organizations, employees who stay late to process work are locked in after the doors are locked at the end of the day.

- Keep copies of all of your forms offsite. One good place could be at your home. Ensure that the documentation includes the home phone numbers of the service people you can rely on, such as your insurance agent, plumber, and electrician.

- Plan for frequent testing. You can perform these tests in various ways. Regardless of the testing techniques used, following are some important points to keep in mind:

  - Testing should be successful. Any test that can provide even a small input on improving the plan is worth trying.

  - Every test should have defined objectives and parameters; otherwise, it serves no purpose and actually results in loss of time and money.

  - Create demo tests and carefully document them. These are useful during auditing.

  - Conduct tests regularly. This ensures consistency between the disaster recovery plan and business reality. This does not mean that you should conduct tests strictly per calendar dates. Instead, conduct tests in response to triggers, such as a new business unit, a new technology, or after a staff "rightsizing." In the absence of these triggers, conduct testing at least once every 3–6 months, depending on the organization's requirements.

  - Involve auditors during testing to assess the adequacy of your disaster recovery plan against other IT and business unit audits.

- Remember that some disaster recovery plan consultants specialize in testing and can give valuable suggestions—at a price, of course.

Last but not least are some questions that you can ask yourself when you are finished preparing a disaster recovery plan for your organization:

◆ Is another person with full authority for disaster recovery available in case the usual person in charge is not available?

◆ Do the fire and police departments that service each of your locations have your phone number as well as that of your alternate?

◆ Have you tested the disaster recovery plan?

◆ Can your alarms work without main power? (Do they have battery backup?)

◆ Is a binder that has a copy of every form you use and the phone number of the place where you get them available offsite?

◆ Are your records safe from fire?

◆ Are you aware of the street addresses of your local radio stations? This is required in the event that telephones are not working and you need to get there to make announcements.

◆ Do you have access to a list of all employees' voicemail passwords? This is required to retrieve messages when an employee is suddenly ill or incapacitated.

◆ Does your location have emergency cabinets that contain at the minimum a first-aid kit, candles, matches, flashlights, and a radio?

◆ Do all your locations have at least one exit that employees can use without a key? In some industries, up to 30 percent of sites lock in their employees after public hours.

Appendix B

FAQs

Q. What is disaster recovery planning?

A. *Disaster recovery planning* (DRP) is the process used to create a disaster recovery plan. The disaster recovery planning process enables organizations to develop policies and procedures to bring about quick, efficient, and cost-effective resumption and recovery of their business operations regardless of the nature of the disaster.

Q. Who must participate in disaster recovery planning?

A. A DRP organization structure should be created, often called the crisis management or disaster management team. Such a team includes members from all the departments of an organization. In addition, the executives, managers, and other employees of the organization must contribute to the formulation of the disaster recovery plan.

Q. When should I start planning for disaster recovery?

A. There is no set time to start the disaster recovery planning process. The time to plan for disaster recovery is not when a disaster occurs. Ideally, the entire process of disaster recovery planning should be performed to your best capacity well before a disaster occurs.

Q. How do consultants perform their activities?

A. Although consultants rarely create a disaster recovery plan, you can use their expertise and experience to create a disaster recovery plan. An organization chooses consultants to perform the initial steps in the disaster recovery planning process. Some activities that consultants perform include the following:

◆ Reviewing documents regarding disaster recovery, such as emergency evacuation procedures.

◆ Conducting onsite interviews of key personnel.

◆ Conducting a walkthrough of the physical facilities of the organization.

◆ Interviewing the organization representatives to gain insight into the unique challenges or risks that the organization faces.

◆ Contacting local agencies and other resources to obtain information on the natural hazards in the area.

◆ Providing an estimate for the services for which the expertise of consultants might be required.

◆ Presenting their findings while highlighting the effort required in the planning process.

Q. **What are the various levels of assistance that consultants provide?**

A. Consultants provide varied assistance. The various levels of assistance provided include these:

◆ **Consulting and software.** Some consultants provide consulting as well as software related to business continuity planning and management.

◆ **Consulting and hardware.** Some consultants provide consulting as well as hardware, such as mobile-site or hot-site facilities.

◆ **Consulting and Internet e-commerce continuity.** Some consultants provide consulting as well as rapid recovery solutions and high-availability networking.

◆ **PC-based planning tools.** Almost all hot-site vendors provide a PC-based disaster recovery plan development tool.

Q. **What considerations must I keep in mind while employing a consultant?**

A. Although the field of recovery consultancy is not governed by standards, you must keep certain considerations in mind when selecting a consultant. Some of these considerations include the following:

◆ The consultant's certification

◆ The clients for which the consultant has worked

◆ The consultant's practical experience in disasters

◆ The consultant's current standing

◆ The consultant's reputation in the industry

Q. **What considerations should I keep in mind while involving external support in the disaster recovery process of my organization?**

A. While involving external support in the disaster recovery process, you must ensure that vendors are able to deliver and provide the promised resources and assistance in times of disaster. The resources and assistance should be made available in the required quantity and timeframes.

Q. **How much time is typically taken to create a disaster recovery plan?**

A. Planning for business continuity is an ongoing process, but at the same time, the organization has to attain a basic level of continuity that should be enhanced over time. Typically, the creation of a disaster recovery plan will take one and a half to two years. It is wise to invest time in the creation of the plan.

Q. **How significant is management support for disaster recovery planning?**

A. Management plays a significant role in the disaster recovery planning process. Therefore, you must seek the support and involvement of management in the planning process as well as throughout the creation and maintenance of the plan. Management provides financial support and allocates its personnel to the planning task. Management also coordinates the implementation and maintenance of the disaster recovery plan to ensure its effectiveness throughout the organization. Management's underlying support for disaster recovery planning ensures the necessary involvement of all the departments and the employees of the organization.

Q. **How do I calculate risks that cannot be measured in terms of monetary loss?**

A. When it is not possible to measure risks quantitatively, you must use qualitative risk analysis. In qualitative risk analysis, you describe the elements of risks in qualitative terms. The categorization of risks as low, medium, and high forms the basis of qualitative risk measurement. Qualitative risk measurement advocates the use of descriptions and includes the analysis of threats, vulnerabilities, and security measures.

Q. **What important guidelines should I keep in mind while performing risk analysis?**

A. Keep the following guidelines in mind while performing risk analysis:

- Set up a risk analysis team.
- Ensure that management actively participates in risk analysis.
- Conduct risk analysis during the initial phases of disaster recovery planning.
- Consider all the functional areas of an organization and the interdepartmental dependencies.
- Decide the level of risk acceptance at the beginning of the process.

◆ Define all the baselines for deciding the priorities in the beginning.

◆ Conduct risk analysis whenever a significant change occurs.

◆ Document the results of all the phases.

Q. **An organization already identified and listed the risks to its assets last year. Can I use the same list for disaster recovery planning?**

A. To start with, it is advisable to ignore the existing list of risks. It is likely that the organization has acquired new assets, opened new branches, or moved to a new location during the intervening period since the old list was prepared. In such circumstances, the existing list is redundant. Of course, you can validate and update the existing list; but it would be better if you prepared a new list.

Q. **What is business impact analysis?**

A. The process of determining the critical business functions and their associated requirements, such as resources, time period, and priorities, is known as *Business Impact Analysis* (BIA).

Q. **Should the disaster recovery plan for my organization be a general plan or consist of individual plans devoted to the major departments or sectors of the organization?**

A. The decision to create a single plan for the entire organization or create individual plans for each department of the organization depends on the nature and complexity of the organization and the ease of planning. As such, there is no rule to decide whether you should have a comprehensive single plan for the entire organization or have sectioned department-wise plans. The latter approach is advisable if the organization is large with well-defined departments. In such a case, you can create individual plans devoted to each department. You can also create separate plans for individual components of an organization, such as network recovery plans.

Q. **When should I review a disaster recovery plan?**

A. It is recommended that the reviews take place at least on a yearly basis. However, you should also review the plan whenever a significant change is made to the organization in its structure, asset acquisitions, or business operations. This is to ensure that all changes to an organization are identified and that the disaster recovery plan is modified accordingly.

Q. **How necessary is it to test a disaster recovery plan?**

A. A disaster recovery plan is incomplete until it's tested. A disaster recovery plan is tested to ensure that it works as it was designed. Testing identifies all the areas that are not discussed or are inadequately mentioned in the plan. Another important purpose of testing is to promote awareness in the employees about the disaster recovery plan.

Q. **What is an active test?**

A. An *active test* is used to test a disaster recovery plan. In the test, a technical exercise is conducted to execute scripts and provide hands-on experience to the disaster recovery personnel.

Q. **What are the different types of drills involved in testing a disaster recovery plan?**

A. Typically, three types of drills are available to test a disaster recovery plan. An organization can implement any or all of these, but it is advisable to implement all the drills:

◆ **Walk-through drill.** The walk-through drill is designed to test disaster response procedures. The drill is similar to a tabletop review, but it is more thorough and involves more people.

◆ **Functional drill.** The functional drill is designed to test specific areas of the disaster recovery process. For instance, you can test disaster notification and communication procedures. It is not necessary that these procedures be tested simultaneously. The results of the tests help to identify the areas that have not been considered in the procedures and are a potential source for the failure of recovery from disasters.

◆ **Evacuation drill.** The evacuation drill is conducted to check the efficiency of procedures at a disaster recovery center. During the drill, all the participants prepare notes of the risks that are likely to occur during evacuation and the inadequacies at the disaster recovery center.

◆ **Full-scale exercise.** The full-scale exercise is designed to test disaster recovery by simulating a real-life disaster scenario. Management, disaster response personnel, employees, and local government agencies participate in this drill.

Q. **What is remote journaling?**

A. *Remote journaling* refers to the periodic online transmission of transaction data to backup system. Remote journaling minimizes data loss as well as recovery time.

Q. **How detailed should a disaster recovery plan be?**

A. A disaster recovery plan should include all the procedures and information required for a successful recovery from a disaster. To this effect, the plan can include sections devoted to the responsibilities, recovery strategies, plan administration, and so on.

Q. **What are the different procedures involved in the successful recovery of an organization?**

A. The successful recovery of an organization involves various procedures, as follows:

◆ Procedures to detect disaster and perform an initial assessment of the disaster

◆ Procedures to escalate and recommend recovery

◆ Procedures for recovery preparation

◆ Procedures to assign administrative responsibilities

◆ Procedures to restore the primary site

Q. **What time period considerations should I keep in mind while planning for recovery?**

A. Following a disaster, you must plan for two time periods:

◆ **Limited-operation time period.** During the limited-operation time period, immediate and disorganized recovery happens. This time period can extend for up to a week or more.

◆ **Makeshift-operation time period.** During the makeshift-operation time period, recovery from a disaster is prolonged until all activities of an organization are resumed. This time period can last for several months.

Q. **What is the range of recovery for critical systems and operations that I must aim for during a disaster?**

A. The recovery of critical systems can range from interim processing for a few days to full redundancy. It is likely that the resources required to resume operations will involve hardware, software, physical facilities, office equipment, funding, application software, backup data, vendor support, interagency support, staff, communications, security, and acquisitions. All these might not be available in adequacy or be available at all. In such a case, you should resume the critical systems and operations to a degree in which a disruption will not severely impact the organization. However, your aim must be to resume critical systems and activities to the fullest as soon as possible.

Q. What is an alternate site?

A. An *alternate site* is a location (other than the original premises of an organization) that is used to ensure the continuance of the critical activities of that organization in the event of a disaster.

Q. What considerations should I keep in mind when selecting a hot site?

A. Keep the following considerations in mind when selecting a hot site:

◆ Adequate floor space

◆ Relationship with vendors for immediate replacement or assistance

◆ Voice or data communications

◆ Availability of skilled personnel

◆ Security

 NOTE

The requirements stated in the preceding list are only some of the minimum requirements that you need to ensure when considering a hot site. In addition to these requirements, you must consider issues that are specific to your organization.

Q. The process of disaster recovery often involves the use of the term bare metal restore. What does it mean?

A. *Bare metal restore* is a recovery method that automates the recovery of the operating system and the data as one process.

Q. Who are the leading vendors of disaster recovery solutions?

A. Some of the leading vendors of disaster recovery solutions include the following:

◆ **BM Business Continuity and Recovery Services (a business unit within IBM Global Services).** This vendor offers services for risk analysis and disaster avoidance. Additional services such as recovery centers including hot sites are also offered.

◆ **SunGard Recovery Services.** This vendor provides facilities for business continuity and disaster recovery, such as fully equipped computer facilities in more than 30 centers with hot sites supporting multiple platforms. Cold sites and mobile data centers are also offered. In addition, SunGard offers planning and consulting services software, such as PreCovery.

Q. **What is a call tree?**

A. A *call tree* refers to the hierarchical flow in which communication should happen in the event of a disaster. A call tree details who calls whom when a disaster occurs. This helps to keep track of people and ensure a systematic disaster recovery.

Q. **Is it essential to test a call tree?**

A. Yes, it is critical to test a call tree to help retain the importance of the list. Testing identifies changes in contact numbers and helps suggest better ways to ensure that the required individual can be contacted at the time of a disaster.

Q. **What kind of contact information should be stored?**

A. Store all the information that can be useful to contact an individual during a disaster. For this purpose, you can store the pager numbers and work and personal e-mail addresses. In addition, you can store the home and office telephone numbers or any other telephone numbers of destinations that the individual frequents.

Q. **Are there any standards that enforce planning for disaster recovery?**

A. Yes, standards are available that enforce disaster recovery and its planning. Some of these include the following:

◆ **ISO/International Electrotechnical Commission (IEC) 17799:2000 – Code of practice for information security management.** This includes a section that emphasizes countering interruptions to business activities and critical business processes from the impact of disasters. Another section emphasizes the protection of assets.

◆ **National Institute of Standards and Technology (NIST) Special Publications (SP) 800 Series.** This emphasizes the need for plans for contingency, disaster recovery, and continuity of operations.

Q. **What state and government considerations must I keep in mind while ensuring recovery from disasters?**

A. Identify all the applicable federal, state, and local regulations, such as environmental regulations, fire codes, and transport regulations, while ensuring recovery from disasters.

Q. **How can I check if a disaster recovery plan is integrated into organizational operations?**

A. The integration of a disaster recovery plan into organizational operations forms an important task toward ensuring successful recovery at the time of a disaster. You can use multiple methods to identify whether the plan is integrated into organizational operations, some of which include the following:

◆ Management's support for the plan and the responsibilities specified in the plan

◆ Awareness of the employees about disaster recovery

◆ Involvement of all levels of the organization in the evaluation and updating of the disaster recovery plan

Q. **What are the possible challenges to the success of a disaster recovery planning project?**

A. As with any project, a disaster recovery planning project faces numerous challenges, such as these:

◆ A broad scope of the project

◆ Vague objectives of the project

◆ Unrealistic target deadlines

◆ Lack of accountability

◆ Lack of commitment from management

◆ Budget constraints

◆ Inadequate communication facilities

◆ Insufficient testing

◆ Poor maintenance

Q. **Are there any disaster recovery certification programs?**

A. Yes, disaster recovery certification programs are available. Various organizations offer these programs. Following are some of the certifications and the organizations that provide them:

◆ **Certified Business Continuity Professional (CBCP) from DRI International.** This is the basic certification level for individuals who have a minimum of two years of experience as a disaster recovery planner.

◆ **Associate Business Continuity Planner (ABCP) from DRI International.** This certification is for individuals who have a minimum knowledge in disaster recovery planning.

◆ **Master Business Continuity Professional (MBCP) from DRI International.** This certification is for individuals who have significant knowledge and skill in the industry and a minimum of five years of experience as a disaster recovery planner.

◆ **Certified Recovery Planner from Harris Recovery Institute.** This certification is for individuals who have been directly associated with the recovery responsibility for a minimum of two years.

 NOTE

For further information on the certifications, you can access the respective Web sites.

Q. **Where can I get more information about disaster recovery planning?**

A. Following are some sources of information on disaster recovery planning:

◆ **http://www.dr.org.** This is the site of Disaster Recovery Institute International DRI International.

◆ **http://www.drj.com.** This is the site of the *Disaster Recovery Journal*.

◆ **http://www.thebci.org.** This is the site of Business Continuity Institute.

Appendix C

In the Wings

The ongoing developments in the industry determine the future of any concept or technology. Past events also affect the future of disaster recovery.

The recent spurt of terrorist attacks has brought about an unprecedented awareness of the need to have a disaster recovery process in place. No one could have imagined the scale of disaster that was witnessed in the September 11, 2001 terrorist attack. This attack has led all major organizations to review and rereview their disaster recovery plans for completeness, feasibility, and durability. Not only has it become imperative for organizations to review and strengthen their disaster recovery plans, but it also has become important for disaster recovery vendors to evolve new and better means of handling disasters.

If you analyze the September 11 disaster, you will realize that many of the communication systems that were until then presumed to work during a disaster could and did go off course when a massive disaster did strike. Cell phones ceased to work, as did the dial-up connections to the Internet. Road traffic came to a standstill, as New York City was closed to all external traffic. Therefore, if an organization is relying on transshipment of communication and IT equipment by road to the disaster site, such a provision in its recovery plan needs to be re-examined.

You need to consider the use of an alternate site for business operations in case the primary location becomes inaccessible. Future disaster recovery plans are likely to increasingly work in this direction. The following list spells out some of the new trends in disaster recovery planning:

◆ **Increase in frequency of data backup.** Organizations are likely to use high-speed Internet connections to regularly back up data at the alternate location in case data at the primary location is destroyed. Increasing the frequency of updating the backed up data also merits consideration. Some organizations make backups every hour or even more frequently. The volume of business data that is generated in a given timeframe also has to be considered in this context.

◆ **Increase in use of hot sites.** The use of hot sites for reestablishing business operations is likely to increase. In the September 11 disaster, certain hot sites were unable to service some of their clients because of the high number of requests. Therefore, hot site vendors are likely to improve their customer-to-service ratio.

◆ **Enhanced role of Application Service Providers.** An Application Service Provider (ASP) offers services to enterprises that they can utilize instead of establishing their own infrastructure. ASPs are likely to play an important role in disaster recovery planning because of their ability to establish virtual data centers and provide customized solutions to enterprises.

◆ **Increased use of Web-based disaster recovery planning tools.** Web-based tools can automate the process of disaster recovery. Their application is likely to increase in the near future.

◆ **Improved prediction of natural calamities.** The best way to cope with a disaster is to know about its possible occurrence in as much advance as possible. By improving prediction of natural calamities such as earthquakes and tornadoes, it is possible to provide the disaster recovery planning team the extra time to get recovery systems in place. Therefore, more work is likely to be done for accurate and timely prediction of natural calamities.

Disaster recovery planning programs are generally considered expensive because infrastructure facilities must be replicated. However, if you go by the statistics, Strategic Research Corporation has estimated the cost of corporate downtime to be as high as $6.6 million per hour in lost revenue and services. This cost does not include costs incurred in replacing damaged equipment or in relocating employees. It follows, therefore, that organizations can really afford the cost of disaster recovery planning and should invest more into it to avoid the massive losses occasioned by disasters. Disaster recovery planning is bound to become a major area of expertise in the near future.

Appendix D

**Common Modes
of Attack and
Intrusion
Detection
Systems**

This Appendix discusses some of the common methods that hackers use to attack an organization's computing resources. It also lists some important Intrusion Detection Systems (IDSs) that are available in the market.

Common Modes of Attack

Three commonly employed attacks by hackers are IP spoofing, sniffing, and Denial of Service (DoS) attacks. These attacks are described in this section.

IP Spoofing

IP spoofing is used to deceive the target server about the origin of the TCP/IP packets. To the server, it appears that the data packets have originated from an authentic IP address. Actually, these packets are sent from a client that is using an impersonated IP address. The cracker normally uses an IP address that the server trusts as the spoof address. Therefore, the cracker takes advantage of the trust between the target system and the spoofed system.

To understand IP spoofing, consider the following scenario:

- ◆ **Server IP address.** 201.13.12.1
- ◆ **Client IP address.** 202.45.12.2
- ◆ **Spoofed IP address.** 180.74.5.2

In this scenario, the target server with IP address 201.13.12.1 is led to believe that the data packets come from the client with the IP address 180.74.5.2, whereas the actual originator of the packets is the client with the IP address 202.45.12.2. The server, in this case, trusts the spoofed address.

To understand IP spoofing, you first need to look into the concept of the three-way handshake. The three-way handshake is the process used to establish a TCP session between the server and the client. The three-way handshake between a client and a server involves the following steps:

1. The client sends an SYN packet to the server to establish the connection. This TCP packet only has the SYN flag active. The SYN flag indicates a request for connection. This packet also contains the Initial Sequence Number (ISN) of the client, which tracks the connection.

2. The server responds to the client request with an SYN/ACK packet by sending its own ISN to the client.

3. The client acknowledges the server's SYN with an ACK packet.

Upon completion of the preceding steps, the connection is established for data exchange between the client and the server. The cracker uses the spoofed IP address to establish a similar connection. The cracker uses the following process:

1. The client sends an SYN packet to the server with a fake source address.

2. The server replies with an SYN/ACK packet to the fake address. The fake address must not be accessible; otherwise, the client IP address will reply to the packet and the spoofer's attack will be foiled.

3. The client sends a fake SYN packet to the server after some time, in response of the SYN/ACK packet. The cracker must determine the correct sequence number to be used for the response because the SYN/ACK packet is sent to the fake address and the cracker never receives it. The server believes that the response has come from the fake address and the connection is established.

IP spoofing can be checked to some extent by using other authentication tools on the server and not relying only on IP trust relationships. Following are two solutions to prevent IP spoofing:

◆ Using random ISNs to prevent crackers from guessing the sequence number of the packet sent to the fake address

◆ Configuring router firewalls to reject packets from the Internet that claim to have an internal IP address

Sniffing

Sniffing is the process of capturing network packets to intercept communication that is not meant for the sniffer. Sniffing involves the use of software that is normally used to monitor and diagnose the network, such as the network monitor.

Sniffing is carried out by putting the network card in a promiscuous mode so that it can listen to all broadcast messages on the particular network segment on which it resides. The network packets are analyzed for confidential information, such as usernames and passwords. Passwords obtained by such means can be used later for disruptive purposes.

 TIP

Normally, only the first few bytes of the packets are captured because these are the bytes that contain user and password information.

You can use the following means to prevent sniffing:

◆ **Compartmentalizing a network.** A network that is compartmentalized to a greater degree through the use of routers, switches, and bridges is less prone to sniffing attacks. This is because sniffers sniff data only on the network segment on which they reside.

◆ **Using encryption technologies.** Use of encryption technologies also discourages sniffing. Although the data might be sniffed, it is incomprehensible to the sniffer. The encryption technology must be strong enough to resist cracking. Secure Shell (SSH) provides a secure environment for Telnet sessions by using strong encryption.

DoS Attacks

DoS attacks involve incapacitating the target server or network from serving legitimate clients. Attackers flood the target system with packets and consume the available memory space. As a result, the target system becomes incapable of serving legitimate clients for a certain period of time until recovery is effected.

DoS attacks might be brute force attacks, in which the attacker attempts to clog all resources of the target system, or they might exploit certain vulnerabilities in the TCP/IP and IPv4 implementations.

Let us look at some DoS attacks that hackers commonly employ.

Ping of Death

The ping of death attack used to be a popular form of attack, but almost all systems today are secure against this vulnerability. This attack involves pinging the target system with a data packet that is larger than the maximum number of bytes allowed by TCP/IP. This normally causes the target system to stop responding or restart.

Teardrop Attack

The teardrop attack involves using overlapping offset fields in the TCP headers of the data packets. This attack seeks to destabilize the target system when it tries to reassemble the data packets, which causes the target system to stop responding or restart.

SYN Attack

The SYN attack is a form of IP spoofing. The attacker sends a number of SYN requests to the target system with a fake IP source address. The target system replies with SYN/ACK packets and waits for the ACK packets from the non-existent clients. As a result, the requests are queued up at the target system. This ultimately chokes up the resources of the target system.

Smurf Attack

A smurf attack aims to flood the target networks with packets. A large number of spoofed address packets are sent to a target system, which is normally the router. These spoofed addresses have the addresses of internal systems of the target network. The router echoes back the reply to all these messages, resulting in the target network becoming flooded.

Distributed DoS Attacks

Distributed DoS attacks use smaller and less protected networks as platforms to attack more secure networks. The hackers first hack and gain control of smaller networks and then use these networks to launch DoS attacks against the target network. By following this strategy, the hacker also makes it difficult for the network administrators of the target network to trace the hackers because the hackers can easily manipulate the logs of intermediate networks, which are less secured.

Intrusion Detection Products

Before selecting an IDS, you should first determine if the requirements of the organization are being met. Vendors advertise about a lot of features in their products. However, before you finalize a product, you must ascertain whether the product fulfils the core requirements of the organization.

The after-sales support that a vendor provides is an important factor when selecting the product. Vendors must be committed to supporting and up-grading the product in the future because IDSs need to be constantly updated with new signature patterns to keep current.

Before we look at some of the intrusion detection products available in the market, we will describe the qualities to look for in an intrusion detection product.

Selecting an Effective Intrusion Detection Product

An intrusion detection product needs to rate high on the following parameters:

- Scale of protection
- Reduced false alarms
- Scalability and architecture
- Front-end interface and usability
- Regular updates
- Flexibility

Let us examine each of these parameters in detail.

Scale of Protection

The scale of protection that an IDS offer is an important consideration when choosing a product. An IDS might have an attractive and easy-to-use application interface. It also might have a robust database architecture. However, these features are secondary when compared to the scale of protection offered.

For example, a Network Intrusion Detection System (NIDS) must be capable of recognizing a wide array of attack patterns. If the NIDS is not capable of recognizing newer attacks, it is barely useful. Similarly, a Host Intrusion Detection System (HIDS) must be capable of more than simply analyzing a few logs. Advanced HIDS products can even look for Trojan codes and end rogue processes.

The IDS also must be compatible with multiple platforms in case your organization uses diverse platforms. Otherwise, the usability of the system becomes limited.

Reduced False Alarms

Accurate products are always desirable. Testing helps establish how prone a system is to false alarms, especially for NIDS. False alerts impose additional overheads on the system administrator and should be reduced to a minimum.

Scalability and Architecture

An IDS product must have a robust front- and back-end architecture and should be scalable to changing business requirements. For example, an NIDS should have a backend database engine capable of handling increasing amounts of alert data that are fed in by the sensors.

The NIDS also should be able to support high bandwidth environments if the organization envisions these in the near future.

Front-End Interface and Usability

An IDS must be able to present the logged and alert data in a way that facilitates easy analysis by the network administrator. Otherwise, the use of the IDS would be limited in spite of its capabilities. The IDS management framework should be tested in a managed environment if possible.

The learning curve that is associated with the product should not be too long. Administrators cannot always spare time for difficult-to-use products.

Regular Updates

Vendors for intrusion detection systems provide upgrades that are usually deployed to fix identified security patches or to counter newly discovered security threats. You should schedule your intrusion detection system to check for regular updates and deploy them for the security of the network.

Flexibility

Some administrators need the IDS product to be customizable so that they can tailor it to the needs of the organization. For example, certain administrators might seek the facility to add custom signatures to an NIDS.

Intrusion Detection Products

Having examined the qualities of an intrusion detection product, let us now look at some of the intrusion detection products in the market.

Cisco Secure IDS

Cisco offers a number of NIDS products, which include these:

- ◆ Cisco 4210 for x86-based platforms
- ◆ Cisco 4230 for industrial-strength implementation
- ◆ Cisco intrusion detection "blade" for the Catalyst 6500 series of switches

The Cisco Secure IDS suite has its foundation in NetRanger. Cisco acquired the NetRanger NIDS in the late 1990s. With the launch of the new interface, Cisco Security Policy Manager (CSPM), Cisco has raced to the forefront of the industry. This interface can handle numerous events and offers a scalable solution for large organizations. You can access Cisco products on their Web site at http://www.cisco.com.

NFR Security IDS

NFR offers an NIDS product that offers a high degree of flexibility. You can customize this product by using a scripting language called ncode. NFR was also one of the first companies to address the common NIDS vulnerabilities in its product. NFR products are suitable for low-bandwidth environments and can detect packet-mangling techniques designed to dupe NIDSs. NFR is accessible at http://www.nfr.com.

Anzen Flight Jacket

Anzen offers an NIDS product based on the NFR engine. Anzen has added more signatures to the NFR base product. Many of the NFR product advantages and drawbacks are found in the Anzen products as well. Find more details about Anzen products at http://www.anzen.com.

Axent/Symantec NetProwler and Intruder Alert

NetProwler is an NIDS product that runs on Windows NT. It is packaged with the HIDS known as Intruder Alert. Intruder Alert can support most operating systems.

NetProwler is prone to some of the NIDS evasion strategies that hackers use. However, it includes some features, such as the user-friendly application interface, that other IDSs in the market do not possess. The Axent Web site is http://www.axent.com.

CyberSafe Centrax IDS

CyberSafe offers an integrated NIDS-HIDS product. The product uses a single management console for both the NIDS and the HIDS. Centrax works well on Windows systems and also has some support for specific UNIX platforms.

CyberSafe's HIDS offering is one of the best in the industry. However, its NIDS engine lacks in a number of attack signatures and its design is not robust. CyberSafe's Web site is http://www.cybersafe.com.

ISS RealSecure

ISS was one of the foremost companies to provide an integrated host and network-based system. The integrated management console is simple to use. RealSecure runs on Windows NT and many UNIX versions. It, however, is not efficient in high-bandwidth environments. You can query about ISS products at http://www.iss.net.

Open Source IDS Solutions

Snort is an example of a popular Open Source IDS solution. It has a large bank of signatures and is suitable for the UNIX platform. You can obtain details about Snort at http://www.snort.org.

TIP

IDS is still an evolving technology and new players come into the market every day. Therefore, it is prudent to research the players in relation to your requirements before choosing a product.

Appendix E

**Evaluating
Available
Firewall
Products**

You learned about firewalls in Chapter 5, "Baseline Measures." This Appendix looks at some of the important considerations to remember when you purchase a firewall. In addition, it examines a cross-section of firewall products from different companies.

An organization must determine its requirements before selecting a firewall. It should map its requirements to a specific firewall architecture and should be clear about the other services required from the firewall. After the organization determines the requirements, the number of firewalls that match the organization's requirements narrows. It becomes easier to select a firewall from this smaller list of products.

The organization must have a sound security policy in place before it searches for a firewall product. Firewalls must be a part of a larger security solution; they are not the security solution themselves.

An organization needs to consider the following questions when deciding on a firewall:

- What authentication is used in the security policy?
- What is the level of logging that is required?
- Which firewalls are required?
- Do you need an out-of-the-box solution or a customizable solution, in which you can define filters, rules, and so on?
- What services would you require from the firewall?
- Is the firewall required to handle DNS? Is it required to act as the SMTP server as well?
- Is the firewall required to act as the Web server?
- Would the firewall be a separate entity? In other words, will there be a clear demarcation between network services and the firewall?

After an organization has defined its security policy and clearly identified the services required from the firewall, it can proceed to selecting a firewall.

Let us now look at a broad cross-section of firewall products serving various needs. For additional information on the firewall products discussed in the following sections, check out the URLs that are listed for the product vendor.

Router (Stateless Packet-Filter Based) Firewalls

In some routers, a set of filter rules, referred to as Access Control Lists (ACLs), can act as a firewall. These firewalls are referred to as router-based firewalls. This section describes some router-based firewalls available in the market.

Cisco 2500 Series

The Cisco 2500 series of routers incorporates packet-filtering capabilities. All Cisco 2500 series routers run the Cisco IOS software. This software is particularly useful for small organizations or for those organizations that have a small number of multiuser systems. Following are the two Cisco routers that you can use as firewalls:

- ◆ **Cisco 2514.** This router has two LAN interfaces and two WAN interfaces. These interfaces allow Cisco 2514 to be used as a firewall.
- ◆ **Cisco 2501.** This router is suitable for smaller organizations because it has only a single WAN and a single LAN interface. It is also cheaper than other Cisco routers that can be used as firewalls.

The advantage of using router-based firewalls is that they can be configured as the administrator requires. The administrator must have a sound understanding of configuring ACLs because incorrectly configured firewalls are the leading source of intrusions.

One disadvantage of using most router-based firewalls, which includes Cisco products, is that they have little or no logging capabilities.

Livingston FireWall IRX

The Livingston FireWall IRX firewall is more suitable when greater logging capabilities are required. It is a multiprotocol router firewall that has logging facilities and a powerful rule set. The Livingston FireWall IRX firewall allows logging to a host on the network. Firewall IRX uses the UNIX syslog facility for logging. The ACLs in Livingston also have a well-designed syntax and are easier to learn and use for the network administrators.

FireWall IRX has two LAN ports and one WAN port. Therefore, you can use it as a connection router to the Internet and as a firewall connecting two branch offices of the company. The rule sets of FireWall IRX are powerful enough to detect attacks, such as IP Spoofing, that can deceive most routers.

The Security Router

Network Systems Corporation (NSC) has a multiprotocol router-based firewall product named The Security Router. This firewall can support more protocols than the FireWall IRX. This firewall also provides a facility for secure IP tunnels.

All routers can provide only the basic firewall capabilities. However, stateful packet filter-based and proxy-based firewalls have greater capabilities than these firewalls. We discuss them in the next section.

Stateful Packet Filter-Based Firewalls

A stateful packet filter-based firewall operates in the application layer. This type of firewall not only scans a traversing data packet for its source and destination, but also scans the packet for information contained in it. As a result, this type of firewall provides better protection and filtering than stateless packet filter-based firewalls. This section describes a few commonly used stateful packet filter-based firewalls.

BorderManager

BorderManager is a stateful packet-filter-based firewall primarily used in Novell Netware environments. You can use this firewall to provide internal firewall capabilities in an organization. For example, BorderManager can separate department boundaries. It offers high-speed real-time analysis of network packets as well as a centralized management facility. You can obtain more details about this firewall from http://www.novell.com/products/bordermanager/index.html.

Firewall-1

Firewall-1 is a popular stateful firewall because of its myriad features. Firewall-1 supports Windows NT and UNIX. Manufactured by Check Point Software Technologies Ltd, it has the following features:

- ◆ It is an effective means of content screening in addition to packet filtering.
- ◆ It guards against IP Spoofing attacks.
- ◆ It has a real-time scanning facility for viruses.
- ◆ It includes VPN options.

The drawback with Firewall-1 is its high-end pricing. Details about Firewall-1 are available at http://www.checkpoint.com.

PIX Firewall

PIX firewall is available in the form of an appliance. PIX supports IPSec and can be remotely administered through Telnet or encrypted SSH sessions. Because PIX is a Cisco product, you can administer it using the Cisco Security Policy Manager (CSPM). The URL for PIX Firewall is http://www.cisco.com/warp/public/cc/pd/fw/sqfw500/index.shtml.

GNAT Box Firewall

GNAT Box Firewall is similar to the PIX firewall. It is a stateful packet filter-based firewall. You can administer it either through the command line or through a Web-based interface. You can get more information about GNAT Box Firewall at http://www.gnatbox.com.

NetScreen Firewall

NetScreen Firewall is a stateful packet filter-based firewall appliance. Manufactured by NetScreen Technologies, Inc, NetScreen Firewall supports IPSec, DES, and triple DES encryption schemes. You can learn more about this firewall at http://www.netscreen.com.

Guardian Firewall

Guardian Firewall is a stateful packet filter-based firewall that is suitable for a Windows NT platform. It filters traffic based on IP source and destination addresses, port, network interface, and protocol. Manufactured by NetGuard, Inc., Guardian Firewall can be accessed at http://www.netguard.com.

Application Proxy Firewalls

Application proxy firewalls are deployed at the application level and are based on applications rather than routers. This section describes some common application proxy firewalls.

Firewall Server

Firewall Server is a proxy-based firewall that BorderWare manufactures. It works on proprietary operating systems that run on Intel hardware. You can learn more about Firewall Server at http://www.borderware.com.

Raptor Firewall

Raptor Firewall, which is manufactured by Axent, is meant for Solaris and Windows NT. Symantec acquired Axent in December 2000. The URL for this firewall is http://enterprisesecurity.symantec.com/default.cfm.

Sidewinder

Sidewinder is a proxy-based firewall meant for UNIX platforms. It is manufactured by Secure Computing. You can get more details about the Sidewinder firewall at http://www.securecomputing.com.

Index